THE SURVIVAL OF THE SMALL FIRM 2

Employment, Growth, Technology and Politics

THE SURVIVAL OF THE SMALL FIRM 2

Employment, Growth, Technology and Politics

Edited by
JAMES CURRAN
JOHN STANWORTH
DAVID WATKINS

Gower

Published by
Gower Publishing Company Limited,
Gower House,
Croft Road,
Aldershot,
Hants GU11 3HR
England

Gower Publishing Company,
Old Post Road
Brookfield
Vermont 05036
U.S.A.

British Library Cataloguing in Publication Data

The survival of the small firm.
    1. Small business
    I. Curran, J.   II. Stanworth, John
    III. Watkins, D.S.
    338.6'42   HD2341

Library of Congress Cataloging-in-Publication Data

The survival of the small firm.
    Contents: V. 1. The economics of survival and entrepreneurship –
    V. 2. Employment, growth, technology, and politics.
    1. Small business – addresses, essays, lectures.
    2. Self-employed – addresses, essays, lectures.
    3. Small business – employees – addresses, essays, lectures.
    I. Curran, James.   II. Stanworth, John.   III. Watkins, David, 1947-.
    HD2341.S87   1986   338.6'42   85-27035

    ISBN 0-566-00726-6 (Hbk)   0-566-05223-7 (Pbk) (V. 2)

Typeset in Great Britain by Graphic Studios (Southern) Limited, Godalming, Surrey.
Printed in Great Britain at the University Press, Cambridge

Contents

Part II THE SMALL FIRM, GROWTH AND TECHNOLOGY

Part III THE STATE, POLITICS AND THE SMALL ENTERPRISE

List of Figures

List of Tables

Notes on Contributors

Arnold C. Cooper is Professor at the Krannert Graduate School of Management, Purdue University in the United States. He has also served on the faculties of the Harvard Business School, Stanford University and the Manchester Business School. He has authored or co-authored five books and a number of articles on entrepreneurship, strategic planning and the management of technology. His current research interests are in entrepreneurship and strategic planning.

James Curran is Reader in Industrial Sociology and Director of the Small Business Research Unit at Kingston Polytechnic. He has been involved in research on the small enterprise for well over a decade and has published widely on the subject. He is currently researching the impact of environmental influences such as government policies and local labour markets on small firms in the electronics and printing industries.

John McHugh is Senior Lecturer in Politics at Manchester Polytechnic. He has conducted research on housing policy in Britain, on petite bourgeoisie representative groups and is currently completing research on working class political movements and organisations.

S.M. Miller is Professor of Sociology and Economics at Boston University in the United States. He has been a visiting scholar at the Centre for Environmental Studies and at the London School of Economics. He is currently adviser to a multi-country study of the welfare state co-ordinated by the European Centre for Social Welfare in Vienna. He has written extensively, his most recent book being *Recapitalizing America* (Routledge and Kegan Paul).

Alistair Rainnie was, until December 1984, Research Associate in the School of Occupational Studies at Newcastle upon Tyne Polytechnic. He has done research on industrial relations in small textile firms and is at present doing research on the same topic in the printing industry.

Roy Rothwell is Senior Research Fellow at the Science Policy Research Unit at the University of Sussex and a former physicist and design engineer in the telecommunications industry. His main research interest is in technological innovation, management and policy and he has co-authored four books and a large number of papers on these subjects. His work is well known abroad and he is an expert consultant to the OECD.

Michael Scott is Lecturer in Small Business Studies at the Durham University Business School. Besides a long-established interest in industrial relations in the small firm, he is currently involved in education for enterprise projects and the development of self-employment programmes for people in higher education. Part of his current work is sponsored by Shell UK Ltd.

John Stanworth is Professor and Director of the Small Business Unit at the Polytechnic of Central London. He was a pioneer of research on the small business in Britain and has recently completed a major study of the franchised small enterprise. He has written several books and a large number of articles on various aspects and varieties of the small firm.

David Storey is Senior Research Associate at the Centre for Urban and Regional Development Studies at the University of Newcastle upon Tyne. He has authored and edited books on the small firm including *Entrepreneurship and the New Firm* (1982) and *The Small Firm: An International Survey* (1983) as well as several articles.

David Watkins is Director of the New Enterprise Centre at the Manchester Business School where he has taught entrepreneurship and small business courses for the past eight years. He was principal author of the *Small Business Kit* which accompanied a major television series for entrepreneurs in Britain, and has co-edited three major research-based books on the small enterprise, and, more recently has been conducting research on the female entrepreneur.

Ava Westrip was until recently Research Officer at the Small Business Unit of the Polytechnic of Central London and has been a researcher with several other organisations. Currently she is a freelance researcher and writer on employment policy and the small firm.

Preface

Volume One of this collection concentrated on three of the wider issues featuring in current discussions of the survival of the small firm: its fate in the complex economies of advanced industrial societies, the persistence of motivational impulses towards self-employment and the variety of types of small enterprise, especially those which appear to be emerging as a result of recent economic and social changes. In the second volume the approach is somewhat less general, focusing on three specific issues relating to the survival of the small firm which have been the subject of much debate recently. None, however, has been selected simply as a fashionable issue of the moment. Rather, they deal with less obvious aspects of the context of the small enterprise which are, nevertheless, in one way or another, fundamental to its continuing existence.

First, we have selected several contributions which discuss the until recently neglected topic of employment in the small firm. Much of the literature on the small enterprise gives the impression that the only human figure involved is the owner-manager. But around one-third of the United Kingdom labour force, and often as many as a half or more in other industrial societies, find employment in small firms. Their experiences have been largely disregarded or presented in an idealised fashion yet one key to understanding the small business as an economic and social entity must lie in the opportunities afforded to employees by its continued existence.

For policy-makers, the labour market created by small employers has become increasingly central in formulating solutions to the persistent unemployment problem of present-day industrial societies. A lively literature has developed concerning the employment-generating potential of the small enterprise sector of the economy but academic views on this topic are mixed. An understanding of some of the subtleties of this debate is a prerequisite for sensible, effective policy-making.

Working in the small enterprise is a distinct form of employment experience which contrasts with similar kinds of employment in the large enterprise. Small firms, for example, have their own industrial relations patterns which differ from those in the larger enterprise and public sectors of the economy. In other words, we cannot be concerned simply with the creation of jobs in small firms, we also need to know something about the quality of these jobs and the reactions of those who fill them, if we are to assess the potential of the small firm for employment.

The second issue with which this volume is concerned is small firm growth and relations between the small firm and new technology. Growth is a perennial topic in the literature on the small enterprise. How do small firms grow, why do some grow and not others, what are the barriers to growth and, conversely, what can we do to stimulate growth? These recurring questions are examined at some length. Paradoxically, the statistical data on small firms in industrial societies actually shows that, in fact, relatively few small firms do grow to any considerable extent, which might suggest that the extensive literature on this topic is either disproportionate to the phenomenon it addresses or has been singularly ineffective in promoting an increase in small business growth. Alternatively, it may be that the processes involved are much more complex than first imagined and important questions on the nature of small business growth have too often been begged.

The impact of new technology on the economy generally has been a central concern in all industrial societies as they undergo rapid and massive restructuring consequent upon the introduction of new forms of technology whose broader implications can even now only be dimly envisaged. Its impact on the small firm is part of this wider discussion. Whether new technologies will destroy or enhance the future of the small enterprise is the basic question addressed in this debate. Again, however, academic thinking has produced mixed results although, of late, it has become more optimistic on the opportunities offered to small enterprise by new technology. Like the analysis of growth, the relations between technology and the small enterprise have emerged as highly complex and, to the extent that the full impact of new technology on the economy as a whole is far from clear, equally, there remains a large area of the unknown in relation to its promise for the small enterprise.

The final issue examined in this volume is politics and the small enterprise. At first sight, relations between the small firm and the political order might seem tenuous. What has the busy owner-manager, struggling to make a go of his or her business, often too busy even to vote, got to do with political parties and governments? The answer is that, however remote the political order might appear from the back-street engineering subcontractor, corner shop or even the small high-technology electronics firm, the survival of the small enterprise is closely bound up with the political process. This is not simply a matter of the heavy bureaucratic hand of government imposing increasingly severe restraints on the freedom of action of owner-managers. Small firms symbolise fundamental values and the way in which the small business owning class influences, directly or indirectly, the fortunes of the main parties affects the wider political process. In some industrial societies, politicians ignore the voices of the numerical minority involved in small-scale enterprise to their cost. The small enterprise survives not by economic criteria alone — the political dimension may be even more important in survival or at the very least, may successfully counteract many of the economic forces which threaten the small firm.

Our thanks are again due to the authors contributing to this volume. Those who have written original papers as well as those who have allowed us to edit and reprint their previously published work (not forgetting their original publishers) have enabled us to maintain the high standards achieved in Volume One. Together, the two volumes offer, we believe, an optimistic answer to the implied question in the overall title we have selected for this collection. The survival of the small firm seems assured: what appeared as death and decline to commentators only a decade or so ago, is now seen to be more accurately interpreted as metamorphosis. Change offers opportunities for new forms of small enterprise and old forms show more potential to survive than doubters assumed. Survival is a permanent struggle for the small firm but no economic endeavour, however large or powerful, is ever free from such struggle — the small enterprise in all its forms has already shown its mettle in this respect.

James Curran
John Stanworth
David Watkins

PART I
SMALL FIRMS,
THE LABOUR MARKET
AND
SOCIAL RELATIONS

Introduction

The four papers in the opening section of this volume explore various aspects of employment in the small enterprise. There has always been a tendency in the small firms literature to ignore the fact that a large proportion of the labour force (including the self-employed themselves) in many industrial societies earn their living through employment in various kinds of small firm. In Britain, for example, this proportion is roughly one-third, in the United States 40 per cent would be a conservative estimate, depending on the definition adopted (Thompson and Leyden, 1983) and in Japan the majority of the labour force work in small firms (Anthony, 1983). Other mature industrial societies tend to be closer to the upper end of this range (EIU, 1983). Recently, the traditional neglect of the small firm as an employer has been partly remedied by the 'discovery' by policy-makers of the small firm as a source of employment.

On the whole, small firms tend to be labour-intensive whereas large firms tend to be more capital-intensive. Even where the large enterprise does employ large amounts of labour, more and more frequently production is being located in Third World countries where labour is cheaper and less likely to be unionised. Unemployment resulting from the relocation of plants outside national boundaries, from technological changes and the cyclical downturn in economic activity since

3

the mid-1970s, have all induced policy-makers to exploit the job-generating potential of the small firm. Small firms are not only more labour-intensive than their large counterparts, they are also often located in labour-intensive areas of economic activities such as services. Overall, therefore, the small firm has been given an important role in countering unemployment.

Researchers have been quick to investigate the underlying assumptions and likely results of policies promoting more jobs in small firms. The best known study here is the highly influential American research by David Birch (1979) which was optimistically interpreted as demonstrating conclusively that small firms are a major source of new employment. However, some researchers in Britain attempting to replicate Birch's findings have been sceptical about whether the job-generating potential of the small enterprise was quite as straight-forward as Birch was seen as implying. The opening paper in this section by David Storey shows how some of this scepticism emerges and how the analysis required to examine the employment effects of the small enterprise needs to be wider and deeper than was originally assumed.

For instance, Storey shows that in the northern region of England where he collected data, the overall size structure of industry is a considerable influence on new firm formation rates and hence on the job-creating potential of small firms. In other words, the presence of a high proportion of *large* firms in the region indirectly shapes the employment potential of the small firm sector since entrepreneurial activities are often on a lower level in such regions. It seems that those who work in large firms are less likely to consider embarking on their own business than those with experience of working in smaller enterprises. In other regions where the size distribution is more favourable, the job-creation potential of small firms, *ceteris paribus,* will be greater.

The second paper in this section switches attention to the subjective aspects of working in the small enterprise. Too often, the experience of small firm employment has been reported by those whose direct knowledge was limited and who frequently had a vested interest in offering a somewhat rosy view. When, however, small firm employees are allowed to offer their own views a rather different picture emerges. Curran and Stanworth's paper reflects the views of male small firm employees in the printing and electronics industries and directly compares these data with those collected from a sample of large firm employees in the same two industries.

The paper's findings concentrate on social relations within the enterprise, that is, relations between fellow employees and those between employees and owner-managers. Some of the findings are, at first sight, unexpected. For example, while small firm employees do overall perceive their work place as friendlier than they would expect to be the case in a large firm and while more of these relations were continued outside work, the latter difference disappears when marital state is controlled for. The researchers suggest that this results from the fact that, on average, small firms have younger work-forces than large firms, containing more unmarried employees. Amongst married small firm employees, levels of out-of-work contacts with fellow employees fall to about the same as among married workers in larger firms.

On vertical relations, Curran and Stanworth report that shopfloor worker–supervisor relations are more closely related to type of industry than size of enterprise. On relations between employees and owner-managers — often thought to be especially close — the authors conclude that employees see social relations with owner-managers as rather distant and were well aware that the interests of themselves and their owner-managers might not always be the same.

The following paper by Alistair Rainnie and Michael Scott, especially written for this collection, examines industrial relations in the small firm in detail. This is again a subject about which there is a great deal of well-voiced opinion but which has received little serious attention from researchers. Probably the most accepted view stresses the harmonious relations between employer and employee in the small firm; the firm is often seen as a 'family' with the owner-manager taking a close and paternalistic interest in the welfare of employees in and outside work. Yet there is also another paradoxical theme in historical and current accounts of the small enterprise — the small firm as a 'sweatshop'. More recently, these views have been added to by the 'small is beautiful' movement stressing the vritues of small size as a work environment for all those involved. Statistics on the relationship between size of establishment and the likelihood of industrial action appears to support the harmonious, positive views as do those concerning the relationship between size of establishment and the likelihood of unionisation.

But, as Rainnie and Scott point out, neither frequently asserted views nor statistical correlations can be taken as a proper analysis of the nature and character of industrial relations in the small enterprise. First of all, the small enterprise, like its large counterpart, is an economic unit which, for its owners, primarily exists to make a profit in the sense that failure in this aim will more or less quickly bring about the dissolution of the unit and the loss of the owner's assets. The employment relationship and worker–management relations are embedded in this wider economic framework. Thus, employees' opportunities to work in one kind of firm rather than another, to work in small or large firms, are primarily determined by their position in the wider labour market.

Small firm owners themselves are often in a very insecure position in the wider economic system. This, in turn, limits their freedom in relations with employees. Labour costs are an important element in the overall cost structure of the enterprise and labour has to be carefully controlled and utilised. Owner-managers have often been shown to be autocratic, antipathetic to trade unions or other forms of worker representation and as resenting strongly any idea that they do not know what is best for their employees.

Trade unions, on the other hand, find it difficult to recruit and service members in small firms. Employer resistance, high rates of labour turnover (typically, small firms have higher levels of labour turnover than large firms) and having to negotiate for small groups of workers rather than large numbers or even a whole industry, combine to make life difficult for trade unions. Small firms often employ a higher proportion of women than large firms and, in the past, trade unions have not been very sensitive to their needs. The weakness of trade unions in small firms often in itself weakens the appeal of the trade union to potential members in small firms — a self-reinforcing pattern.

In other words, Rainnie and Scott are suggesting that industrial relations patterns in the small enterprise are dependent upon a number of complex factors which lead them to take on a different form than in the large firm. The simple picture of owner-manager paternalism and harmony or, alternatively, of the small firm as sweatshop, are inadequate for providing a proper understanding of what goes on inside the enterprise. In particular, they do not take into account the wider environment of the small enterprise — its situation in the industry and economy, the kinds of experiences of those who own and manage the small enterprise as well as those who are employed in it, and, not least, the characteristics of the large firm economy with which the small business sector co-exists.

The final contribution in this section examines another subjective aspect of employment in the small enterprise — levels of job satisfaction. Accepted views — supported by a considerable amount of academic theorising and some research — claim that the small firm offers a higher level of job satisfaction than is obtainable in the large firm. This is seen to be especially the case with regard to intrinsic aspects of job satisfaction — for example, satisfying social relations, more varied and interesting work and opportunities to identify with the enterprise as a whole.

However, the most sophisticated recent studies of job satisfaction in the small enterprise — those which have attempted to take into account both the results of objective measures and the subjective responses of small firm employees as well as carefully comparing these data with those obtained for workers in comparable large firm employment — have not entirely supported accepted views. Curran and Stanworth, reporting findings on subjective aspects of job satisfaction from the study reported in the second paper in this section, show that any straightforward assertion on absolute levels of job satisfaction in the small firm is likely to be, at best, superficial.

Job satisfaction patterns among small firm workers cannot, it seems, be described in terms of any simple set of assertions which show the unequivocal superiority of the small firm work environment. The type of industry in which the firm is located, marital status, worker expectations and workers' appreciation of their labour market situation all enter into the determination of small firm employee perceptions of the satisfaction to be derived from their work and firm. Again, as Rainnie and Scott argue in the previous paper in this section, small firm employee attitudes, behaviour and experiences can only be interpreted fully by extending the analysis beyond the firm itself.

Together, the four papers in this section on employment in the small firm, examine both objective aspects — the economist's analysis of the job-generating potential of small firms and the structural framework of small firm industrial relations — and the subjective dimension, the experience of small enterprise employment. This discussion counter-balances to some extent the more familiar concern (reflected in most of the other sections in both volumes of this collection) with the role, problems and personalities of those who actually own and manage small firms.

References

Anthony, D. (1983). 'Japan' in D.J. Storey (ed.), *The Small Firm, an International Survey*, Croom Helm, London.

Birch, D.L. (1979). *The Job Generation Process*, MIT Programme on Neighbourhood and Regional Change, Cambridge, Mass.

Economist Intelligence Unit (1983). *The European Climate for Small Business, a Ten Country Study*, Economist Intelligence Unit, London.

Thompson, J.H. and Leyden, D.R. (1983). 'The United States of America' in D.J. Storey (ed.) *The Small Firm, an International Survey*, Croom Helm, London.

1 New Firm Formation, Employment Change and the Small Firm: The Case of Cleveland County*

DAVID STOREY

The northern region of England has suffered rates of unemployment which have persistently exceeded the average for the United Kingdom. Traditionally, this has been attributed to the dominance of heavy manufacturing industry in the area, demand for the products of which has been declining. This structural explanation of the employment difficulties faced by the region was developed by the Northern Region Strategy Team (NRST 1977a, b) who also felt that entrepreneurship was less developed than in the country as a whole. A relative absence of small businesses, the prevalence of branch plants, the absence of top level managerial and administrative functions were thought to characterise the region. It was, in the opinion of the NRST, the poor supply capacity of the region which restricted the transition of an economy based on shipbuilding, coal mining, chemicals and heavy engineering into one capable of self-sustaining growth in technologically advanced industries.

NRST were, however, unable to provide any evidence on comparable rates of new firm formation in the region and elsewhere. They were also unable to determine the importance of wholly new firms to employment change, or offer any new insight into the contribution of small firms to job creation in the region.

---

* Reprinted from: *Urban Studies*, vol. 18 (1981), pp 335–45.

This paper presents information for the county of Cleveland, which contains one-quarter of the region's manufacturing employment. It contrasts new firm formation rates in Cleveland with those of the East Midlands, an area which has a large number of new firms per head of population, and which has experienced rates of unemployment below the national average. The purpose is to estimate the number of manufacturing jobs that might be created if Cleveland were to have a new firm formation rate similar to that of the prosperous East Midlands.

A number of writers have tried to explain differences in entrepreneurship — in this case defined to be synonymous with new firm formation — between regions or between groups of individuals. Some have emphasised psychological or motivational factors such as the need for achievement, whilst others have offered sociological explanations. NRST felt the relative absence of small firms in the North could be attributed, at least in part, to the social traditions of the area. This paper, however, questions the relevance of 'social' explanations by showing that, statistically, much of the difference in the rates of new firm formation between Cleveland and the East Midlands can be 'explained' by differences in firm size in the two areas. Where there is a higher proportion of the total labour force employed in very small firms, within comparable industries, it is that area which has the higher rate of new firm formation.

Throughout the paper, the size structure of the existing stock of firms is argued to be a major determinant of rates of new firm formation, and hence prosperity. The effect of British regional policy, as it has affected Cleveland, has been to encourage large manufacturing plants to move into the area, and arguably to act as a factor depressing local rates of new firm formation. In our conclusion, we speculate on the effect of a variety of policy measures in assisting new firm formation in areas with apparently low entrepreneurial potential.

The employment performance of small firms

There has recently been an increased emphasis placed by British policy-makers upon the role of small firms as creators of jobs. Their importance in the United States is reported by Birch (1979) who demonstrated, from a study of employment change in 5.6 million US establishments (or 82 per cent of all private sector establishments), that 66 per cent of net new jobs were created in establishments employing less than 20 people. The word, 'net' however, is frequently omitted from descriptions of Birch's findings, suggesting that two-thirds of *all* new jobs are created by small firms.

Even when correctly interpreted, Birch's results are more ambiguous than they appear at first sight. Birch showed that total employment in all US establishments rose between 1969 and 1976, with an increase in employment in all establishment size bands. Hence it is valid, for example, to express net growth in employment in the 1–20 size band as a proportion of total employment growth. Unfortunately, US employment in the manufacturing sector alone, fell slightly between 1969 and 1976, with a large net fall in employment in large establishments and a net increase in employment in small establishments. For manufacturing it is therefore impossible to derive a single measure of the proportion of new jobs created in the different sizes of establishment.

Table 1.1

Net employment change by size of establishment: USA, East Midlands and Cleveland

Establishment size	0–20	21–50	51–100	101–500	500+	Total
USA (1969–76)	+3.2	+0.5	−0.2	−1.5	−2.9	−0.9
East Midlands (1968–75)	+2.7	+2.3	+1.5	−2.2	−5.9	−1.5
Cleveland (1965–76)	+4.0		+0.9	+1.6	−16.0	−9.5

Sources: The top two lines are taken from Fothergill and Gudgin (1979), Table 13. The Cleveland data are derived from the Cleveland County Council Establishment Data Bank.

Where there are net job losses in a size category, Table 1.1, following Fothergill and Gudgin (1979), takes net job change in each size sector, expressed as a percentage of the numbers employed in that sector in the base year. It shows that manufacturing employment in the US and in two British regions, declined in large establishments, and increased most rapidly in small establishments. The pattern in the three areas is basically similar, indicating that, at least for manufacturing, small firm employment growth in Britain in manufacturing differs only marginally from that of the United States.

Even these data, however, require careful interpretation. To facilitate comparison, the British data follow Birch by placing firms in existence in the base year in the size category of that year. New firms, however, are placed in their final year size category. This may result in an underestimate of the contribution of openings to employment change, especially in the very small sector.

Small firm employment performance in Cleveland 1965–76

This section assesses the contribution to manufacturing employment change made by establishments of different sizes in Cleveland between 1965 and 1976. The ambiguities of the measures used by Birch mean that it is better to compare the different rates of employment growth of only those establishments which existed in the base year, in this case 1965. Given that an establishment could either increase or decrease its employment, or close before 1976, the employment performance of different establishment sizes in Cleveland is shown in Table 1.2. It shows that only the group of establishments which in 1965 had under 50 employees showed a *net* growth in employment with the most rapid growth among those establishments with less than ten employees, which grew by an average of 56.1 per cent. All other establishment sizes showed a decline.

To examine whether the above results were due to the inclusion of the traditional heavy industries of Cleveland — shipbuilding, chemicals and allied and metal manufacture — these sectors were excluded. Figure 1.1 shows that, of the establishments which declined in employment size, the largest proportionate decline was in the largest establishments and the smallest proportionate decline was in the smallest establishments.

The pattern for establishments which increased in employment is erratic in the middle range, although clear at the extreme points of the size distribution. The average increase for the smallest establishments which increased was 87 per cent, whereas the average increase for larger establishments (over 500 employees in 1965) was only 2 per cent. In the middle range of 100–249 and 250–499 employees, growth rates increased before plunging in the 500+ employees category. This is due to the existence in 1965 of a number of recently established branch plants which were building up to full employment.

These results however, can be subjected to two major criticisms. The first is that there is a major bias in the measures of employment created by the small establishment. The second is that the analysis does not distinguish between the small *firm* and the small *establishment*.

The bias in favour of the small firm sector can be seen by taking the case of firm *i* currently employing 8 people. If it goes out of business, the sector loses eight jobs, but if it prospers there is no upper limit to

11

Table 1.2
Changes in employment of different-sized manufacturing establishments in Cleveland 1965–76

Establishment size	1–9	10–49	50–99	100–249	250–499	500–999	1000–1999	2000+
Gross in-situ gain	+596	+2133	+590	+1364	+1551	+311	+510	+729
Gross in-situ loss	−61	−474	−572	−1346	−1352	−2106	−3318	−15615
Closures	−181	−1014	−872	−2241	−1376	−2071	−2194	0
Total	+354	+645	−854	−2223	−1177	−3866	−5002	−14886
% change	+56.1	+16.3	−28.3	−28.2	−14.9	−34.6	−31.1	−23.3

Source: Cleveland County Council Establishment Data Bank

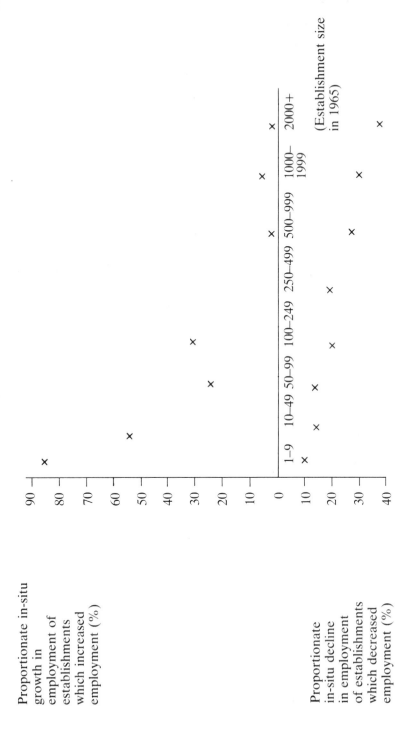

Figure 1.1 In-situ employment change by establishment size, excluding Orders IV, V, VI, X, as a proportion of 1965 employment, 1965–76.

the number of jobs which it can create. Hence, one very successful firm will, in an arithmetic sense, compensate for job losses through a large number of small firm closures. It is, of course, much more difficult for the large firm sector to compensate for job losses. The arithmetic mean, therefore, which is used in Table 1.2 as an index of the performance of the various sectors, is misleading since it takes no account of the spread of performance and, as we shall show in Table 1.3, it would be wholly wrong to assume that the typical small firm employing either less than ten workers or less than 25 workers, grows either by 56.1 per cent or 16.3 per cent, respectively.

Table 1.3 shows that although the cohort of firms in the 1–49 employees group had a positive rate of employment growth, this was due to the remarkably high growth of a few firms. Reading across the rows of Table 1.3, it is possible to see that for firm i employing less than ten people in 1965, there was a probability of 0.26 that it would no longer be in business in 1976. The probability that firm i would still be employing less than ten people in 1976 is 0.61. Hence, although this sector grew in aggregate by 56.1 per cent, the probability that firm i would have moved into a higher size category was only 0.13. This emphasises that although most new firms are small, the vast majority of small firms are not new. It also shows that the performance of small firms as a group is strongly influenced by a very small number of exceptionally fast growers, which upon inspection do not have common industrial or ownership characteristics (although two were branch plants new in Cleveland in 1965).

Table 1.3 also shows that, in general, death rates of firms are higher in small establishments, but the association is imperfect, since rates are substantially higher in the 25–99 employee than in the 1–24 employee categories.

The above analysis does not, however, distinguish between firms and establishments. A large firm could have a very small establishment and so, in examining employment change, the effect of size and ownership form are treated simultaneously. To isolate the effect of ownership, Table 1.4 examines the employment performance of the single-plant independent firm. Much the same characteristics are apparent as for all establishments. For the single-plant independent firm employing less than ten people in 1965, the probability that it will either go out of business or still employ less than ten people in 1976 is 0.86. Only 14 per cent of that stock of firms in 1965 showed any significant growth. For single plant independent firms employing between 10 and 24, only 19 per cent showed any growth, and only 8 per cent and 7 per cent of those employing between 25 and 49 and between 50 and 99, respectively, showed growth. In addition, there is

Table 1.3
Deaths and movements between size bands — all 1965 establishments in Cleveland (per cent)

Employment size band in 1965	Deaths	Employment size band in 1976							
		1–9	10–24	25–49	50–99	100–249	250–499	500–999	1,000+
1–9	26	61	9	2	1	0	1	0	0
10–24	19	15	6	15	3	0	1	1	0
25–49	32	5	12	34	9	8	0	0	0
50–99	31	2	0	20	38	9	0	0	0
100–249	26	2	0	8	20	34	6	4	0
250–499	27	0	0	0	4	23	31	11	4
500–999	27	0	0	0	6	6	17	44	0
1000+	5	0	0	0	0	0	9	9	77

Table 1.4
Deaths and movements between size bands: single-plant independent firms in Cleveland (per cent)

Employment size band in 1965	Deaths	Employment size band in 1976						
		1–9	10–24	25–49	50–99	100–249	250–499	500–999
1–9	27	59	12	1	1	0	0	0
10–24	18	13	49	15	4	0	0	1
25–49	22	3	19	48	8	0	0	0
50–99	35	0	0	27	31	7	0	0
100–249	25	0	0	19	25	31	0	0
250–499	25	0	0	0	0	0	50	25

no consistent inverse relationship between death rate and size, with the highest death rates being in the 50–99 group, and the lowest in the 10–24 category.

The role of different ownership forms on aggregate employment change in Cleveland is shown in Table 1.5. It shows that the single-plant independent firm was one of the few sources of net employment growth in the county — the other was the branch plant. The single-plant firm was, however, the only major source of in-situ growth.

Table 1.5
Manufacturing employment change by ownership:
Cleveland County 1965–76

	Openings*	Closures †	In-situ change †
1 Single-plant independent firm	+1902	−2169	+681
2 Independent locally controlled headquarters	+91	−309	−3563
3 Independent locally controlled branch	+200	−259	−4297
4 Independent non-locally controlled plant	+944	−2968	−5793
5 Single-plant subsidiary firm	+1508	−2542	+181
6 Headquarters of locally controlled subsidiary	+195	−1390	+148
7 Branch of locally controlled subsidiary	+223	−20	+28
8 Branch of non-locally controlled subsidiary	+10283	−294	−4439
Total	+15346	−9951	−17054

Note: †1965 classification
 * 1976 classification
Source: Cleveland County Council Establishment Data Bank

These results suggest that the large enterprise has generally been a net shedder of labour in Cleveland during the 1965–76 period, whilst the small, locally owned firm has shown a net increase in its employment of labour. Much of this, however, is due to the exceptionally rapid growth of a very few firms.

New firm formation rates: Cleveland and the East Midlands

The Northern Region Strategy Team regarded lack of entrepreneur-ship as 'one of the remaining weaknesses of the Northern economy' and by implication suggested that raising the rates of new firm formation would make a significant impact upon employment in the region. During the 1965–76 period, indigenous new firm formation in manufacturing contributed approximately 2000 out of 15 000 gross new jobs created in Cleveland through openings, possibly indicating support for the NRST hypothesis. To test whether raising these rates would have a major impact upon employment we compare wholly new manufacturing indigenous firm formations in Cleveland with the East Midlands.

The East Midlands is selected for comparison because, by contrast with the North, it has been characterised by a relatively rapid rate of new firm formation. Gudgin (1978) showed that two-thirds of the increase in manufacturing employment which occurred in the East Midlands between 1948 and 1967 was attributable to wholly new indigenous firms. In addition, data were made available to the author to enable comparisons between the two areas to be made. Clearly, other regions could have been chosen for comparison, but the East Midlands is the most appropriate because its tradition for new firm formation contrasts with that of Cleveland.

To compare these areas, an index of new indigenous firm formation rates is used, which takes the number of surviving new firms at the end of the period and expresses them as the number per year, per 1,000 employees at the start of the period. Given a new firm formation rate for the East Midlands, and given Cleveland's employment in each industry at a base date, we can estimate the number of new firms that would have existed in Cleveland at the end of the time period, if it had a formation rate identical to the East Midlands, taking account of its industrial structure, i.e. an 'expected' number. This can then be compared with the actual number. The results are shown in Table 1.6, but the reader's attention is drawn to a large number of qualifications to be made before direct comparison of these data sources can be made.[1] Bearing in mind these qualifications the table gives a reason-ably accurate picture of firm formation rates by sector in the county.

Table 1.6 shows the total number of surviving wholly new indigenous manufacturing firms formed in Cleveland between 1965 and 1976 was 183, whereas given its industrial structure, the expected number was 572, indicating a rate approximately one-third that of the East Midlands. Much of the difference is explained by shipbuilding, which is not, in any way, comparable in the two areas. Differences in

Table 1.6
New indigenous manufacturing firm formations in
Cleveland 1965–76 (actual and expected)

Industry	Actual Number	Expected Number
Chemicals and metal manufacture	9	144
Shipbuilding	3	201
Engineering: mechanical, electrical, instrument, vehicles and metal not elsewhere specified	104	120
All other manufacturing	67	107
Total	183	572

the chemical and metal manufacturing industries explain much of the remaining difference in total new firm formations. Again it is difficult to regard the Cleveland steel and chemical industries which specialise in the 'heavy' end as truly comparable to those of the East Midlands where emphasis is more on 'upstream' products.

Comparisons between the engineering and light metal goods sector are, however, more valid and these show that the rates of new indigenous firm formation are not significantly different between the two regions. Table 1.6 shows the 'expected' number of firms only exceeds the 'actual' by 16 or about 15 per cent.

An examination of all other industrial sectors shows that the 'expected' exceeds the 'actual' by 40 firms, or by about 60 per cent. Hence, excluding shipbuilding, chemicals and metal manufacture, where comparisons are difficult, Cleveland has a surviving new indigenous manufacturing firm formation rate about 35 per cent below that for the East Midlands.

If we make the extremely optimistic assumption that public policy could raise overnight the rate of new firm formation in Cleveland to that of the East Midlands, in those industries where comparison can be made, this would create a maximum of 1000 new jobs over an 11-year period. Although it is not possible to make direct comparison for the shipbuilding, metal manufacturing and chemical and allied industries between Cleveland and the East Midlands, the larger establishment size of firms in Cleveland, in these industries, suggests the true expected rate of new firm formation should be zero. This is because those industries in the East Midlands with a comparable average establishment size, also show a zero rate of new firm formation. Hence it seems highly unlikely that more than 1000 new jobs over 11 years could be created by raising the rate of new firm formation in Cleveland to that of the East Midlands. This has to be placed in the context of the net loss of 16 704 jobs, over the same period, through in-situ decline. Assumptions about the role of establishment size in this context are critical and we now discuss them in greater detail.

The effect of size on new firm formation

In the above it has been shown that:

1   The cohort of firms employing less than 50 people increased employment, whereas other cohort sizes showed a net reduction.
2   The growth of the small firm cohort was primarily attributable to the growth of very few firms.
3   Wholly new indigenous manufacturing firms made only a minor contribution to employment change in the county, and a massive change would have to occur for new firms to make a major impact on employment, in Cleveland, within a decade.

If small manufacturing firms are the only source of net new manufacturing jobs in the economy, then an area such as Cleveland is likely to be at an increasing disadvantage compared to areas such as the South-East and the East Midlands, because it has a higher proportion than most areas of large firms which, as a group, are contracting their labour force.

In this section, however, we argue that Cleveland suffers the additional disadvantage that large firms generate relatively few individuals who start their own businesses, so that areas with an initially large stock of small firms are likely to add more rapidly to their stock, and hence to employment, than will areas dominated by large establishments.

Kilby (1971) suggests that economic models of entrepreneurship have distinguished between 'supply' and 'demand' factors. The 'demand' factors are the observed rate of profit in industry i, and whether the individual feels post-entry market price will enable him to obtain a satisfactory return. Traditional barriers-to-entry literature such as Bain (1956) or Mansfield (1962) demonstrates that price may persistently exceed LRAC (Long run average cost) without inducing entry, but these 'supply' barriers, instead of being framed solely in terms of LRAC or product differentiation, can also be examined in terms of knowledge on the part of the potential entrepreneur considering entry. For example, an individual currently working in industry i is more likely to identify a potential market in i than, *ceteris paribus,* an individual working in j. Secondly, the individual working in a large firm is unlikely to have the breadth of knowledge of an otherwise comparable individual working in a small firm. The large firm manager is more likely to have specialised in particular functions such as sales, accountancy, production, and so on, rather than being involved, on a day-to-day basis, with the totality of the business.

'Supply' factors also suggest the small firm employee is more likely to establish his own firm than his large firm counterpart. Working in a large company is almost certainly better paid and has greater job security than employment in small firms. The risk involved in establishing a company, for the individual currently working in a small firm may be only marginally greater than continuing in paid employment.

It therefore seems likely that new firms are more likely to be formed by those working in small firms, and that the greater the number of small firms in an area, *ceteris paribus,* the larger the pool of potential entrepreneurs. Extensive empirical support for this hypothesis has been provided by Cooper (1971), Fothergill and Gudgin (1979), Johnson and Cathcart (1979a, b) and by Cross (1981). This however does not necessarily prove that the size of the incubator firm is important, since the sample includes new firm founders in a variety of industries. If the majority of entrepreneurs were in industries where there were many small firms, higher formation rates might merely reflect the height of entry barriers in that industry rather than the role of small firms within that industry. Only by demonstrating that, within *each* industry, small firms have higher spawning rates can firm size be shown to be an important factor in entrepreneurial supply.

Table 1.7 compares, within each industry, the rates of new firm formation in Cleveland with those of the East Midlands. It shows that there is a significant positive correlation between relatively high rates of new firm formation in industry i and a relatively high proportion of the work-force in i employed in very small establishments. It shows the correlation is stronger with the proportion of employment in very small establishments — less than ten employees — than with those establishments having 11–49 employees. This supports the small firms incubator hypothesis that the propensity to form a new firm of an individual working in a very small establishment was markedly higher than that of an individual employed in a medium-sized establishment. The Table also shows these results do not depend upon the presence of essentially non-comparable industries in the two areas, i.e. the ship-building, metal manufacture and chemical and allied industries. Even when these are removed, similar results are obtained.

Table 1.7

Correlation between new firm 'deficiency' and percentage of employment in small establishments: Cleveland and the East Midlands

D_X	D_Y
$E_1 = 0.8678$	$E_3 = 0.7404$
$E_2 = 0.4819$	$E_4 = 0.4845$
n = 15	n = 12

Notes

$D_X =$ Deficiency in new firms in Cleveland, i.e. actual minus expected, where expected = East Midlands new firm formation rates for industry i × Cleveland employment in i, in 1965.

$D_Y =$ As D_X above, but excluding Orders, IV, V, VI, & X.

$E_1 =$ Differences in proportion of employment in industry i in establishments employing 1–10 persons (Cleveland minus East Midlands)

$E_2 =$ Differences in proportion of employment in industry i in establishments employing 11–49 persons (Cleveland minus East Midlands)

$E_3 =$ Differences in proportion of employment in industry i in establishments employing 1–10 persons (Cleveland minus East Midlands), excluding Orders IV, V, VI & X.

$E_4 =$ Differences in proportion of employment in industry i in establishments employing 11–49 persons (Cleveland minus East Midlands), excluding Orders IV, V, VI & X.

This Table combines Orders IV and V, and Orders XII and XIII.

Conclusions

Firstly, it has been shown that manufacturing firms employing more than 50 people are net shedders of labour whilst firms employing less than 50 people are net job generators, with the performance of the very small firm sector being determined by the rapid growth of a very few firms. Secondly, the paper shows that wholly new manufacturing firms create relatively few jobs in Cleveland but this is unlikely to be due to a lack of 'entrepreneurial spirit' or to industrial structure, but rather to the inherent nature of the new firm, i.e. its instability and its tendency to create very few jobs in its early years. Thirdly, it is argued that the existing size structure of the industry is a powerful 'explanation' of differences in new firm formation rates between regions, i.e. more new manufacturing firms are formed in areas with a higher proportion of the manufacturing labour force in small firms. Fourthly, the paper suggests that since a high rate of new firms formation is a necessary (but not sufficient — see Howick and Key 1980) condition for self-sustaining employment growth, the entry into Cleveland, during the 1965–76 period, of large firms, although it created the bulk of the new jobs in the area, may actually have depressed the rate of new indigenous firm formation. It has resulted in the large externally-owned branch plant coming to the area. This type of firm produces relatively few entrepreneurs from within its work-force, and it buys relatively little from local companies and offers little opportunity for the development of local managerial talent. Hence although the entry of large establishments has been a major source of new jobs in the past, it is questionable whether, even if it were possible, basing job creation upon attracting the branch plant is likely to lead to self-sustaining employment growth in future. Continued reliance on the entry of large manufacturing firms may, if anything, lead to a depressing of indigenous rates of new firm formation, which, in turn, has been shown to be a necessary condition for prosperity.

This should, however, not be interpreted as unqualified support for policies based upon the small indigenous firm. It is unclear whether the superior employment performance of such firms derives from demand or supply-side factors, i.e. whether it is due to small firms supplying primarily a local market where competition is less fierce (possibly due to the protection offered by local tastes or transportation costs) or whether, as the Bolton Committee suggested in 1971, demand for the type of 'one-off' products produced by small firms is highly income-elastic. If the latter is the more powerful explanation then reliance upon small firms to regenerate the economy might have merit. Alternatively, if the small firm has prospered because of local protection, not available to larger firms, then the opportunities for expanding the small firm sector are limited.

Policies to assist the small manufacturing firm in an area such as Cleveland will make only a limited impact upon employment in less than a decade. The area therefore faces a major dilemma: in the long term raising the rate of new firm formation seems an essential prerequisite to achieving a self-sustaining rate of employment growth; in the short to medium term, however, reductions in state assistance to larger firms will mean both a reduction of employment at existing plants and a reduced in-movement of such plants.

The real issue raised in this paper is that of the ability of an economy to adjust and respond to changes in the demand for its commodities. The indigenous Irish economy, for example, has reacted to the entry of large externally-owned manufacturing branch plants by providing an increasing proportion of inputs to these plants. In the North of England, despite nearly 50 years of regional policy, the last 15 of which have seen the entry of a substantial number of large plants to the area, indigenous industrial performance, if anything, appears to have been depressed rather than stimulated. In chronicling these events, perhaps more questions are raised than answered.

Note

1. Data for the East Midlands are derived from the records kept by the Factory (Health and Safety) Inspectorate, which inspect all manufacturing premises. Data for Cleveland are taken from the Annual Census of Employment. The HSI and ACE data may differ in coverage, especially of very small establishments. The HSI data also give employment data on manual employees — white collar staffs are separately recorded, but because HSI are primarily interested in manual staffs, white collar employment is less accurate. Since HSI visits may only be once every four years, not all establishments have their employment records taken in the same year. In addition, there are substantial problems in comparing data derived by different researchers on numbers of new firms, since apparently 'new firms' may, in fact only be changed in name and/or location. They may also be new branches of subsidiary companies rather than wholly new establishments. Hence the total number of 'new' firms (defined as wholly new indigenous manufacturing enterprises) in an area depends critically upon the care, precision and local knowledge of the researchers. At the margin it may also depend upon somewhat arbitrary decisions exercised by the researchers. To enable comparisons to be made between regions, where the classification has been conducted by different individuals, one must be broadly satisfied that similar judgements have been exercised. In the case of Cleveland and the East Midlands, we have adjusted the Cleveland data to take account of the slightly broader definitions of new firms used by Fothergill and Gudgin (1979). The data are now as comparable as possible.

References

Bain, J.S. (1956). *Barriers to New Competition,* Cambridge, Mass.: Harvard University Press.
Birch, D.L. (1979). *The Job Generation Process,* MIT Program on Neighbourhood and Regional Change, Cambridge, Mass.

Bolton, J.E. (1971). *Report on the Committee of Inquiry on Small Firms,* Cmnd. 4811, London: HMSO.

Cooper, A.C. (1971). 'Technical entrepreneurship: What do we know?', *R & D Management,* vol. 3, pp. 59–64.

Cross, M. (1981). *New Firm Formation and Regional Development,* Farnborough: Gower Press.

Fothergill, S. and Gudgin, G. (1979). *The Job Generation Process in Britain,* London: Centre for Environmental Studies, Research Series no. 32.

Gudgin, G. (1978). *Industrial Location Processes and Regional Employment Growth,* London: Saxon House.

Gudgin, G. and Fothergill, S. (1979). 'The East Midlands Industrial Data Bank: A Guide to Sources, Methods and Definitions', CES (Centre for Environmental Studies) Working Note WN 559.

Howick, C. and Key, A. (1980). 'Small Firms, Entrepreneurship and the Industrial Regeneration of Inner Cities', paper given at conference on 'Problems and Prospects for Stimulating Small Firms', Manchester Business School.

Johnson, P.S. and Cathcart, D.G. (1979a). 'The Founders of New Manufacturing Firms: A Note on the Size of Incubator Plants', *Journal of Industrial Economics,* vol. 28, pp. 219–24.

Johnson, P.S. and Cathcart, D.G. (1979b). 'New Manufacturing Firms and Regional Development: Some Evidence from the Northern Region', *Regional Studies,* vol. 13, pp. 269–80.

Kilby, P. (ed.) (1971). *Entrepreneurship and Economic Development,* New York: The Free Press.

Mansfield, E. (1962). 'Entry, Gibrats Law, Innovation and the Growth of Firms', *American Economic Review,* vol. 52, pp. 1023–52.

Northern Region Strategy Team (1977a), *Strategic Plan for the Northern Region, vol. 2, Economic Development Policies,* N.R.S.T. Newcastle upon Tyne.

Northern Region Strategy Team (1977b), 'Small Firms in the Northern Region', N.R.S.T. Working Paper no. 12, March.

2 Worker Involvement and Social Relations in the Small Firm

JAMES CURRAN AND JOHN STANWORTH*

A recurrent theme in the literature on small firms is that workers in such firms escape many of the deprivations experienced by workers in larger enterprises. In the small firm, social relations both between workers themselves and between workers and their employers are frequently seen as mutually satisfying and conflict-free.[1]

Perhaps the best known formulation of these ideas is that of Schumacher[2] whose somewhat romantic view of social relations in the small firm is summed up in his catch-phrase 'small is beautiful'. The government-sponsored Committee of Inquiry on Small firms, which reported in 1971, made similarly optimistic assumptions:

> In many respects the small firm provides a better environment for the employee than is possible in most large firms. Although physical working conditions may sometimes be inferior in small firms, most people prefer to work in a small group where communication presents fewer problems: the employee in a small firm can more easily see the relation between what he is doing and the objectives and performance of the firm as a whole. Where management is more direct and flexible, working rules can be varied to suit the individual.[3]

* From: *The Sociological Review*, vol. 27, no. 2 (May 1979).

Sociologists studying the small firm worker have largely supported these views. The most important study here is undoubtedly that of Ingham whose interpretation of social relations in small firms is closely linked to his view that small firm workers manifest what he terms a *non-economistic expressive orientation* to work. Workers with this orientation place a relatively low emphasis on economic rewards and a high emphasis on non-economic rewards such as interesting work and satisfying social relations with others in the enterprise, especially superiors.[4] This orientation may be contrasted with an *economistic-instrumental orientation* held by workers who attach overriding importance to material rewards and who are willing to sacrifice a wide variety of intrinsic rewards in order to achieve them.[5]

Since, in Ingham's view, the small firm provides an environment most congruent with a *non-economistic-expressive orientation*, workers with the latter orientation will, *ceteris paribus,* choose to work in small firms. Those with strongly materialist orientations, on the other hand, will tend to work for large firms which, on the whole, pay better than small firms but offer lower levels of intrinsic rewards. Further, small firm workers are seen as forming close relations with fellow shop-floor workers because lower levels of rational organisation allow more informal interaction: 'Thus, size is likely to be inversely related to the level of potential rewards from peer relationships.'[6] Similarly, vertical social relations in the small firm are also seen as more rewarding for workers because they promote direct and close associations with owners and managers in ways which are virtually impossible in the large firm. This is said to be further reflected in feelings of moral involvement in the enterprise and identification with management goals.[7]

Research by Batstone[8] provides the other major recent contribution to the sociological study of social relations in the small firm. The general argument and findings are, at first sight, broadly in line with those of Ingham. Again we have the notions of self-selection amongst small firm workers, of their involvement in shop-floor social relations and their strong concern with intrinsic aspects of the job.[9] However, Batstone's arguments are not entirely consistent with those of Ingham. For example, he notes that social relations among large firm workers may be stronger because of the greater choice of possible friends. A large firm will contain more workers of a similar age and position in the life-cycle and more people doing similar jobs.[10]

On vertical social relations, Batstone found that small firm workers had more frequent and more diffuse relations with owner-managers which were sometimes continued out of work. Moreover, they valued these contacts and the overall atmosphere which interaction of this kind generated. However, because he was living in the community in which his research was being carried out, Batstone felt unable fully to explore management–worker relations for fear of offending owner-management respondents.[11]

One important point brought out by Batstone is that of worker–management relations (and relations between workers) being related to type of community. Banbury, the town in which Batstone's small firms were located, had elements of a traditional social order. Both workers and owner-managers lived within this order and out-of-work contacts were important influences on relations within the firm. Local businessmen dominated local politics and in the past, when these businessmen conflicted with the landed gentry, their employees had often sided with them. Overall, these wider social relations formed part of an 'ethos of small town capitalism'[12] and it was the latter which most influenced vertical social relations in the small firm. In the present study, relations between shop-floor workers and owner-managers outside work were non-existent and the wider social order lacked any indications of a traditional social community.

There is sometimes an assumption that close physical proximity between worker and employer will, in itself, produce close social relations and worker identification with his employer's aims.[13] This assumption is present in both Ingham's and Batstone's interpretation of social relations in the small firm and, in addition, Ingham provides a clear example of obvious methodological weaknesses in examining these relations. Ingham's interview schedule lists only four main questions directly concerned with this issue and two of these refer to management's strictness in enforcing rules.[14] Worker respondents were asked if they ever saw the firm's directors on the shop floor and, if so, did they think it was a good thing and, finally, did they ever talk to them? None of these questions, it may be argued, was likely to test adequately the character of the social relations concerned.

A sample of small firms in two industries

The present paper is based on tape-recorded interviews with 145 male shop-floor and supervisory workers in eight small firms in the printing and electronics industries and 88 interviews with a control sample of equivalent workers in two large firms, one in each of the industries. In addition, 40 executives in the firms were interviewed on their views on workers and social relations in the firm. All interviews with workers and supervisors were carried out in respondents' homes or other non-work venues. The interview programme lasted from late 1974 to early 1976. In no firm did the response rate fall below 70 per cent of those invited to participate in the research.

All the firms were located in or around the northern half of Surrey, an economically buoyant area with an unemployment rate of about half the national average. The two industries in the study were chosen for their sharp contrast. Printing is a traditional, craft-based industry which, until comparatively recently, has experienced a slow rate of technological change. It is a small firm industry *par excellence* with over 95 per cent of workers located in establishments employing less than 100 people.[15] It is also, unusually for an industry dominated by small firms, highly unionised.[16]

The electronics industry, in contrast, is a young, science-based industry which dates back only to the 1930s in terms of providing substantial employment.[17] Although it is difficult to define the exact boundaries of the industry, it has many more large firms than printing and is much less unionised.[18] The firms in the present research were chosen from areas in the industry specialising in technologically sophisticated products, often on a short-run basis. This ensured that workers would be more likely to be involved in skilled work and that there would be fewer women workers making the firms more comparable with those drawn from the printing industry in terms of sex composition and skill levels. The main reason for specifically choosing firms from two industries was to allow for an examination of the influence of industrial sub-culture on social relations within the firm. Previous research on small firms had tended to ignore this issue and mixed samples from different industries as if the meanings, definitions and attitudes shared by those working in particular industries were of little importance in discussing social relations.

Ingham and Batstone both adopted '100 employees or less' as their criterion of the small firm.[19] The Bolton Committee adopted a definition of '200 employees or less' for manufacturing industry[20] and the present research adopted this latter definition but also ensured that the firms selected were spread across the size spectrum of 1–200 employees with some emphasis on the 1–100 size category.

The large printing firm studied employed 450 people, making it one of the 2 per cent of establishments in the industry employing over 200 people. The large electronics firm, on the other hand, employed 1600 people but this is an industry where large establishments are much more common.[21]

Background differences between the small and large firm worker samples

That those who own and manage small firms are socially distinct from their counterparts in large firms is now well established.[22] The relatively poor educational background and socially marginal character of the small firm owner-manager is linked with a distinct world-view. His managerial style tends to be autocratic and to show a reluctance to delegate in everyday decision-making.[23] This can have a profound effect on social relations in the firm, given the normative and material sanctions normally at the disposal of the person occupying this role. This may be all the more so where, as is often the case, small firm employees are not unionised.

Batstone, however, noted that his sample of small firm workers had a lower average age than his large firm workers, a finding confirmed in the electoral register sample investigated at the same time in Banbury.[24] In the present study it was found that small firm workers were, on average, nine years younger than their large firm counterparts. These age differences were naturally associated with other differences such as the proportions of married and single respondents. Equally important, however, were the further findings that small firm workers were less well qualified, less experienced and had a higher frequency of unstable previous employment histories than large firm workers even after age differences were allowed for.

These background differences were also related to employers' selection practices. For example, personnel departments in large firms are more likely to insist on workers having had a conventional training and history of stable employment. This mainly reflects the more bureaucratised administrative practices of large firms.[25] Small firm owner-managers, on the other hand, are more particularistic in their relations with employees. They more frequently recruit workers with less conventional previous work histories and no trade union card who are usually also cheaper to hire.[26]

Horizontal social relations

Previous views on social relations among shop-floor workers in small firms have not always been in agreement. One view is that such relations are closer and more friendly than in comparable large firms. In the more relaxed atmosphere of the small firm, it is argued, people have a greater opportunity to develop face-to-face relations with those with whom they work.[27] On the other hand, others (including those in the Marxist tradition) have argued that frequent contact between worker and employer prevents the formulation of close attachments with fellow workers and the emergence of an awareness of shared interests.[28]

The data from the present research supported the view that peer relations were perceived as somewhat friendlier by the small firm workers than by the workers in the large firms.[29] However, when shop-floor workers were asked whether they regarded any of their workmates as *close* friends, differences between small and large firm workers disappeared and, indeed, a slightly higher proportion of large firm workers claimed to regard a fellow worker as a close friend. A more stringent measure of the quality of these relations was the extent to which close friends were seen outside work. Among small firm workers, nine out of ten saw close friends outside work compared to three-quarters of the large firm workers. But the extent of such relations was related to marital status. Married workers were much less likely to have close friends they saw outside work, so that part of the difference between small and large firm workers disappears when marital state is controlled for, since fewer small firm workers were married.

Since the small firm contains, by definition, fewer workers it will also tend to contain fewer people of similar age, outlook and tastes from the point of view of any particular individual and, therefore may actually be a less likely source of close friends than a large firm. The lower labour stability rates among small firm workers may also be unfavourable to the formation of close personal relations.

Overall, levels of out-of-work contact between shop-floor workers were lower than in some previous studies. For example, Goldthorpe *et al.* reported that 55 per cent of their manual workers had a work-mate they regarded as a close friend[30] which compared to 38 per cent in the present study. What is particularly interesting in this comparison, however, is that Goldthorpe and his colleagues saw the level of out-of-work contacts they found as an indication of a privatised lifestyle. The latter involved a sharp separation of work and non-work lives and low expectations of satisfying social relations with fellow workers. In the present study, the balance of the findings reported above indicates that, if anything, the small firm workers are *more* privatised than their large firm counterparts, suggesting that the idea of the small firm acting as a major source of satisfying social relations — the thrust of Ingham's interpretation — is highly questionable, as is the notion that privatisation is an inevitable adjunct of employment in the large-scale bureaucratic enterprise.

Vertical social relations

As Table 2.1 indicates, there were no apparent relationships between size of firm and workers' perceptions of their relations with first line supervisors. While the small electronics firm workers appeared most enthusiastic about relations with supervisors, the small printing firm workers were the least enthusiastic. If the favourable responses are amalgamated this again produces no consistent size relationship although, if anything, the large firm shop-floor workers appear rather more satisfied overall with their relations with supervisors.

Ingham reported that *all* his small firm workers, without exception, claimed to get on 'very well' or 'quite well' with their supervisors, while among his large firm control sample between 87 per cent and 95 per cent claimed a similar close relationship.[31] Not finding a single small firm worker who felt he got on badly with his supervisor seems, on the face of it, rather implausible and possibly results from the smallness of the sample. Ingham, however, attributed the apparently closer relations between shop-floor workers and supervisors to the expectations and orientations of the small firm workers who, he argued, preferred a 'human relations' style relationship with their supervisors as compared to the large firm workers, whose orientations to work led them to prefer a low frequency of interaction and an affectively neutral relationship with supervisors.[32]

Clearly, this argument is not supported by the findings from the present study but, further, it does not take account of a number of other organisational and industrial sub-cultural differences which may be related to worker–supervisor relations and which, it is argued, provide a fuller interpretation of these relations. As Table 2.1 shows, while overall there are few differences between small and large firm workers when favourable responses are aggregated, there remains a very large difference between the two small firm sub-samples when the responses indicating the highest levels of enthusiasm are compared.

In printing, the shop-floor worker is, ideally, a 'journeyman' or craftsman, a status gained after a long, formal training. In the industrial sub-culture, the journeyman is self-directing and relations with the supervisor should be minimal. The large printing firm department approximates more closely to this since the supervisor has less opportunity to violate this ideal. The department tends to be bigger and the workers are more likely to be highly skilled and thus require less supervision than in the small firm. In the latter, the small size of the typical department throws workers and supervisors together more often constraining the supervisor to violate workers' expectations. The more varied skill levels of workers *and* supervisors in the

Table 2.1
Shop-floor workers' estimate of how well they got on with their first line supervisor

	Small printing firm workers		Small electronics firm workers		Large printing firm workers		Large electronics firm workers		All small firm workers		All large firm workers	
	no.	%	no.	%	no.	%	no.	%	no.	%	no.	%
Very well	14	21.9	27	50.0	17	41.5	17	40.5	41	34.7	34	41.0
Pretty well or fairly well	38	59.4	18	33.3	19	46.3	19	45.2	56	47.5	38	45.8
Sub-total	52	81.2	45	83.3	36	87.8	36	85.7	97	82.2	72	86.8
Not very well	6	9.4	5	9.2	1	2.4	3	7.1	11	9.3	4	4.8
Badly	4	6.2	—	—	—	—	3	7.1	4	3.4	3	3.6
Other/could not state	2	3.1	4	7.4	4	9.8	—	—	6	5.1	4	4.8
Total	64	100.0	54	100.0	41	100.0	42	100.0	118	100.0	83	100.0

Percentages may not add up to 100 because of rounding.

small firm further increases opportunities for interpersonal conflict.

In the electronics industry, on the other hand, worker–supervisor relations are grounded in a very different industrial sub-culture. Shop-floor workers do not, despite the industry's advanced technology, receive much formal training as compared to printing workers. Yet those who work in the industry are very conscious of their connections with science and scientific research. Partly, this is a reflection of the exceptional rate of technological innovation in the industry over the last 30 years.[33] As Burns and Stalker pointed out in one of the few previous studies of social relations in the industry,[34] electronics firms tend to have much less rigid organisational structures and a relative absence of the sharp distinction between shop floor and management typical of manufacturing industry in Britain.

Supervisors in the electronics industry are, on the whole, more qualified and experienced than the workers they supervise, and these considerations are important in promotion to supervisor. Given the less authoritarian and relaxed character of social interaction in the industry, the relationship between the worker and supervisor is much more 'consultative' than in printing: shop-floor workers define the supervisor as a technological resource and defer to his expertise. The ideal relationship here, however, is more likely to be realised in the small firm than the large firm since the larger size of department and wider span of control of the large firm supervisor makes it more difficult for workers and supervisors to achieve this consultative relationship fully.

In other words, size of firm was related to worker–supervisor relations in these two industries but not in terms of workers' orientations. The relationship is a more complex one in which industrial sub-culture meanings interact with organisational constraints related to size. In one instance, the result is rather less happy worker–supervisor relations in the small firm than in the large firm but, in the other, these relations are more successful in the small firm. This interpretation was fully borne out by the reasons given by respondents in the small and large firms for their views on relations with supervisors.

Workers and owner-managers

A second aspect of vertical social relations in the firm — those between shop-floor workers and the owner-manager/director — has often been seen as the most distinctive aspect of social relations in the small firm and is the way in which such relations most profoundly differ from those in large firms. Small firm respondents were initially asked how well they felt they knew the managing director of the firm. As Table 2.2 indicates, overall, rather less than one in three small firm workers felt they knew the managing director of their firm 'very well' and a similar proportion reported a more distant relationship.

Table 2.2
Shop-floor workers' estimate of how well they know the managing director (small firm workers only)

firm workers	Small printing firm workers		Small electronics firm workers		All small firm workers	
	no.	%	no.	%	no.	%
Very well	6	9.4	1	1.8	7	5.9
Fairly well	17	26.6	9	16.7	26	22.0
Sub-total	23	36.0	10	18.5	33	27.9
Not very well	25	39.1	16	29.6	41	34.7
Hardly/not at all	14	21.9	26	48.1	40	33.9
Sub-total	39	61.0	42	77.7	81	68.6
No Response	2	3.1	2	3.7	4	3.4
Total	64	100.0	54	100.0	118	100.0

Percentages may not add up to 100 because of rounding.

This finding is in strong contrast to those of previous studies but, as suggested earlier, Batstone's sample of small firm workers lived in a community where workers and their bosses had more or less strong social relations outside as well as inside work, each reinforcing the other. This was not the case for the present sample. Ingham, on the other hand, did not specifically ask his small firm workers how well they felt they knew their managing director but rather whether they ever spoke to him.

The small firms in the present study often had more than one owner-manager and some workers felt they knew one rather better than the other(s) but the overall strength of social relations between shop-floor workers and the top level of management shown in Table 2.2 held. A particular director might be better known because his managerial function brought him into frequent contact with the particular worker or he had superior social skills as compared to his fellow directors but this variation was never sufficient to alter the general perceptions of a clear social distance between workers and management.

It will be noted that Table 2.2 indicates greater social distance between owner-managers and shop-floor workers in the small electronics firms than in the small printing firms. The reasons for this again appear connected to differences between the industrial sub-cultures. In the electronics industry the greater technological complexity, greater rate of technological change and need to be more market-orientated, constrain owner-managers and directors to concern themselves more with these areas. This leaves less time for interaction with the ordinary shop-floor worker than in an industry like printing where technological and market considerations are more straightforward.

While the present findings suggest that the closeness of social relations between workers and owner-manager/directors in small firms is easily exaggerated, there may well also be a tendency to exaggerate the impersonality of shop-floor worker–management relations in large firms. The present study included only two large firms but it was noticeable that in both there were managers at the level of production manager (that is, either directly above first-level supervisor or one level higher) who had social relations with shop-floor workers at least as close as those between workers and owner-managers in the small firms. In each case, the individual filling the role had considerable social skills and was not averse to using more senior management as scapegoats for unpleasant decisions, thus strengthening relations with shop-floor workers. The fact that the latter often centred their meanings and definitions of work not on the firm as a whole but on the department in which they worked, further strengthened social relations with middle managers. It is also possible that those chosen for this kind of management role are selected on their known human relations skills.

Two further tests of the quality of relations between workers and senior management were provided by questioning workers on the extent to which they felt management kept them informed about how the firm was doing and about their willingness to transcend the cash nexus relationship by seeking management help or advice on personal problems. In both instances the findings were entirely in accord with the earlier findings on social distance between workers and management and the influences of industrial sub-cultures.

A final indication on social relations between employers and shop-floor workers was provided by data from a question asking the latter whether they viewed industry in 'teamwork' or 'conflict' terms. This question has been asked in a number of studies of manual workers.[35] As can be seen from Table 2.3, overall, there is little difference between the main small and large firm samples on this question in the present study.

This result again goes against conventional views of small firm worker–management relations or the alleged special involvement or identification of the small firm worker with the firm and management suggested in some previous sociological interpretations such as that of Ingham. Yet is replicates the similar findings of Batstone[36] who also found little difference between his small and large firm samples on this issue. He did, however, find a much higher level of agreement with the teamwork view as compared to that among the present sample. The latter, in fact, offered one of the lowest levels of support for a teamwork view among the studies where this question has been put but, as Cotgrove and Vanplew have shown,[37] agreement with a teamwork view may vary sharply with geographical location of the establishment, suggesting that wider community influences may be of considerable importance here. This would again be consistent with Batstone's higher level of general support for a teamwork view in a community with a strong traditional element in its social relations.

Again, there are some interesting differences between the sub-samples in Table 2.3. Unexpectedly, perhaps, the large printing firm workers, the most unionised sub-sample, were also the most prone to choose a teamwork view of industry while the large electronics firm workers, of whom under half were trade union members, offered the lowest level of support. The interpretation suggested for this is that the large printing firm workers felt they were on more equal terms with management *because* they had the backing of a strong union. Instead of seeing teamwork in terms of a consensus on the aims of everybody involved in the firm — the conventional meaning attributed to this view by researchers — these workers recognised differences of interests of workers and management but felt that their mutual participation in the enterprise could still be viewed in teamwork terms on the basis of the relative bargaining power of each.

Not only were the small firm workers' responses on the teamwork view of worker–management relations sandwiched between those of the large firm sub-samples, but they also displayed a relationship to age. Younger small firm workers favoured a teamwork view to a greater extent than respondents aged 30 and over. Among those aged 29 or under, 26.8 per cent chose a conflict view as compared to 40.4 per cent of those aged 30 and over. But since, as noted earlier, the small firms contained a much higher proportion of younger workers than the large firms, this implies that, if the age distributions of the small and large firm work-forces had been more nearly the same, then we might have expected a lower proportion of small firm workers to select a teamwork view.

Thus, these findings, supported by those from Batstone's research,

Table 2.3

Views on worker–management relations in industry (shop-floor workers only)

	Small printing firm workers		Small electronics firm workers		Large printing firm workers		Large electronics firm workers		All small firm workers		All large firm workers	
	no.	%	no.	%	no.	%	no.	%	no.	%	no.	%
A firm is like a football side — it is a team and good teamwork means success which is to everybody's advantage	34	53.1	33	61.1	29	70.7	18	42.9	67	56.8	47	56.6
Teamwork in industry is impossible – because employers and men are really on opposite sides	26	40.6	13	24.1	10	24.4	23	54.8	39	33.0	33	39.8
No response/other	4	6.2	8	14.8	2	4.9	1	2.4	12	10.2	3	3.6
Total	64	100.0	54	100.0	41	100.0	42	100.0	118	100.0	83	100.0

Percentages may not add up to 100 because of rounding.
Note: Respondents were given a card with the two statements printed on it and asked which came closest to their own view of industrial relations.

strongly suggest that, contrary to the implications of Ingham's argument and other writings such as the Bolton Report, small firm workers are no more likely to see worker–management relations in harmonious terms than workers in large firms.

Conclusion

The present study shows that to construct a more adequate sociological interpretation of the small enterprise a consideration of its capitalistic basis and the industrial sub-culture in which the firm is located is required in addition to the more social-psychological concern with the orientations of the actors involved. The previous overemphasis on the latter has simply led to interpretations which, consciously or otherwise, have reinforced the more widespread romantic view of the small firm offered in the media and by those with a strong ideological interest in promoting the small firm.

References

1. See, for example, G.K. Ingham, *Size of Industrial Organization and Worker Behaviour,* Cambridge University Press, Cambridge, 1970; and E.F. Schumacher, *Small is Beautiful, a Study of Economics as if People Mattered,* Blond and Briggs, London, 1973; J.E. Bolton, *Report of the Committee of Inquiry on Small Firms* (Bolton Report), Cmnd 4811, HMSO, London, 1971.
2. Schumacher, *Small is Beautiful.*
3. Bolton Report, p. 21.
4. Ingham, *Size,* Chapter 3, especially pp. 46–53.
5. Ingham sees this orientation as well exemplified by the workers in J. Goldthorpe, D. Lockwood, F. Bechhofer and J. Platt, *The Affluent Worker: Industrial Attitudes and Behaviour,* Cambridge University Press, Cambridge, 1968.
6. Ingham, *Size,* p. 38.
7. Ibid., p. 39.
8. E.V. Batstone, 'Deference and the Ethos of Small Town Capitalism' in M. Bulmer (ed.), *Working Class Images of Society,* Routledge and Kegan Paul, London, 1975; and 'Aspects of Stratification in a Community Context: A Study of Class Attitudes and the Size Effect', PhD thesis, University of Wales, 1969.
9. Batstone, 'Deference', especially pp. 122–4.
10. Batstone, 'Aspects of Stratification' pp. 112–13 where he also cites

I.C. Cannon, 'Ideology and the Occupational Community: A Study of Compositors', *Sociology,* vol. 1, no. 2 (1967), pp. 165–185; and S.M. Lipset, M. Trow and J.S. Coleman: *Union Democracy: The Internal Politics of the International Typographical Union,* Free Press, Glencoe, 1956, as reporting similar findings.

11. Batstone, 'Aspects of Stratification', p. 167.

12. Batstone, 'Deference', especially pp. 127–8.

13. This assumption has been severely questioned in H. Newby: 'Paternalism and Capitalism' in R. Scase (ed.): *Industrial Society: Class, Cleavage and Control,* Allen and Unwin, London, 1977.

14. Ingham, *Size,* Appendix B, questions 6 and 7, p. 157 and questions 3 and 4, p. 162.

15. *Report of the Census of Production 1973, General Printing and Publishing,* HMSO, London, 1977, Table 4.

16. R. Price and G.S. Bain: 'Union Growth Revisited: 1948–1974 in Perspective', *British Journal of Industrial Relations,* vol. XIV, no. 3 (1976), Table 3, p. 342.

17. For brief histories of the electronics industry see T. Wilson, 'The Electronics Industry' in D. Burn (ed.): *The Structure of British Industry,* Cambridge University Press, Cambridge, 1964, vol. II, pp. 130–83; and G.C. Allen, *British Industries and Their Organization,* Longman, London, 1954 (5th edn, 1970), Chapter 9.

18. The problems of defining the electronics industry are discussed in: *Annual Statistical Survey of the Electronics Industry,* National Economic Development Office, 1975, p. 5. The equivalent publication for 1972, Appendix I, has a longer discussion. For the reasons mentioned later in this paragraph, all the firms in the present study were in the sections of the industry covered by: *Report of the Census of Production 1973, Radio, Radar and Electronic Capital Goods* and *Report of the Census of Production, 1973, Scientific and Industrial Instruments Systems,* HMSO, London, 1977. The level of unionisation in the electronics industry is difficult to estimate because no trade union exclusively recruits members in the industry and because no official data exist on the distribution of union membership by industry. However, it is very unlikely that it reaches the average level in manufacturing industry. See the general discussion of industrial variations in union membership in Price and Bain, 'Union Growth Revisited'.

19. Ingham, *Size,* p. 65; Batstone, 'Aspects of Stratification', p. 10.

20. Bolton Report, Table 1.1, p. 3.

21. See the data on size of establishment distributions in the electronics industry in Ingham the *Census of Production* reports above.

22. Much of literature on the psychological and social characteristics of owner-managers is reviewed in M.F.R. Kets de Vries, 'The Entrepreneurial Personality: A Person at the Crossroads', *Journal of Management Studies*, vol. 14, no. 1 (February 1977). See also M.J.K. Stanworth and J. Curran, *Management Motivation in the Smaller Business*, Gower Press, Epping, 1973, especially Chapter 2; and C.W. Golby and G. Johns, *Attitude and Motivation*, Committee of Inquiry on Small Firms Research Report No. 7, Cmnd. 4811, HMSO, London, 1971.

23. Kets de Vries, 'Entrepreneurial Personality', p. 57.

24. Batstone's research formed part of the larger study of Banbury reported in M. Stacey, E. Batstone, C. Bell and A. Murcott, *Power, Persistence and Change, A Second Study of Banbury*, Routledge and Kegan Paul, London, 1975. The electoral register sample was the main sample of 1449 people interviewed in this larger study.

25. Trade unions are also more likely to be present in large firms and to insist that new workers have had a specific previous work history.

26. The exact differences in earnings levels in small and large firms are not easy to arrive at but it is widely accepted that small firm workers earn less. The Bolton Report, p. 21, suggests that the difference 'is of the order of 20 per cent'. See also Table 2.XX, p. 22 of the Report.

27. See, for example, Acton Society Trust, *Size and Morale, Part II, A Further Study of Attendance at Work in Large and Small Units*, London, 1957, p. 27; and Ingham, *Size*, p. 38.

28. See for example, D. Lockwood: 'Sources of Variation in Working Class Images of Society', *Sociological Review*, vol. 14 (November 1966), pp. 249–67; F. Parkin: 'Working Class Conservatives: A Theory of Political Deviance', *British Journal of Sociology*, vol. XVIII, no. 3, (September 1967), pp. 278–90. See also K. Marx: *Capital*, vol. I, Chapter XIV, Lawrence and Wishart, London, 1970.

29. It is recognised that there are problems in comparing responses concerning qualities of human relations since these depend to some extent on respondents' expectations about such relations. However, this finding should be considered in relation to the further findings in this section.

30. Goldthorpe, Lockwood, Bechhofer and Platt, *Affluent Worker*, pp. 55–7. Of course, an allowance must be made for the fact that the sample in the present study almost certainly lived over a wider geographical area than the Luton workers, making out-of-work contacts more difficult. The present workers also changed jobs more often but the sample of Goldthorpe *et al.* were all married which, in the present study, reduced out-of-work contacts as compared to the level among unmarried workers.

31. Ingham, *Size,* Table 8.8, p. 102.

32. Ibid., pp. 102–4.

33. See on this, Wilson, 'Electronics Industry'; and Allen, *British Industries.*

34. T. Burns and G.M. Stalker, *The Management of Innovation,* Tavistock, London, 1961.

35. See, for example, Goldthorpe, Lockwood, Bechhofer and Platt, *Affluent Worker;* D. Wedderburn and R. Crompton, *Workers' Attitudes and Technology,* Cambridge University Press, Cambridge, 1972; S. Hill, *The Dockers,* Heinemann, London, 1976; S. Cotgrove and C. Vanplew, 'Technology, Class and Politics: the Case of the Process Workers', *Sociology,* vol. 6 (May 1972); and R. Brown and P. Brannen, 'Social Relations Among Shipbuilding Workers: a Preliminary Statement', *Sociology,* vol 4 (May 1970). The question was also put to respondents in Batstone's study of small firm workers in Banbury. As Ramsay has pointed out, there are problems in interpreting respondents' answers to this question but in the present instance the important finding is of the similarities in the responses of the small and large firm samples and their implications for accepted views of worker-management relations in small firms; see H. Ramsay, 'Research Note, Firms and Football Teams', *British Journal of Industrial Relations,* vol. XIII, no. 3 (1975).

36. Batstone, *'Aspects of Stratification',* p. 74.

37. Cotgrove and Vanplew, 'Technology, Class and Politics'.

3 Industrial Relations in the Small Firm*

ALISTAIR RAINNIE AND MICHAEL SCOTT

The study of industrial relations in small firms presents a paradox. On the one hand, we have a view going back to the early days of the Industrial Revolution which associates small enterprises with the term 'sweatshop', the location of the worst excesses of exploitation and degradation of the worker. Through the 1950s and 1960s the drive towards the concentration of British industry into ever larger units to achieve technical and managerial economies of scale enhanced the view of the small enterprise as anachronistic, inefficient and belonging to an earlier age. One consequence of this was that the smaller firm became unfashionable as a location for organisational research, and in some respects became invisible.

The re-emergence of the small enterprise in a quite different guise, summed up in Schumacher's phrase 'small is beautiful', can be dated to the late 1960s and particularly to the publication of the Bolton Report (Bolton 1971: 21).

* The authors would like to acknowledge the support of the Economic and Social Research Council, Grant HR 8603, for work on related issues, on which this chapter draws extensively.

In many respects the small firm provides a better environment for the employee than is possible in most large firms. Although physical working conditions may sometimes be inferior in small firms, most people prefer to work in a small group where communication presents fewer problems: the employee in a small firm can more easily see the relation between what he is doing and the objectives and performance as a whole. Where management is more direct and flexible, working rules can be varied to suit the individual. Each employee is also likely to have a more varied role with a chance to participate in several kinds of work and better opportunities to learn and widen his experience. No doubt mainly as a result of this, the turnover of staff in small firms is very low and strikes and other kinds of industrial dispute are relatively infrequent.

The decade following the publication of the Bolton Report saw the development of a largely untested view of the small enterprise as 'harmonious' in terms of its labour relations. Indeed, it can be argued that one of the reasons behind the shift in government policy in favour of regeneration of the small firm sector is the latter's apparent success in dealing with those industrial relations problems, and especially strikes, to which large organisations have appeared particularly prone.

For the drive towards merger and concentration of the 1950s and 1960s had failed in two significant respects: firstly it failed in its attempt to make 'British' capital large enough and strong enough not only to compete at an international level, but also to survive a world-wide economic recession; and secondly, because it was in the large-scale, core sections of the economy that the 'problems' of autonomous work-place union organisation (the informal system berated by the Donovan Commission) were most evident.

The paradoxical view of industrial relations in small firms appearing on the one hand to be the product of the sweatshop, and on the other of being 'harmonious', can be resolved if we examine the source of the currently fashionable view that 'labour relations are less of a problem in small firms than large' (Bannock 1981: 10), and if we clarify exactly what we mean by industrial relations.

The conventional wisdom of harmony

There is no doubt that the ideology of paternalist capitalism runs deep in our culture, and sees the individual entrepreneur as folk hero (see Figure 3.1). There is a whole genre of 'let us now praise famous businessmen' texts from Samuel Smiles in the mid-nineteenth century

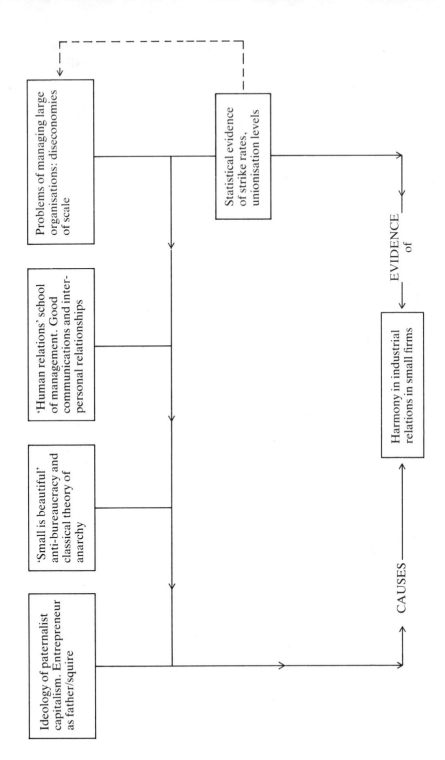

Figure 3.1 Sources of the conventional view of harmony

onwards. The use of the family as a role model for other collectivities in society has an even longer tradition: there is therefore a cultural imperative for those in charge of work organisations to behave as if they were responsible 'fathers'. Leaving aside reality, there is no doubt that this ideology has been unquestioningly accepted and research into the attitudes of the owner-managers of small firms typically produces self-images of the caring paternalist (Bolton 1971; Scott 1980; Bannock 1981). The impact of this ideology may be to blind the owner-manager to the very possibility that he has industrial relations problems: many small enterprises are indeed 'family' firms, and for the others there is often a significantly higher degree of personal involvement by the owner-manager than would be the case for a manager in a large organisation.

A second strand is associated with the philosophy of 'small is beautiful'. In its original formulation (Schumacher 1974) this involves a retreat from the dehumanising developments of large-scale western industrialisation. The alternative technology movement (Dickson 1974) stresses the improvements in the quality of life consequent on a return to smaller-scale and culturally appropriate technologies. These views stress self-sufficiency and the return of control to the individual within a small group, and address issues of alienation not from the Marxist but rather from a classical anarchist standpoint. A restructuring of industrial life (for example, through the development of 'cottage electronics') involving a shift of power nearer to the individual is central to this view of the world.

A third strand derives from the influence of social psychology on management theories, and can be said to involve the depoliticisation of work-place relationships. A typical example would be the human relations approach to management which stresses the importance of good inter-personal relationships and the need for open communications within organisations. These imperatives stem from the work of Elton Mayo (See Roethlisberger and Dickson 1949) and his followers, who emphasise the role of the small face-to-face work group in the determining of work-place behaviour. The underlying assumption is that man's inherent social needs cannot be satisfied in large-scale, bureaucratised, impersonal settings, which give rise to 'feelings' of anomie and alienation. This essentially psychological view of work life plays down power relationships and sees conflict as pathological.

It was particularly the latter views which were influential in informing the views of the Bolton Committee. However, it was specifically the work of Ingham (1970) upon which the committee drew heavily. Ingham's work stresses non-bureaucratic relationships, ease of communication, the fact that 'informal organisations at work and more extensive management–worker interaction in the small firms provided structural conditions for a relatively high level of moral involvement' (Ingham 1970: 143), leading to the substitution by workers of high non-economic gains for low economic rewards.

Together, these strands form a powerful rationale for the encouragement by government of small businesses. The independence and individual responsibility of the entrepreneur are seen as an example whereby a solution can be found to 'the institutional, attitudinal and cultural ills of present-day western societies' (Scase and Goffee 1980: 11). Perhaps more explicitly, the ideological content can be seen in Edward Du Cann's address to the 1975 Conservative Party Conference when he said that small businesses 'were the seedcorn of our future prosperity, lively, ingenious, self-reliant, an anti-Marxist barrier, conservatism in practice and the true picture of free enterprise, honourable, patriotic and acceptable' (Jones 1980: 138). The image of the folk hero, the individual entrepreneur, with his retinue or family of followers pursuing common goals in harmony is a powerful one, especially in the context of a culture which portrays the large impersonal bureaucracy as the location of 'mindless' industrial conflicts.

The key question is, of course, whether there is any truth in the foregoing. The answer is that statistical evidence can be compiled which indicates a relationship between certain kinds of industrial action and size of organisation. Table 3.1 shows the breakdown of industrial action by manual workers by size of establishment. It can be seen for example that an establishment with over 1000 full-time employees is nearly three times as likely to have experienced industrial action as one employing between 50 and 99 workers.

There is an underlying assumption behind the quoting of these figures that workers in small enterprises are less concerned about

Table 3.1
Establishments experiencing any type of industrial action, by number of manual workers

Size of establishment	1–9	10–24	25–49	50–99	100–199	200–499	500–999	1000+
Percentage experiencing any form of industrial action	2	8	13	27	33	50	74	77

Source: Daniel and Millward (1983: 218)

Table 3.2
Proportion of establishments that recognised manual unions in
relation to independence (per cent)

	Total	1–24	25–49	50–99	100–199	200+
			(Private sector only)			
		Number of manual workers employed				
All establishments	50	25	43	63	78	91
Independent establishments	31	16	24	50	66	67
Establishments that were part of a group	58	28	55	68	81	92

Source: Daniel and Millward (1983: 25)

organising themselves to protect their interest than their counterparts in large-scale units. Low rates of unionisation (Table 3.2) are therefore taken as a proxy measure of harmony. One should of course be most careful not to confuse correlation with causality. (There is a statistical correlation between the number of fire engines attending a fire, and the amount of damage caused by that fire. No one would make the mistake of saying that fire engines *cause* fires; yet the correlation between size of firm and strike proneness and unionisation rates, *is* all taken as causal.) More significantly, other statistics, which would equally act as proxy measures, are often neglected as evidence for potential conflict and these include figures for rates of pay, incidents of accidents, labour turnover and references to industrial tribunals for unfair dismissal.

The definition of industrial relations

The selective use of statistics to support the notion of harmony in labour relations in small enterprises gives a clue to the way that the conventional wisdom has developed. Put simply, our view of industrial relations has been heavily oriented towards large-scale settings. Industrial relations has been seen to be about collectivities such as trade unions and employers' associations; about the rules and practice of collective bargaining; and about the breakdown in these formal structures. It has focused on large-scale settings and the key indicators it has sought have inevitably been concerned with rates of unionisation and measures of overt conflict activity such as strikes. Moreover, and this has something to do with the ease of access to industrial organisations, research in industrial relations has been heavily biased towards settings which have been male dominated and typically in heavy engineering technologies. In short, our knowledge of industrial relations is especially coloured by large-scale manufacturing activities.

From this standpoint, it is relatively easy to contrast the apparently 'better' situations of small organisations. Smallness is itself seen as the determining variable. And smallness fits with the ideology already described. It is our contention, therefore, that an understanding of industrial relations in small enterprises requires a fundamental recasting of the above view of industrial relations. Put simply, we must take a broader view of the subject matter. Such a wider definition would see industrial relations as being concerned with 'the process of control over the employment relationship' (Palmer 1983: 2). This definition allows us to examine the whole of the labour process, and moreover to deal with settings in the service sector, and in particular with those parts of the economy which employ women, the young, and racial minorities. This opens up a whole new set of factors which need to be considered if we are really to understand the processes of industrial relations in firms of all sizes. Figure 3.2 maps out the key items necessary for this analysis.

The labour process

The employer's interest in the employment relationship is a by-product of his pursuit of more primary objectives (Palmer 1983: 35). Since these objectives require the effort of employees, it follows that the employer has to recruit staff, and build an organisation to manage and control that staff, so that the employer's plans are carried through. Simply going to the labour market to buy labour power is insufficient, for this is merely the purchase of labour potential. In order to turn this potential into something of value to the employer, labour needs to be directed, organised and controlled (Palmer 1983). Put simply, the employer's primary objectives are the extraction of surplus value from individual workers. For Marx (1976: 769), this was the defining characteristic of capitalism:

> Labour power is not purchased under this system for the purpose of satisfying the personal needs of the buyer, either by its service or through its product. The aim of the buyer is the valorisation of his capital, the production of commodities which contain more labour than he paid for, and therefore contain a portion of value which costs him nothing and is nevertheless realised through the sale of those commodities. The production of surplus value or the making of profits is the absolute law of this mode of production.

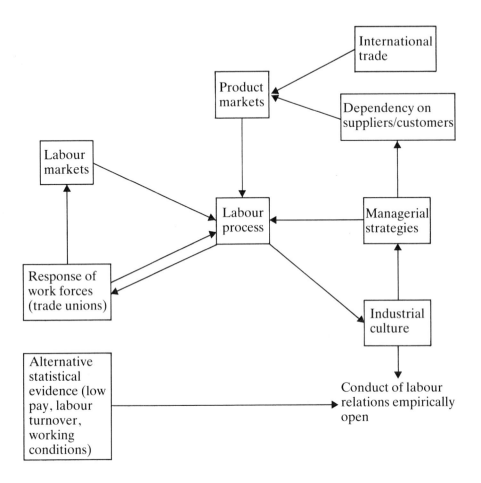

Figure 3.2   Factors involved in an alternative view of industrial
relations in small firms

What follows from this is that 'the capital–labour relation is antagon-istic because it is based on exploitation. Exploitation is, in turn, the result of the need of the capitalist to extract production from the worker such that the value of the product is greater than the value of the wage' (Edwards 1983: 6A). The fact that the labour process is objectively exploitative underlies the following analysis, although with the caution that 'the fact a relationship is exploitative says nothing directly about the ways in which exploitation will be experienced or made effective' (Edwards 1983: 9).

The study of industrial relations in small firms has therefore to take account of the following:

(a) the development of the labour process within and between different industrial sectors;
(b) the operation of the labour market;
(c) the development of dependency relationships between small and large firms with implications for the range and nature of managerial strategies;
(d) the response of workers to the labour process and the special difficulties which collective action encounters in small firms.

Explanations for labour relations in small firms, we would argue, can only be found in the interrelationships of the above factors, in conjunction with wider issues external to the work-place including class relations in general, and industry specific factors including the role of international trade. From this it will be clear that any attempt to treat the small firm sector as homogeneous will be doomed to failure, a point to which we shall return later.

The labour process comprises the various methods used to convert purchased labour power into valuable work for the employer (Palmer 1983: 39). The revival of interest in this process begins with the reanalysis of the work of F.W. Taylor particularly by Harry Braverman (1974) (see also Thompson 1983). Braverman's thesis, simply, is that work has been deskilled, using techniques developed by Taylor and others, as a deliberate strategy used by employers to enable them to hire cheap semi- or unskilled workers and exercise tighter controls over how the work is performed. Before the advent of Taylorism, workers controlled their own work methods and had skills which they could sell to employers as a valuable asset. Scientific management enabled this to be broken down ('the removal of intelligence from the shop floor'). The newly designed jobs could be performed by cheaper labour which could be hired and fired as required, and whose costs could be precisely matched to rewards.

Braverman's work has been extensively criticised on the grounds that he exaggerates the universality of this employer strategy, and that he neglects the role of labour itself in the structuring of the labour process (Elger 1979). However, Braverman has directed our attention to the dynamics, and the dialectical nature, of the labour process, points which have been taken up by subsequent writers. Edwards (1979) and others (e.g., Kyneston-Reeves and Woodward 1970) have suggested a simple developmental typology of managerial strategies to control the labour process:

1   Personal control. The employer personally organises and allocates work and imposes checks through direct supervision.
2   Bureaucratic control. Based on impersonal rules and a system of administrative controls, regulating recruitment, hours of work, effort levels, wages, etc. It is further possible to distinguish (Littler 1982: Chapter 4) between bureaucratic control over personnel policy (hiring, firing and rewarding) and bureaucratic control over task performance (the design of jobs and direction and monitoring of work). Taylorism is a typical example of the latter.
3   Technological control. Impersonal control based not on rules but on mechanical means, for example, in the design of machinery and automated process plant.

For Braverman, the increasing complexity of work organisations was sufficient to bring forth the development of Taylorist principles. Other writers, for example Elger (1979), argue that it was a major crisis in the extraction of surplus value which constituted the driving force behind attempts to reorganise production through the intensification of labour and through technical reorganisation. Burawoy (1979) contrasts the labour process of early competitive capitalism with that under the later monopoly capitalism. Throughout there is a need for employers both to secure and to obscure the generation of surplus values. However, in the former stage attempts were made to use coercion, for instance by tighter personal control to speed up output. Whilst this may secure increased surplus value it also generates tensions since it does not obscure the process. At the later stage, at least some employers are able to provide what Burawoy calls 'consent producing measures' at the point of work, such as the provision of limited autonomy, careers ladders, and so on. These can successfully obscure the extraction of surplus value.

Although there are problems with both the simple typologies of Edwards' and Burawoy's notion of consent, they should alert us to the need to be aware of the variety of experiences which exist in relation to the labour process. Whilst personal control is typically found in small organisations, there is in fact nothing determining about size. Any understanding of industrial relations in small firms has therefore to take account of the empirical realities of the labour process in the particular organisation. This will of course include the age and previous history of the organisation including the response of the work-force (Rainnie 1984).

Segmented labour markets

Attempts have been made to link the development of the labour process with the operation of the labour market (Edwards 1979). Edwards argues that 'capitalists have attempted to organise production in such a way as to minimise workers' opportunities for resistance and even alter workers' perceptions of the desirability of opposition. Work has been organised then, to contain conflict' (Edwards 1979: 16). The development of large monopolistic organisations enabled the creation of internal labour markets in which workers are typically recruited to the large firm and then experience the whole of their working life within that or similar organisations: they do not enter the general labour market again. Monopoly profits enable the large organisation to provide better working conditions and rewards, including career progression, and at the same time locking in the skills acquired by the work-force. Whether or not this was a conscious conspiracy on the part of employers (a basis for criticism by Rubery (1980)), the other side of this coin is that in those sectors of the economy where the drive to concentration and centralisation into monopoly structures did not have immediate effect, in those sectors particularly dominated by smaller enterprises, workers typically remain under simple control and do not have the benefits accorded to those employed in internal labour market situations. The distinction is made between primary sector and secondary sectors both within, and between, firms. The primary sector refers to internal labour markets. The secondary sector comprises the rest of the work-force, including those persons who are more open to exploitation, for example women, racial minorities, and young people. They are typically employed in smaller organisations (a point made clear but misinterpreted in terms of 'work orientations' by the Bolton Committee). Most importantly, as Curran and Stanworth (1979) have shown, it is difficult for an individual to move from one sector to another, and in particular entry to the more favoured primary sector is effectively closed after the initial rung of a ladder, access to which is anyway controlled by educational and training barriers. For workers in the majority of small firms, therefore, the reality of the labour market is that they face lifetime careers in less well-rewarded jobs with greater chances of unemployment.

The extent to which any small firm can operate its own internal market is of course empirically open. A few small businesses, typically in areas of high technology and generating high levels of profit, may indeed be able to generate internal markets. The majority of small businesses are however unlikely to fit this thrusting, dynamic, entrepreneurial image. In particular, at any time there will be small firms suffering decline, as they age (Boswell 1973: 121) or as they face new competition (Scott and Rainnie 1982). These situations are likely to result in downward pressure on wages and working conditions and the creation of 'sweatshops' (Turner *et al.* 1977).

Dependency and managerial prerogative

There is a link between the operation of the labour market and the development of the labour process, as they affect small firms, in that management style and the circumstances within which a particular firm operates are inextricably linked. It has been argued that the 'world view of the owner manager has been repeatedly found to stress independence, antipathy towards large external organisations and a dislike of theory as opposed to practice' (Curran and Stanworth 1979: 427). Scase (1982) in discussing the work of Poulantzas (1975) argues that small firms in the modern economy can fulfil a number of functions:

> They often operate, for example, in sectors characterised by low profits and high risks, and those which 'service' large corporations. They may also function as a 'staging post in the process of subjecting labour-power to monopoly capital', and as a means whereby prices may be set at a level which allows monopoly capital larger profit margins because of its cheaper production costs (Scase 1982: 154).

In general this calls into question the supposed independence of the small business owner. Scase quotes Bechhofer and Elliott (1981) as arguing that 'small capital is menaced from above and below . . . in all circumstances it is a dependent stratum, dependent first and foremost on the dominant groups and institutions. It is their decisions, their interests that do most to affect the size and circumstances of the stratum.' The relationship between 'dominant groups and institutions' not only affects the size and circumstances of the stratum, but also the conduct of industrial relations within the particular firm. The Commission on Industrial Relations (1974: 7), for example, has commented that:

> The degree of dependence of a small firm on a larger can be a further factor in its industrial relations. It can bring with it considerable risks and uncertainties for the small firm which is rarely in a strong bargaining position, but it can also bring economic security and stability. It can also entail an upheaval in management's approach, depending on the demands made by the large firm . . . In some cases links of this nature are not unlike those between a parent and subsidiary company.

Friedman (1977) has argued that a high degree of dependency means that the small owner-manager cannot afford to allow any large section of the labour force the degree of latitude available to the manager in a large firm. In other words, management style will be limited to the control of the adaptability of labour through close supervision and the allowing of minimal responsibility — a managerial style that Friedman characterises as direct control, and which contrasts with the granting of 'responsible autonomy' to workers in primary sector organisations. Direct control is described as an attempt to 'limit the scope for labour power to vary by coercive threats, close supervision and minimising individual worker responsibility . . . [and] . . . to limit its particularly harmful effects and treats workers as though they were machines' (Friedman 1977: 78).

Friedman's hypothesis is *not* directly concerned with small business but simply any business in a dependent relationship. However, recent work on the clothing industry (Rainnie 1983) would suggest that small firms in that sector, at least, exhibit all the symptoms that Friedman analyses. This study quotes one manager of a small clothing firm on the subject of his relationship with Marks and Spencers as saying 'when you've got all your eggs in one basket, and they pull out, you've lost your contracts. They've got you and they know it.' This analysis of what has been described as 'the western world's most tightly controlled factory-to-shop system' (*Sunday Times*, 19 June 1983) highlights the intense competition between suppliers to retain the desperately sought after contracts from large retail outlets. Competition between the retailers intensifies the pressure on small suppliers, both forces bringing pressure to bear on prices. Clothing production is relatively labour-intensive. Therefore, firms can only survive by keeping wage costs down, relying on cheap female labour and brooking no interference in work systems. This study showed how in particular management actively resisted any union interference in the bonus system. Although espousing a belief in the family atmosphere in their business, managerial style was found to be highly authoritarian. For example, women watching a needle all day had to put their hands up before being allowed off the line to go to the toilet, and no talking other than to a supervisor was allowed. Yet this industry is not perceived as having 'labour problems', and is relatively strike-free.

The extent to which any particular management will be under competitive pressure will again be empirically open. However, decline and competitive pressure have been found to have a direct effect on industrial relations. Turner *et al.* (1977) found an inverse relationship between the size of a plant's share of its products market and its provision of welfare and fringe benefits, and a direct relationship between market share and incidence of days lost from disputes. The authors concluded that 'the degree of competition to which establishments were exposed . . . imposed limits on the power of managements to offer benefits to or concede claims from their employees' (Turner *et al.* 1977: 53). They go on to conclude that despite the relationship between size of market share and strike incidence, 'the biggest single factor in the differing dispute experience of firms relates to the circumstances (historical, institutional and economic . . .) of the particular industries in which they operate, rather than the qualities of particular managements' (Turner *et al.* 1977: 54).

Working in a small firm

There has been justifiable disagreement with the utopian view of happy small business families. The Commission on Industrial Relations called into question both the ease of communications, given the highly individualistic nature of small businessmen and the effectiveness of such communications as did actually take place. Communications tend to be *one* way, because, as the report said of small businessmen, 'it is not in their nature to consult' (CIR 1974: 31).

Nash (1980) has stressed that the team spirit notion is usually only expressed by those looking from the top; and that the views of owner-managers tend towards the high unitarist end of the spectrum. The argument of the employee then is that *he* is 'just as much in need of safeguards as anybody else. Often he is more vulnerable than workers in larger concerns since his firm is less likely to be unionised and he has no support in raising matters directly with the employer . . . [the owner] may resent interference in the running of something that he regards as his own possession. Such an employer may have the interest of his employees at heart, but he personally is not necessarily the best judge of them' (Henderson and Johnson 1974: 31).

However, in terms of the capital – labour relation, matters may not be so clear cut. The experience of working in a small firm *may* be different from that in a large firm.

Murray quotes an apprentice in a tiny engineering firm in Turin as saying 'here, they exploit you, but you're part of town, your place. You're treated badly, slapped around, but in that place, you see yourself in the work you do' (Murray 1983: 94). Closer to home, the *Financial Times,* in a report on the dispute between the National Graphical Association and Eddie Shah's newspaper group, quoted one of Mr Shah's workers as saying 'I know it sounds corny but we are a family firm and people seem to want to work hard . . . We have regular meetings. Eddie's door is always open for anyone who wants to talk. He might swear at you sometimes but he's very popular' (*Financial Times* 2 December 1983).

Paternalism is a powerful pervading influence in such firms, coupled with a strong motivation on the manager's part to resist any incursion into areas of managerial prerogative. 'It is factory despotism without the large factory and implies the reproduction of the mass, but non-collective, worker at a higher stage of the real subordination of labour to capital where the labour process is fragmented between many small production units, or into the minute division of labour between outworkers and artisans who supervize their own exploitation' (Murray 1983: 94).

Now this should not be taken as arguing that elements of paternalistic control and worker compliance combine to halt all manifestations of labour–capital conflict. However it does mean that there are serious implications regarding the limits and possibilities of trade union organisation in small firms.

Trade unionism in small firms

Trade unionism is not absent from small firms, it is simply less prevalent than in large firms. Table 3.2 showed that in 50 per cent of independent establishments with 50–99 employees trade unions are recognised. These are not inconsiderable numbers, but they are much lower than those for large-scale industry and they pose the question 'why'?

John Edmonds, General Secretary of the GMBATU addressing the 1983 Conference of the Institute of Personnel Management, argued that 'the trend towards smaller plants with fewer people doing similar jobs and towards white collar rather than manual work meant both a reduction in traditional labour solidarity and an increase in the pressure of work on union officials' (*Financial Times* 22 October 1983).

There are two factors at play in this statement. Firstly, it identifies a move to decentralisation as large companies increasingly contract out all but their core activities, and the pressure that this brings on management to resist any interference, for example by trade unions. Secondly, it is far easier for unions to deal with a large number of workers in one place, rather than the same number scattered over many small places where the cost and logistics involved are seen to be prohibitive (Rainnie 1983).

The prevalence of high labour turnover in some industries characterised by small firms can cause problems for unions in that 'workers who formed the core of nascent collective challenges to managerial control tended to leave rather than pursue the challenge' (Edwards and Scullion 1982: 328). This abandonment of trade unionism to its fate can actually be reinforced by the activities of trade unions towards some of their members, in particular women.

It has already been noted that women tend to be over-represented in small firms, and it is now becoming more widely accepted that unions have a poor record as far as women's rights and women's issues are concerned (Coote and Kellner 1980). A study of small clothing firms (Rainnie 1983) has concluded that apathy towards the union and the resulting low levels of union organisation were due to the following factors:

(a) the weakness of the union in question, both objectively and in terms of the perceptions of its members;
(b) the isolation of shop stewards from the union structure;
(c) the negative attitude of male full-time officers to female shop stewards;
(d) the difficulties women have in combining their dual role of wife/mother and worker with active trade unionism.

Pollert (1979; 1981) has concluded that in these circumstances women do not need bossing because they have got their hands tied anyway, 'tied by the incorporation of trade unionism into capital through a complex web of centralised procedures which were as distant as the stars and filtered their effects through an invisible unknown bureaucracy. Power and decisions were somewhere "out there" never in the factory let alone on the shop floor' (Pollert 1979). These feelings can only be exacerbated by working in a factory that is deemed too small to warrant much attention by the union officialdom.

Conclusion

By now it ought to be obvious that any attempt to seek a monocausal explanation for the apparent labour quiescence in small firms is doomed from the start. What we have sought to demonstrate is that clues exist to a more meaningful analysis of industrial relations in small firms. This involves:

(a) an awareness of the labour process;
(b) an awareness of the industry-specific culture of each setting;
(c) an awareness of the heterogeneity of the small firms sector.

If one accepts that the process of extraction of surplus value means that the capitalist labour process is inherently antagonistic, at least in terms of the capital–labour relation, then one has to explain why this objective antagonism does not translate directly into subjective, perceived antagonism on the part of those who suffer under it, that is, the work-force.

There is a debate as to whether worker consent to the operation of the capitalist labour process is manufactured solely within the work-place (Burawoy 1979) or conversely that the 'arenas of influence and control may be the school, the family and other non-work social institutions, such that workers come to the factory gates prepared to contribute effort in terms of customary standards and even beyond the bounds of organisational rules and works specifications' (Littler 1982: 28). The discussion of the ties that bind women workers would seem to suggest the latter approach.

The point is that the harmony hypothesis disappears, to be replaced by a search for the factors that intervene between workers and their perception of exploitation. This, not size *per se,* provides the answer to the apparent paradox between the image of the small firm on the one hand as 'sweatshop' and on the other as 'beautiful'.

References

Bannock, G. (1981). *The Economics of Small Firms,* Basil Blackwell, Oxford.

Bechhofer, F., Elliott, B. and Rushford, M. (1971). 'The Market Situation of Small Shopkeepers', *Scottish Journal of Political Economy,* vol. 18, pp. 161–80.

Bechhofer, F., and Elliott, B. (1981). *The Petite Bourgeoisie: Comparative Studies of the Uneasy Stratum,* Macmillan, London.

Bolton, J.E. (1971). *Report of the Committee of Enquiry on Small*

Firms, (Bolton Report) Cmnd 4811, HMSO, London.

Boswell, J. (1973). *The Rise and Decline of Small Firms,* Allen & Unwin, London.

Braverman, H. (1974). *Labour and Monopoly Capitalism,* Monthly Review Press, London.

Burawoy, M. (1979). *Manufacturing Consent: Changes in the Labour Process under Monopoly Capitalism,* University of Chicago Press, Chicago.

Commission on Industrial Relations (CIR) (1974). *Small Firms and the Code of Industiral Relations Practice,* Report no. 69, HMSO, London.

Coote, A. and Kellner, P. (1980). *Now Hear This Brother,* New Statesman Report no. 1, London

Curran, J. and Stanworth, J. (1979). 'Self-selection and the Small Firm Workers. A Critique and an Alternative View', *Sociology,* vol. 13, no. 3, pp. 427–44.

Daniel, W. and Millward, W. (1983). *Workplace Industrial Relations in Britain,* Heinemann, London.

Dickson, D. (1974). *Alternative Technology,* Fontana, London.

Edwards, P.K. (1983). 'Control, Compliance and Conflict: Analysing Variations in the Capitalist Labour Process', paper presented to the Organization and Control of the Labour Process Conference, Manchester.

Edwards, P. and Scullion, H. (1982). 'Deviance Theory and Industrial Praxis: A Study of Discipline and Social Control in an Industrial Setting', *Sociology,* vol. 16, no. 3.

Edwards, R. (1979). *Contested Terrain,* Heinemann, London.

Elger, T. (1979). 'Valorisation and Deskilling: A Critique of Braverman', *Capital and Class,* no. 7, Spring.

Friedman, A. (1977). *Industry and Labour,* Macmillan, London.

Henderson, J. and Johnson, B. (1974). 'Labour Relations in the Smaller Firm', *Personnel Management,* December.

Ingham, G.K. (1970). *Size of Industrial Organization and Worker Behaviour,* Cambridge University Press, Cambridge.

Jones, P. (1980). 'The Thatcher Experiment: Tensions and Contra- dictions in the First Year' in *Politics and Power II: Problems in Labour Politics,* Routledge & Kegan Paul, London.

Kyneston-Reeves, T. and Woodward, J. (1970). 'The Control of Manufacture in a Garment Factory' in J. Woodward, *Industrial Organisation, Behaviour and Control,* Oxford University Press, Oxford.

Littler, C. (1982). *The Development of the Labour Process in Capitalist Societies,* Heinemann, London.

Marx, K. (1976). *Capital,* vol. 1, Penguin Books, Harmondsworth.

Murray, F. (1983). 'The Decentralisation of Production — the Decline of the Mass Collective Worker', *Capital and Class,* no. 19, Spring.

Nash, M. (1980). 'Industrial Relations in the Small Firm', *Employee Relations,* vol. 2, no. 4.

Palmer, G. (1983). *British Industrial Relations,* George Allen & Unwin, London.

Pollert, A. (1979). 'Resistance and Control', *Socialist Review,* no. 13.

Pollert, A. (1981). *Girls, Wives, Factory Lives,* Macmillan, London.

Poulantzas, N. (1975). *Classes in Contemporary Capitalism,* New Left Books, London.

Rainnie, A.F. (1983). 'Industrial Relations in Small Business: The Case of the Clothing Industry in N.E. England', unpublished PhD thesis, Newcastle Polytechnic (CNAA).

Rainnie, A.F. (1984). 'Combined and Uneven Development in the Clothing Industry', *Capital and Class,* no. 22, Spring.

Roethlisberger, F.J. and Dickson, W.J. (1949). *Management and the Worker,* Harvard University Press, Cambridge, Mass.

Rubery, J. (1980). 'Structured Labour Markets, Worker Organisation and Low Pay', in A. Amsden (ed.), *The Economics of Women and Work,* Penguin Books, Harmondsworth.

Scase, R. (1982). 'The Petty Bourgeoisie and Modern Capitalism: A Consideration of Recent Theories' in A. Giddens, and G. Mackenzie (eds), *Social Class and the Division of Labour,* Cambridge University Press, Cambridge.

Scase, R. and Goffee, R. (1980). *The Real World of the Small Business Owner,* Croom Helm, London.

Schumacher, E. (1974). *Small is Beautiful,* Abacus, London.

Scott, M.G. (1980). 'Independence and the Flight from Large Scale: Some Sociological Factors in the Founding Process' in A.A. Gibb and T.D. Webb (eds), *Policy Issues in Small Business Research,* Saxon House.

Scott, M.G. and Rainnie, A.F. (1982). 'Beyond Bolton — Industrial Relations in the Small Firm' in J. Stanworth (ed.), *Perspectives on a Decade of Small Business Research,* Gower, Farnborough.

Stephenson, G., Brotherton, C., Delafield, G. and Skinner, M. (1983). 'Size of Organisation, Attitudes to Work and Job Satisfaction', *Industrial Relations Journal,* vol. 14, no. 2.

Thompson, P. (1983). *The Nature of Work,* Macmillan, London.

Turner, H., Roberts, G. and Roberts, D. (1977). *Management Characteristics and Labour Conflict,* Cambridge University Press, Cambridge.

4 A New Look at Job Satisfaction in the Small Firm*

JAMES CURRAN AND JOHN STANWORTH

Introduction

There appears to be a widespread popular acceptance of an inverse relationship between size of firm and job satisfaction among shop-floor workers. The small firm is seen as offering a higher level of job satisfaction compared to the large firm and as especially superior in relation to intrinsic aspects of job satisfaction such as satisfying social relations (both with fellow workers and superiors), more varied and interesting work roles, and opportunities for identifying with the enterprise as a whole. These views have been echoed in quasi-official reports such as that of the Bolton Committee (1971) and in popular academic writing on the alleged economic and social advantages of the small enterprise (Schumacher 1973).

Academic reviews of the literature on the relationship between size of firm and levels of job satisfaction among shop-floor workers have been inclined to follow the popular view (Beer 1964; Argyle 1972; Davis 1972; Davies and Shackleton 1975; Hall 1977) although writers have usually been cautious about accepting it without qualification. Sometimes they have also expressed doubts about the conceptual and methodological adequacy of the available research. A glance at the

* From: *Human Relations*, vol. 34, no. 5 (1981), pp. 343–65.

research sources cited shows that a comparatively small number of studies are repeatedly mentioned (Acton Society Trust 1952, 1953, 1957; Revans, 1956, 1958; Talacchi 1960; Indik 1965; Ingham 1970) and close examination indicates that they have indeed been of somewhat variable quality and that there may well be doubts as to whether popular views are strongly supported.

The Acton Society Trust studies asserted that workers in small enterprises showed higher levels of involvement as measured by absenteeism, accident rates, a knowledge of the workings of the organisation, and morale. However, by the standards of modern research, both the methodological strategies and associated levels of conceptual sophistication of these studies were poor. For instance, the researchers relied greatly on company statistical records with only a superficial investigation of the enterprises as social groupings. Yet, when there was an attempt to go beyond simple statistical analysis, as in the 1957 report, the researcher openly admitted that quite a substantial part of the 'size effect' bore little relation to worker satisfaction or identification with the enterprise.

Two further frequently cited studies are those of Talacchi (1960) and Indik (1965). Talacchi examined size of firm and levels of job satisfaction in manufacturing and non-manufacturing organisations. He concluded that the expected inverse relationship held particularly for intrinsic aspects of job satisfaction but was more marked in non-manufacturing organisations. He also suggested the precise links between size of firm and job satisfaction producing the relationship. Larger firms had increased division of labour and specialisation and this led to intrinsic deprivations and a decline in the quality of horizontal and vertical inter-personal relations. However, two serious weaknesses have been identified in this study. Porter and Lawler (1965) pointed out that Talacchi's claimed sample of 93 organisations contained at least 45 plants of five parent companies and Ingham (1967) noted that Talacchi implicitly assumed that all workers have the same expectations and attitudes to intrinsic rewards.

Indik's study reached substantially similar conclusions to those of Talacchi although the suggested links between size and member response are seen in more complex terms. Again, there is particular stress on the decline in intrinsic aspects of job satisfaction as size of organisation increases. Indik's sample ostensibly consisted of 96 organisations of which 68 were industrial or commercial while the other 28 were described as 'voluntary-membership educational-political organizations'. The size range of the voluntary organisations (101–2989 employees) differed from that of the two industrial/commercial sets of organisations (15–61 and 25–132) and 36 of the industrial/commercial organisations were franchised car dealerships of a single manufacturer. Finally, as all members of the voluntary organisations were female while virtually all members of the other two sets of organisations were male, the sample was obviously far from ideal.

Probably the most sophisticated theoretical approach to worker involvement in the small firm is that of Ingham (1970). He argued that, as work experience lengthens, workers develop a distinct set of orientations which, other things being equal, results in self-selection into work environments congruent with those orientations. For example, some workers may combine a desire for high economic rewards with a low desire for non-economic rewards. This *economistic–instrumental orientation*, as Ingham labels it, is normally met by working in a large firm since the latter tends to offer higher financial rewards than the small firm but fewer intrinsic rewards. Ingham also suggested that some workers develop a *non-economistic–expressive* orientation combining a relatively low desire for economic rewards with a strong desire for non-economic rewards. It is workers with this orientation who will tend to gravitate toward small firms since the latter offer an overall reward package most congruent with this orientation. Ingham then went on to offer an extensive set of research findings apparently supporting this interpretation.

In job satisfaction terms, Ingham argued that the typical small firm worker placed a greater emphasis on certain aspects of his work task and social relationships in the firm and positively sought out a work environment which met those wants. Equally, he argued, the small firm itself offered rewards which differed from those of the large firm especially in having a positively intrinsic character, that is, in offering greater opportunities for job involvement and socially and psychologically satisfying relations with others. Conversely, the rewards profile of the large firm which offered relatively high extrinsic rewards (monetary and material rewards) but low levels of intrinsic rewards, would not be attractive to these workers but, rather, would attract workers who defined work highly instrumentally and sought intrinsic rewards mainly in non-work sectors of life.

The overall levels of job satisfaction among the small and large firm workers were very similar according to Ingham. On extrinsic aspects, as measured by monetary rewards, small firm workers were paid less but their expectations were also lower so that the experienced level of extrinsic satisfaction was similar to those reported by large firm workers. On intrinsic aspects, as measured by perceived opportunities for using abilities to the full, results were rather more mixed. Small firm semi-skilled workers were much less satisfied than their large firm counterparts; they had very high expectations on this aspect which the small firms clearly failed to meet. Small firm skilled workers, on the other hand, were rather more frequently satisfied on this aspect than their large firm equivalents although the differences were not so marked as those for semi-skilled workers. The overall levels of intrinsic and extrinsic satisfaction were related, therefore, to the differing expectations in relation to intrinsic and extrinsic rewards and the differing potentials of small and large firm environments to meet these expectations. The ways in which these expectations and rewards balanced out helped to explain the very similar levels of attachment to the enterprise among the small and large firm workers which Ingham took as a further indication of the broadly equivalent levels of overall satisfaction experienced by the two samples of workers.

However, Ingham's formulation and findings immediately suggest a number of doubts. For example, the notion that manual workers gradually develop a clearly defined and stable set of orientations which become increasingly important in their decisions to take or leave jobs, goes very much against the bulk of research and recent theorising on occupational placement (Curran and Stanworth 1979; Roberts 1975; Williams 1974). It assumes that factors such as the personnel selection practices of small and large firms, possible changes in orientations connected with life-cycle position, or differences between industries, have no impact on occupational placement or on workers' job satisfaction. Moreover, despite his detailed presentation of empirical findings, Ingham's sample consisted of only 47 small firm workers all employed in firms involved in light engineering, thus allowing for no assessment of variations between small firm workers in different technological and industrial environments.

The present sample

The research reported in the present paper is based upon tape-recorded, semi-structured interviews with 118 small firm shop-floor workers employed in eight small firms (employing under 200 people) in the printing and electronics industries. A control sample of 83 shop-floor workers doing similar work in two large firms, one in each of the industries, was also interviewed in the same way. Each interview lasted, on average, 1¼ hours and was carried out in the worker's home or other non-work venue. All interviews were carried out between late 1974 and early 1976. Response rates of over 73 per cent of those invited to participate were achieved in all firms.

The two industries selected were chosen for the strong contrast they provided. Printing is a craft industry which, until recently, had a slow rate of technological change. It is predominantly a small firm industry with over 95 per cent of workers located in establishments employing fewer than 100 people (Report on the Census of Production 1978a). It is also, unusually for a mainly small firm industry, highly unionised (Price and Bain 1976). The electronics industry, on the other hand, is a relatively young, science-based industry with few craft traditions and a lower level of unionisation. It has had an exceptionally high rate of technological innovation throughout its relatively short history and contains a higher proportion of large firms than the printing industry (Allen 1970; Report on the Census of Production 1978b).

Research on job satisfaction among manual workers has been very extensive and has spawned a number of theoretical approaches and research strategies. Among the better-known formulations are the two-factor theory of Herzberg (1966) and Herzberg, Mausner and Snyderman (1959), expectancy theory (Vroom 1964) and equity theory (Jacques 1961; Adams 1965). However, for various reasons none of these was thought suitable for the present research. The approach developed by Herzberg et al., for example, has been shown to be of doubtful application to manual workers in the United Kingdom and to raise both theoretical and methodological problems which cast strong doubts on its utility generally (Cotgrove, Dunham and Vanplew 1971; Wall and Stephenson 1970; Guest 1976).

Expectancy theory was rejected because of methodological problems connected with its administration both on statistical grounds and as a research instrument. There are also doubts about its assumptions of a strong future orientation and a highly rational approach to job decisions among manual workers (Warr and Wall 1975). Equity theory was questioned as a basis for the present research because of its lack of clarity in two of the major areas of interest, the importance of qualitative and intrinsic aspects of a job and the relation between the latter and extrinsic aspects (Davies and Shackleton 1975). Given the alleged importance of intrinsic aspects in the motivational patterns of small firm workers and their rejection of extrinsic rewards as the main reward desired from work, this theoretical imprecision was decisive in not adopting this approach.

Two lessons may be derived from the weaknesses which have emerged at the theoretical and methodological levels in these approaches: first, that theorists have a tendency to erect a large number of initial, untested propositions concerning worker orientations and behaviour; and, second, to find, as a consequence, that relatively complex measuring instruments are required. In turn, these weaknesses lead to considerable problems of analysis and to incon-

clusive results which focus subsequent discussions on these methodological considerations rather than the substantive issues promoting the
initial research.

Therefore, in the present research it was decided to adopt an
approach to job satisfaction which made the minimum of assumptions.
Workers were assumed to be capable of recognising their wants in
relation to employment and to be able to form an assessment of their
current firm in relation to those wants. Job satisfaction refers solely to
these expressed wants and assessment. The appropriate research
instrument in relation to this conceptualisation of job satisfaction was
deemed to be a series of semi-structured questions backed up by
neutral probe questions wherever it was necessary to clarify a
respondent's views. These questions formed part of a longer interview
on a wide range of issues connected with work and non-work
experiences conducted in the respondent's home.

The data

Each respondent was asked to say what he thought was most
important about a job from a printed list of fourteen items. (This was
an elaboration of a similar list developed by Goldthorpe, Lockwood,
Bechhofer and Platt (1968) for much the same purpose). Respondents
were also invited to mention anything not on the list if they thought it
most important about a job.

As Table 4.1 indicates, the distribution of respondents' first choices
on expectations about jobs confirmed the view that small firm workers
are more intrinsically minded than their large firm counterparts but
with the electronics workers showing this most clearly. However, the
age distributions and marital status of respondents in the main and
control samples differed significantly, with small firm workers being,
on average, nine years younger than the large firm workers and,
therefore, less likely to be married (54.7 per cent as against 72.7 per
cent).

The importance of age distribution differences in the main and
control samples in relation to job expectations emerged strongly.
Workers aged 25 and over showed virtually no difference in preference
for extrinsic and intrinsic aspects of the job regardless of size of firm
but there was a large difference among those aged under 25. The
stronger preference for intrinsic aspects among the small firm workers
was very much linked to the small firms employing a higher proportion
of younger workers. In a similar vein, if marital state is controlled for,
the difference in preference for intrinsic and extrinsic aspects again

Table 4.1
What is most important about a job: first choice*

	Small printing firm workers		Small electronics firm workers		Large printing firm workers		Large electronics firm workers		All small firm workers		All large firm workers	
	N = 64	%	N = 54	%	N = 41	%	N = 42	%	N = 118	%	N = 83	%
Extrinsic items												
Good pay	14	21.9	9	16.7	11	26.8	15	35.7	23	19.5	26	31.3
Security	9	14.1	4	7.4	5	12.2	3	7.1	13	11.0	8	9.6
A strong and active union	2	3.1	1	1.8	1	2.4	–	–	3	2.5	1	1.2
Full wages if sick	1	1.6	2	3.7	1	2.4	2	4.8	3	2.5	3	3.6
Pension	–	–	–	–	1	2.4	–	–	–	–	1	1.2
	26	40.6	16	29.6	19	46.2	20	47.6	42	35.5	39	47.2
Intrinsic items												
Interesting work	16	25.0	11	20.4	7	17.1	7	16.7	27	22.9	14	16.9
Plenty of variety in the job	6	9.4	12	22.2	3	7.3	4	9.5	18	15.2	7	8.4
Good work-mates	6	9.4	3	5.6	1	2.4	2	4.8	9	7.6	3	3.6
Pleasant working conditions	4	6.2	6	11.1	5	12.2	2	4.8	10	8.5	7	8.4
A boss who takes a real interest in you	5	7.8	5	9.3	1	2.4	3	7.1	10	8.5	4	4.8
Good equipment	–	–	–	–	2	4.9	1	2.4	–	–	3	3.6
Responsibility	–	–	1	1.9	3	7.3	1	2.4	1	0.8	4	4.8
	37	57.8	38	70.4	22	53.7	20	47.7	75	63.5	42	50.5
Other/could not state	1	1.6	–	–	–	–	2	4.8	1	0.8	2	2.4

* There are only five items under the heading 'extrinsic items' because no respondent selected 'good bonus' or 'plenty of overtime' as a first choice. Percentages may not add up to 100 because of rounding off.

disappears. Married workers, given their greater family responsibilities, were more likely than unmarried workers to stress extrinsic aspects of the job. Since small firms employ a much higher proportion of young unmarried workers this helps to account for the higher overall emphasis on intrinsic preferences among the main small firm sample.

However, some differences were also linked to type of industry rather than size of firm. For instance, large firms in the electronics industry are more likely to employ contract workers who are especially attracted by the higher pay they receive for being prepared to be mobile and hence tend to opt for extrinsic aspects of a job. Their greater likelihood of being in a large rather than a small firm helps to increase the differences in the balance of preferences between intrinsic and extrinsic aspects of the job shown in Table 4.1 for the small and large firm electronic worker samples (which was greater than the differences between the small and large firm samples in printing). The greater presence of contract workers among the large electronics firm sub-sample also helps to explain why this is the only sub-sample where unmarried respondents show a more frequent preference for extrinsic aspects of the job than married respondents. Thus again part of the difference between the small and large firm samples, at least for the electronics industry, is tied as much to the employment practices of small and large firms as to workers' job preferences.

After allowing for differences in age, marital status, and the presence of contract workers, it is noticeable that electronics industry respondents show a stronger preference for intrinsic aspects of the job than printing workers. In short, discussing small firm workers without reference to the industry in which they work may easily lead to misleading over-generalisations.

The data from respondents' second choices on what they thought most important about a job substantially paralleled those for the first choices although, of course, individual respondents did not always choose the same kind of item — either extrinsic or intrinsic — in both selections. Overall, 42.4 per cent of small firm shop-floor workers put intrinsic items in both first and second place compared to 32.5 per cent of large firm workers. Again, on this measure, small electronics firm workers were much more intrinsically minded than the small printing firm workers.

Having stated what they thought was most important about a job, respondents were then asked how they rated their present job in relation to these preferences. Table 4.2 reports responses for all workers who had been with the firm for at least six months. Clearly, the most satisfied on this measure were the small electronics firm

Table 4.2
Rating of job at time of interview for first-choice item thought most important about a job

	Small printing firm workers		Small electronics firm workers		Large printing firm workers		Large electronics firm workers		All small firm workers		All large firm workers	
	N = 57	%	N = 34	%	N = 36	%	N = 33	%	N = 91	%	N = 69	%
'Good' and 'pretty good'	31	54.4	24	70.6	24	66.7	17	51.5	55	60.4	41	59.4
'bad'	10	17.5	8	23.5	4	11.1	7	21.2	18	19.8	11	15.9

Table does not include respondents who gave other replies or who had been with the firm for less than six months.

workers while the least satisfied were their large firm counterparts. But this relationship was reversed for the workers in the printing firms.

When the results are aggregated there appears to be little overall difference between the small firm main and large firm control samples. This suggests, in short, that differences between industries may again be greater than those between workers in different-sized firms. Results for second choice items were broadly similar to those for first choices in assessing their current job.

Older workers, those aged 40 and over, were, on the whole, less satisfied with their current job in relation to the aspects of the job they had previously mentioned as important, than younger workers. The findings in relation to marital status follow a similar pattern. Thus, in Table 4.3 well over two-thirds (72.2 per cent) of unmarried small firm workers rated their current job as 'good' or 'pretty good' while 53.3 per cent of married small firm workers did so. Married workers in the large printing firm were the only sub-sample to report a higher level of satisfaction than their unmarried counterparts — no less than 80 per cent against 54.5 per cent. In fact, the level of job satisfaction, measured on this indicator, among the large printing firm married workers was higher than among any sub-sample regardless of marital state, size of firm, or industry.

The interpretation of the above findings may be linked to the special character of the large firm in printing. Several previous studies (Hollowell 1968; Goldthorpe et al. 1968; Shimmin 1962) have indicated a strong relationship between attitudes to work and family life-cycle position. Marriage and a family produce, as noted earlier, a

Table 4.3

Rating of firm on first-choice item on what was thought important about a job, by marital state*

| | Proportions rating the firm 'good' or 'pretty good' | | | | |
| | Unmarried | | | Married | |
	N		%	N		%
Small printing firm workers	27	16	59.3	35	18	51.4
Small electronics firm workers	27	21	77.9	25	14	56.0
Large printing firm workers	11	6	54.5	30	24	80.0
Large electronics firm workers	10	7	70.0	29	13	44.8
All small firm workers	54	39	72.2	60	32	53.3
All large firm workers	21	13	61.9	59	37	62.7

* Respondents who were divorced or separated at the time of interview are excluded.

greater emphasis on extrinsic aspects of work. In the large printing firm the younger, married workers could work in the newspaper composing room where wages were relatively much higher. Young workers still in their apprenticeship could not benefit in this way and older workers tended to prefer the general composing room where, although wages were lower, the pace of work was less demanding. So just at the point in the family life-cycle where extrinsic needs were highest this firm, like other large firms in the industry involved in newspaper printing, could offer higher-paying work. Small printing firms could not do this, hence the lower level of job satisfaction in relation to current jobs among their married workers.

That work in the small firm is less boring than work in the large firm is widely accepted. Small firms are held to offer more varied work roles, responsibility at an earlier age, and few demarcations between work roles. However, data from the present study show no such clear differences indicated in reported levels of boredom. There was little overall difference in the proportion finding their job boring all or some of the time either between firms of different size or between the two industries. Indeed, the only important difference between the samples points toward higher levels of boredom experienced in small firms since small firm workers were over twice as likely to find their job unequivocally boring as large firm workers, again with little difference between industries. It may be, of course, that small firm workers have higher expectations about interesting work than large firm workers but clearly the small firms in which these respondents worked did not meet these expectations.

A final set of questions of interest here concerned levels of material rewards. The Bolton Report (1971), while admitting the great difficulties in comparing earnings levels in different kinds of firm and industry, reiterated the widely asserted point that small firms pay less than large firms, estimating that the difference was 'of the order of 20%'. The difficulties of comparison turn on problems of differences in skill and responsibility levels associated with common job titles, calculating the cash value of various fringe benefits, and on variations in the availability of overtime work. But perhaps even more complex here, and certainly of no less importance, are workers' perceptions of various earnings levels and comparisons they might make between earnings levels in various firms.

Objectively, the large firms in the present study did appear to pay better than small firms even after controlling for age differences. On the other hand, small firm workers themselves showed a certain unsureness of this issue and were roughly evenly divided on this question. Interestingly, although large firm workers were more inclined to say that large firms paid better than small firms, there was nevertheless a substantial proportion (42.1 per cent) who thought that small firms paid the same or sometimes as well as large firms.

Two out of three small firm workers believed their present firm paid better or as well as any other firm they could work for (compared to 76.1 per cent of the large firm workers) and this rather goes against the notion that small firm workers exchange the intrinsic rewards of working in the small firm for the extrinsic rewards which might be obtained working for a large firm. Moreover, their assessment may be entirely accurate when it is remembered that small firm workers are not only, on average, younger than large firm workers but less likely to have successfully completed an apprenticeship or to hold a union card (Curran and Stanworth 1979). Large firms may pay better than small firms but they are selective about who they employ and many small firm workers might stand little chance of obtaining a job in a large firm.

Conclusions

This examination of the relationship between size of firm and level of worker job satisfaction has shown that previously accepted views on the relationship are, at best, over-simple. The notion of straight-forward inverse relationship between size of firm and level of job satisfaction fails to take into account such important factors as the differing characteristics of the labour forces of small and large firms and differences in the characteristics of specific industries which may also be related to size of firm. Particularly important were differences in the age distribution and marital status of the small and large firm labour forces.

The present research was limited to two industries and explored a limited number of aspects of job satisfaction but the results strongly suggest that size of firm should not be treated as a simple or even a main determinant of job satisfaction unless it is carefully related to factors in other segments of the worker's life and factors peculiar to the industry in which the firm is located. What is now required is for this approach to be extended to a wider range of industries, preferably on a longitudinal basis, to determine whether, when these further factors are taken into account, any further generalisations emerge.

References

Adams, J.S. (1965). 'Inequity in Social Exchange' in L. Berkowitz (ed.), *Advances in Experimental Social Psychology,* vol. 2, New York, Academic Press.

Acton Society Trust (1952). *The Worker's Point of View, Studies in Nationalised Industry no. II,* London, Acton Society Trust.

Acton Society Trust (1953). *Size and Morale: A Preliminary Study of Attendance at Work in Large and Small Units,* London, Acton Society Trust.

Acton Society Trust (1957). *Size and Morale Part II: A Further Study of Attendance at Work in Large and Small Units,* London, Acton Society Trust.

Allen, G.C. (1970). *British Industries and their Organisation* (5th edn), London, Longman.

Argyle, M. (1972). *The Social Psychology of Work,* Harmondsworth, Penguin Books.

Beer, M. (1964). 'Organisational size and job satisfaction', *Academy of Management Journal,* vol. 7, pp. 34–44.

Bolton, J.E. (1971). *Report of the Committee of Inquiry on Small Firms* (Bolton Report), Cmnd. 4811, London, HMSO.

Cotgrove, S., Dunham, J. and Vanplew, C. (1971). *The Nylon Spinners: A Case in Productivity Bargaining and Job Enlargement,* London, Allen and Unwin.

Curran, J. and Stanworth, J. (1979). 'Self-selection and the Small Firm Worker. A Critique and an Alternative View, *Sociology,* vol. 13, no. 3, pp. 427–44.

Davies, D.R. and Shackleton, V.J. (1975). *Psychology and Work,* London, Methuen.

Davis, K. (1972). *Human Behaviour at Work, Human Relations and Organizational Behaviour,* New York, McGraw-Hill.

Goldthorpe, J., Lockwood, D., Bechhofer, F. and Platt, J. (1968). *The Affluent Worker: Industrial Attitudes and Behaviour,* Cambridge, Cambridge University Press.

Guest, D. (1976). 'Motivation after Maslow', *Personnel Management,* vol. 8, pp. 29–32.

Hall, R.H. (1977). *Organisations, Structure and Process* (2nd edn), Englewood Cliffs, NJ, Prentice-Hall.

Herzberg, F. (1966). *Work and the Nature of Man,* London, Staples.

Herzberg, F., Mausner, B. and Snyderman, B. (1959). *The Motivation to Work,* New York, Wiley.

Hollowell, P.G. (1968). *The Lorry Driver,* London, Routledge and Kegan Paul.

Indik, B.P. (1965). 'Organisation Size and Member Participation', *Human Relations,* vol. 18, pp. 339–50.

Ingham, G.K. (1967). 'Organisational Size, Orientation to Work and Industrial Behaviour', *Sociology,* vol. 1, pp. 239–58.

Ingham, G.K. (1970). *Size of Industrial Organisation and Worker Behaviour,* Cambridge, Cambridge University Press.

Jacques, E. (1961). *Equitable Payment,* London, Heinemann.

Porter, L.M. and Lawler, E.E. (1965). 'Properties of Organisation Structure in Relation to Job Attitudes and Job Behaviour', *Psychological Bulletin,* vol. 64, pp. 23–51.

Price, R. and Bain, G.S. (1976). 'Union Growth Revisited: 1948–1974 in Perspective', *British Journal of Industrial Relations,* vol. 14, pp. 339–55.

Report on the Census of Production, 1974–75 (1978a). *General Printing and Publishing,* MLH 489, London, HMSO.

Reports on the Census of Production, 1974–75 (1978b). *Scientific and Instrument Systems,* MLH 354 and *Radio, Radar and Electronic Capital Goods,* MLH 367, London, HMSO.

Revans, R.W. (1956). 'Industrial Morale and Size of Unit', *Political Quarterly,* vol. 27, pp. 303–10.

Revans, R.W. (1958). 'Human Relations, Management and Size' in E.M. Hugh-Jones (ed.), *Human Relations and Modern Management,* Amsterdam, North Holland Publishing Co.

Roberts, K. (1975). 'The Developmental Theory of Occupational Choice: A Critique and an Alternative' in G. Esland, G. Salaman, and M. Speakman (eds.), *People and Work,* Edinburgh, Homes McDougal in association with the Open University Press.

Schumacher, E.F. (1973). *Small is Beautiful. A Study of Economics as if People Mattered,* London, Blond and Briggs.

Shimmin, S. (1962). 'Extra-mural Factors Influencing Behaviour at Work', *Occupational Psychology,* vol. 36, pp. 124–31.

Talacchi, S. (1960). 'Organisation Size, Individual Attitudes and Behaviour: An Empirical Study', *Administrative Science Quarterly,* vol. 5, pp. 398–420.

Vroom, V.H. (1964). *Work and Motivation,* New York, Wiley.

Wall, T.D. and Stephenson, G.M. (1970). 'Herzberg's Two Factor Theory of Job Attitudes: A Critical Evaluation and Some Fresh Evidence', *Industrial Relations Journal,* vol. 1, pp. 41–65.

Warr, P. and Wall, T. (1975). *Work and Well-being,* Harmondsworth, Penguin Books.

Williams, W.M. (ed.) (1974). *Occupational Choice: A Selection of Papers from the Sociological Review,* London, Allen and Unwin.

PART II
THE SMALL FIRM, GROWTH
AND
TECHNOLOGY

Introduction

The relationship between growth and the small firm has generated a substantial literature and recently the impact of new technology has been of especial interest to researchers. 'Today's large firms were yesterday's small firms' goes the truism but like most truisms it does not, in fact, take us very far in the analysis of growth processes in the small enterprise. Traditionally, it was widely considered that all small firms tried hard to grow in the hope of becoming the large firms of tomorrow. It was felt that absence of the motivation to grow meant inevitable decline and collapse. Such views are now widely recognised by theorists and researchers as crude and inaccurate. In practice, most small firms stay small and yet can remain successful for decades by meeting the needs of some local or specialised market, as well as those of their owner-managers.

Similarly, the impact of new technology on the small firm has also been the subject of considerable myth and misunderstanding. Some writers, for example, used to adopt the view that the small firm was, by definition, excluded from the world of new technology: small firms were involved only with established, traditional and often declining technologies. The history of the microprocessor and computer industries, the core of much recent high-technology development in industrial society, has demolished this view. The emergence of substantial numbers of high-technology small firms on Route 128 and

Silicon Valley in the United States, Silicon Glen in Scotland and the M4 corridor in England, have demanded a new analysis of how small firms interrelate with new technology.

Stanworth and Curran, in their contribution to the discussion of growth in the small firm, begin by noting how the traditional literature on the topic implicitly assumes that all small firms would grow if possible. They point out that most theories of growth reflect this assumption rather than any observation of how small firms behave in reality. In fact, statistics show that growth is rather an exceptional process — that most small firms stay small. This, they argue, is what requires investigation since it is the norm.

The paper suggests that the key to understanding the frequent lack of growth lies essentially in the motivational and social attitudes of the owner-manager, the dominant figure in the enterprise. Small business owners are predominantly people with strong needs for autonomy and independence, limited formal managerial skills and are often what is termed 'socially marginal', that is, people who feel that, somehow, the often modest employment roles they achieve in society are discrepant with their true talents and ambitions. Such people, the paper argues, may well be reluctant as subsequent business owners to allow their enterprises to grow since the requirements of growth might well threaten their autonomy and independence, expose their lack of managerial skills and expose them to further reminders of their earlier social marginality.

Of course, some small firms do grow. Not all small firm owner-managers share the general characteristics of their economic grouping or perceive that growth may threaten a way of life they have created for themselves by setting up a small enterprise. For instance, some high-technology small firms are set up by people who want to join the big enterprise league as quickly as possible but under their own terms rather than as an employee. But the large firm sector needs very few small firms to grow to replace those large firms which disappear or decline, in order to maintain the large firm sector as a whole. What the authors of this paper stress, however, is that small firm growth is a complex social and psychological process rather than a simple economic process which occurs normally unless specifically prevented from doing so.

Cooper, in the first of two technology papers in this section, reviews the literature on the conditions under which technological entrepreneurship emerged in the United States in the early 1970s. Subsequent research has largely borne out his conclusions and suggested that the same conditions also apply outside the United States.

First, he looks at the technological entrepreneur as an individual.

Research indicates that people who start this kind of small firm, unlike other entrepreneurs, like to be with other like-minded individuals. On the whole, they strike out into entrepreneurship in their thirties after achieving at least a first degree and relevant industrial experience. They are non-conforming, single-minded and, like other entrepreneurs, not especially financially motivated. Cooper also carefully reviews the research on the kinds of organisation likely to incubate technological entrepreneurs. As might be expected, they are usually organisations which provide the basic technological know-how needed and they tend to be small rather than large firms — a point picked up very explicitly by Storey in the research reported in the opening paper in this volume. But these organisations also frustrate the kind of people who later start on their own although the latter often only develop their entrepreneurial ambitions *after* parting company with the incubating organisation. In some respects then, elements of McEvoy and Jones' notions of *exclusiveness* and *exclusion* (see Vol. 1) come into play here.

Interestingly, universities did not emerge as always important in directly fostering technological entrepreneurship even if they are important in creating a local technological environment and a trained work-force.

Finally, the paper examines research on other external factors promoting technological entrepreneurship among which are availability of capital and the presence of a local climate of entrepreneurial-mindedness. Local banks and other business services with a real knowledge of the needs of technological small firms provide encouragement to still more new small technological enterprises. In addition, existing firms may well directly produce further firms, either through partners splitting up and going it alone or through inspiring employees to do the same. Above all, however, the local economy must be expanding and technologically-minded.

The second paper on this topic is by Roy Rothwell who provides a recent view confirming much of the above but extending the analysis in several ways. The paper focuses on the part small firms play in technological innovation. His first concern is to stress that we should stop viewing this issue in terms of small firms *versus* large firms: 'small and large firms do not exist in separate worlds'. Rather, we should adopt a dynamic perspective probing how small and large firms interact in complex ways through the stages of technological development. Such a view shows, for example, that neither small nor large firms have a permanent, innovatory advantage over the other.

Roughly, in the complex processes of technological change, small firms are important where they can make most of their 'behavioural' advantages such as adaptability and flexibility while large firms come to the fore when 'material' advantages are important. But much also depends on the type of industry, entry costs, economies of scale, and the local economy characteristics described by Cooper. What is clear is that small and medium-sized firms in the United Kingdom have been playing an increasingly significant role in technological innovation in recent years. The reasons for this, however, are by no means clear.

Rothwell's detailed examination of research on some of the factors involved in small firm participation in developing new technology and new products concentrates on the small-firm–large-firm complementarities involved. He examines these processes in relation to particular industries such as the United States semiconductor industry and in the newly developing area of biotechnology. In effect, Rothwell's paper also provides an agenda for exploring further facets of small firm involvement in new technology in future research but his overall conclusion is highly positive in relation to the small firm: 'as the world economy moves toward a period of recovery, in which a number of emerging technologies will play a crucial part, there will be many innovatory opportunities for both small and large firms working both separately and together: both are desirable; both are necessary'.

Taken together, the papers in this section strenuously avoid the tendency to oversimplification which has been so common in the discussion of growth, technology and the small firm. The former, in particular, has generated a considerable literature purporting to identify and explain the growth processes of small firms. We have not included a conventional growth paper in this section since most of the published work in this area simply does not possess the theoretical sophistication which has emerged in other areas of analysis of the small enterprise. More importantly, it rarely has the empirical underpinning needed to support the interpretation of a complex process which is relatively rare and, by definition, tends to occur only over a relatively extended period of time.

Both of the issues addressed in this section will increasingly attract attention from both theorists and researchers. The increase in the numbers of small firms and the restructuring of the economy now occurring in industrial societies means that the proportion of small firms growing may be expected to increase (although it is never likely to become a flood). Similarly, the period of rapid technological change which has begun also needs relating to the small firm not only in the fashionable, high-technology areas but also in other, less glamorous economic sectors. After all, there are proportionately many more small firms in these other areas who also face the impact of new technology. What can be said at the moment is that small firm theorising and research has cleared the ground for tackling these issues.

5 Growth and the Small Firm*

JOHN STANWORTH AND JAMES CURRAN

One aspect of the small firm which has received fairly considerable attention is its growth and development. This paper seeks to offer a new perspective on the social processes involved here, and is backed by results from an in-depth longitudinal research programme carried out in a sample of small manufacturing firms from the Surrey area over a six-year period.[1] Other research data, especially from American studies, is used to provide additional empirical support.[2]

Previous views of growth in the small firm

A survey of the literature on growth and the small firm reveals several contributions to theory construction with certain close similarities between them.[3] They reveal a dominant and a minor explanatory theme and a shared consistent overall theoretical perspective. The dominant theme is that of a 'stage' model of growth. The number of stages offered varies, but typically there are three or four, though sometimes as many as ten.[4] The small firm is seen as passing through a

* Extracted from: M.J.K. Stanworth and J. Curran, 'Growth and the Small Firm — an Alternative View', *Journal of Management Studies*, vol. 13, no. 2 (1976) and *Management Motivation in the Smaller Business*, Gower Press, 1973, pp. 171–6.

sequence of growth stages though there is little discussion on whether this is a necessary progression or whether, under certain conditions, one or more stages may be missed out or variations in the sequence occur. The absence of such qualifications almost certainly stems from a lack of empirical underpinning.[5] It is rare for samples of firms to exceed double figures; there is often a tendency to rely heavily on retrospective data or observations at a single point in time instead of longitudinal research strategies, and there is usually insufficient linking with data from other studies.

Stage models, regardless of the number of stages offered, also display certain further similarities. The initial stage, as we might expect, stresses the individual entrepreneur(s) with an idea for a product or service setting up in business. The next stage (or sometimes the next but one), is usually concerned with the division of managerial tasks.[6] The entrepreneur(s) can no longer exercise total managerial control and non-owner-managers are recruited, often because they have skills lacking in the founder(s). The remaining stages tend to concentrate on organisational maturity and stability. The firm becomes more bureaucratic and rationalised and takes on the general character of the larger company. It evolves a board of directors who are essentially managers rather than entrepreneurs; it exploits a wide range of management, production and marketing techniques; and, there is an acceptance that it must develop systematic working relations with other organisations in society such as trade unions and government departments.

These various approaches do contain a considerable element of truth but this derives at least partly from the definitional procedures used in theory construction. For instance, to define the first stage in terms of an individual or small group deciding to exploit a market for a product or service is to go little beyond defining the coming into existence of a new independent economic entity.

Another curious aspect of these stage theories of growth is an implied disregard for the size distribution of firms discussed above. The *Census of Production* data show this to be highly skewed with over 94 per cent of manufacturing firms employing less than 200 people and the typical firm, in a statistical sense, employing less than 30. In other words, most firms do not grow to any considerable size in terms of work-force size (which we may assume is broadly correlated with other dimensions of growth) and that substantial growth is seemingly a rather exceptional process. This is reinforced by the data which suggest that the failure rate among small firms, especially in the years immediately following formation, is very high.[7]

Finally, an inspection of the implied characteristics of the firm's organisational and managerial structure contained within the later stages in most of the models strongly indicates that the authors concerned are discussing a firm which has long since entered the 6 per cent of large firms in our economy.

The minor theme present in theorising on growth in the small firm is the so-called 's-curve hypothesis'[8] which can be seen as a special case of the stage theory. This suggests that the small firm will have a short formative period followed by a period of rapid growth perhaps reaching an exponential rate. The thinking behind this is that after the entrepreneur has developed an idea for a product or service, there is an initial establishing period for the firm which ends with the clear demonstration of a market advantage. This leads to a high rate of investment, to exploit the advantage further, sometimes supplemented by outside capital attracted by the firm's performance in the establishing period. This investment fuels the high rate of growth in the next period of the firm's history.

This exceptional rate of growth, however, tails off as competition is offered by other firms who become aware of the market opportunities. A reduction in the rate of expansion further results from a lowering of investment to more conventional levels due to profit-taking by the owner-managers and a decline in the firm's attraction as an investment for outsiders due to the increased competition.

The consistent overall theoretical perspective which unites both the dominant and minor themes in current theorising concerning growth in the small firm is a highly *positivist* one. The underlying paradigm for theoretical development is an idealised version of that used in the natural sciences. The small firm is seen here as a behaving entity whose elements are related in quantifiable, systematic and highly predictable ways and the object of theory construction is the generation of law-like propositions concerning the growth process.

However, theories of small firm growth, constructed upon this positivist view, fail to meet their self-imposed standards. They seldom, if ever, attain the level of precision required for the development of law-like propositions.[9] Nor are they adequately tested against acceptable samples of small firm histories necessary to define limits and boundaries to the relevance of such propositions. Finally, they appear to be inadequately articulated with our present knowledge of the structure of our economy, particularly with reference to the size distribution of firms. Since, in relative terms, so few small firms grow large, it might be expected that these theories should try to explain the rareness of the process they purport to explain. Their failure to do so suggests a blinkered approach.

The inadequacies of this general theoretical perspective have come in for harsh comment in recent years.[10] The main point made is that the assumption that natural and social phenomena belong to the same category of entities for purposes of theorising and explanation is fundamentally mistaken. The crucial difference stems from the fact that social phenomena *understand* their own behaviour and can act *purposefully* while natural phenomena have neither of these properties.

The entrepreneurial spirit in action perspective

Our alternative, a social action view of the small firm, concentrates heavily on understanding the internal social logic of the small firm as a social grouping. We argue that the key to growth lies in the meanings attached to participation in the firm by the actors involved. The small firm, in this view, is an ongoing social entity constructed out of the meanings and actions of those who participate in the firm or who are 'outsiders' in relation to the firm as a social grouping but nevertheless interact with the participants.

It should be stressed that this is *not* a psychological theory of the small firm. It takes the standpoint that definitions and meanings attached to situations are *socially generated, socially sustained* and, of special interest in the present context, *socially changed.* In other words a social action perspective here links the meanings and actions of the small firm's participants with their wider social environment. Moreover, in order to achieve the necessary level of generality for a *social* view of the small firm, the view cannot be limited to specific individuals but is extended to cover tendencies for certain combinations of meanings and actions to recur after the fashion revealed in various studies of small firms in this country and the United States.

This creates a new dimension for analysis because the researcher cannot now simply adopt a theory which assumes that objects in the situation will behave in a relatively positivist and deterministic manner. Purposeful phenomena cannot be treated in this simplistic way. In seeking to interpret the situation, the researcher must now also endeavour to understand what participation means to those involved and the likely changes in these meanings. Only in this way is an adequate account possible.

The resulting interpretation also differs from positivist explanations in that it does not take the form of law-like 'predictions'. Instead, an interpretation of the social situation is provided based upon a knowledge of both internal and external forces[11] influencing the situation. This allows suggestions as to the probabilities of actors attempting certain lines of action, given their interpretation of the situation, and the social forces affecting the situation which originate from the wider social environment.

Given the very strong influence of the owner-manager on the small firm's organisational style, it is important to examine this key role in some detail. Of particular importance are the new owner-manager's reasons for going it alone. Understanding this aids an understanding of attitudes towards growth later on in the firm's life.

Individuals do not generate meanings in a vacuum for most of their social interactions, but rely on an available stock of meanings, 'culture', to make sense of specific social experiences and provide a framework for anticipated experiences aimed at achieving the actor's ends or avoiding certain outcomes. In our society there is a strong cultural bias favouring individualism, and this finds expression in many ways. Economic individualism, it may be argued, in the form of founding and operating a business of one's own, is one of the most legitimate of all culturally prescribed forms of individualism. Indeed, as Weber argued,[12] economic individualism, in this form, has been given divine sanction in our culture and in fact was closely associated with the genesis of modern industrial society itself. An American writer on the small firm claimed that starting one's own business has:

> always been considered an integral element of the American way of life. Our traditional concept of opportunity has carried and still carries, a heavy emphasis on 'freedom', on 'being on one's own', 'being one's own boss' and 'working for oneself'.[13]

While this cultural bias is not quite so highly emphasised in Britain's culture, survey data[14] show that the ideal of self-employment, in order to increase autonomy and personal self-esteem, is none the less widespread.

However, going into business for oneself is a difficult role transition if only because our educational system and vocational guidance processes operate to minimise the practical consideration of this alternative.[15] Nevertheless, some people, albeit a very small minority, do take on the owner-manager role. It is important to know something about the social backgrounds and orientations of these people, especially first-generation entrepreneurs, if we are to achieve an understanding of the small firm. It is also quite clear from the available data on entrepreneurship in this country and the United States that new entrepreneurs are far from randomly drawn from the population.

As a social category, entrepreneurs tend to share certain characteristics. For instance, they are not, on the whole, well educated. The Bolton Report stated that nearly three-quarters of a sample of small manufacturing firms' chief executives had received no higher education and that only 1 per cent had a management qualification.[16] Other data support this claim for both Britain[17] and the United States[18] though there have been exceptions reported for the latter.[19] The more general conclusion, derived from the study of the backgrounds of new enterpreneurs, is that they tend to be people who consider themselves misplaced by the conventional role-allocation processes of their society.

Our main point here of the special social character of those who embrace the entrepreneurial role is well supported in this quotation from the largest American survey on entrepreneurship:

> Entrepreneurs are men who have failed in the traditional and highly structured roles available to them in the society. In this, as we have seen, entrepreneurs are not unique. What is unique about them is that they found an outlet for their creativity by making out of an undifferentiated mass of circumstance a creation uniquely their own: a business firm.[20]

We can use the term 'social marginality' to refer to this situation in which there is a perceived incongruity between the individual's personal attributes — physical characteristics, intellectual make-up, social behaviour patterns — and the role(s) he holds in society.[21] Social marginality is a common phenomenon due to the very nature of role allocation processes in society — these are far from perfect in allocating individuals to social roles — and also because individuals strive to maintain a sense of personal autonomy in social roles in opposition to social pressures pushing towards conformity. These common forms of social marginality are, however, unlikely to lead to dramatic social responses.

But, for some individuals and in some areas of society, circumstances combine to produce high levels of social marginality. The historical example, *par excellence*, of a group displaying high social marginality has been the Jews. Being a Jew has, regretfully, been something which has made a person an 'outsider' in non-Jewish society regardless of his personal and intellectual characteristics. To some extent Jewish communities developed patterns of social integration to counter these deprivations imposed from the wider society but feelings of social marginality were likely to be present to an extent rare in most other parts of society. For a Jew with only a weak commitment to his religion and community, feelings of marginality were likely to be much more pronounced.

Other common examples of social marginality are the intellectually gifted manual worker and the fully acculturated second-generation coloured Briton. Solutions to intense feelings of social marginality are varied. In some cases it leads to adherence to 'extreme' political or religious ideologies which promise to reconstruct social reality and thus 'solve' the individual's experiences of social marginality. The gifted manual worker may choose to become a full-time trade union official. For some, a solution is setting up their own firm.

Examples of the latter solution from our own research include some not uncommon stories. We discovered social marginality resulting from a promising academic career being shattered by domestic tragedy, or through the war sharply diminishing career prospects in conventional industrial or commercial life. Or again, we came across social marginality occurring in middle age when a successful career in the armed services could not be matched by the attainment of a similarly responsible position in civilian life. Other cases included instances of demonstrated talents being overlooked by large employers due to the individuals' unorthodox attitudes and personal idiosyncrasies.

An action view of growth in the small firm

Our previously published research, as well as that of others, indicates that there is no one single, stereotyped entrepreneurial role and thus, by implication, no single pattern of growth. The classical economists offered a picture of the entrepreneur as a rational profit maximiser and this remains the popular stereotype despite little support from research. An American study for example, reported that, of a sample of 81 newly founded businesses, only six approximated to the classical economists' model of the entrepreneur.[22]

Rather, there are several possible constellations of meanings which may form the core of the entrepreneur's self-definition of the entrepreneurial role. We find it helpful, following Gouldner,[23] to distinguish these constellations of more personal role components from those which may be taken as basic cultural prescriptions by using the concept of 'latent social identity'. Research on the small firm — both the research we have previously reported and studies by others — suggests that three such latent identities occur with some frequency in relation to the role of small firm entrepreneur:

1 *The 'artisan' identity.* Here the entrepreneurial role centres around intrinsic satisfactions of which the most important are personal autonomy at work, being able to pick the persons you work with, status within the work-place and satisfaction at producing a quality product backed with personal service.

These are not the only meanings and goals attached to the role, but they are the ones which predominate. Thus, whilst income is important, as it must be for anybody who works and has no other source of income, it is secondary to intrinsic satisfactions.

2   *The 'classical entrepreneur' identity.* This latent social identity most closely resembles the classical economists' view of entrepreneurship. Earnings and profit become a core component in the entrepreneur's definition of his role and hence in the way he acts out his role. Again maximisation of financial returns (consistent with the survival and possible expansion of the firm), is by no means the sole goal of the entrepreneur, but it is given great importance compared to the intrinsic satisfaction associated with the 'artisan' identity.

3   *The 'manager' identity.* Here the entrepreneurial latent social identity centres on meanings and goals concerned with the recognition, by significant others, of managerial excellence. The entrepreneur structures his role performance to achieve this recognition from fellow members of the firm but, and more especially, from outsiders such as other businessmen. Other goals and values stressed here are security and a concern to ensure that the entrepreneur's children will eventually receive the benefits of his enterprise.

These identities are connected to other aspects of the firm's operations and to processes of growth although it should be stressed again that these links should not be seen in a positivist sense. The links occur through the internal social logic generated out of the ways in which the situation is perceived by those involved and the actions which follow on from these perceptions.[24]

The 'artisan' identity is not very concerned with growth and is most frequently found among people who have only relatively recently adopted the entrepreneurial role. It reflects the feelings of social marginality common among entrepreneurs, and is greatly concerned with intrinsic satisfactions likely to minimise the psychological deprivations associated with recent social marginality. However, successful adoption of this identity must be tenuous. Given the data on the instability of new small firms, survival is always problematic. Equally, for the same reasons, it is unlikely that the goals and values associated with the other two identities will be given prominence at this stage.

On the other hand, a small firm which survives the formative period and enters a period of sustained profitability constitutes a social context conducive to the generation of a 'classical entrepreneur' identity. The goals associated with the artisan identity will have been at least partially realised and the new social and economic situation of the firm is favourable to the possible emergence of a new self-definition for the entrepreneur.

But whether any dramatic take-off into sustained growth is likely, even when the external logic — the economic and market situation of the firm and social relations with outsiders — is highly favourable, is a matter for debate and even scepticism. The internal logic of the firm from the point of view of its chief actor contains certain contradictions. A sustained high rate of growth may change the firm from a solution to social marginality to a situation reinforcing it.

As a firm grows forces emerge, internally and externally, which push it towards a more rational and bureaucratic structure. Management functions have to be delegated as they become too complex and time-consuming for a single person to handle. The need for certain skills, almost certainly not possessed by the entrepreneur, becomes crucial and specialists must be recruited. The social relations among participants can no longer be conducted on a highly personal basis but must be more systematically and bureaucratically ordered. From the entrepreneur's point of view, therefore, the firm comes increasingly to resemble previous social situations which produced the social marginality feelings the firm was established to minimise. Entrepreneurs in our own study who took on the classical entrepreneur identity often claimed, despited financial success, that they were 'beginning to feel like employees in their own firm'.

The emergence of these 'growth effects' depends on a variety of factors, and may not occur until the firm has grown to be of some size. But what is more important is whether the entrepreneur comes to perceive the likely outcomes of these changes and the decisions he makes concerning their desirability as well as his ability to cope with them in terms of the kind of person he has now become. So, again, we return to the internal social logic of the small firm, seen from the point of view of its main actor, and the possible outcomes which can develop.

Some small firm enterpreneurs will have little hesitation in deciding that growth is desirable or even necessary for survival. Having established that they can maintain a high-profit growth company, they may come to redefine their entrepreneurial role in terms of the 'manager' identity. In addition to the elements listed above, other behaviour patterns indicative of the presence of this identity are an increased interest in management training and development, employers' organisations, using management consultants, and attempts at taking over other firms and merging with larger companies or attempting to go public. Finally, it should be noted that the adoption of this new self-definition of the entrepreneurial role does not, of itself, give immunity against possible contradictions which may emerge as a result. The re-emergence of socially marginal feelings may occur but the entrepreneur, having embarked on a course of action, may find that it is extremely difficult to halt, let alone reverse, the outcomes.[25]

But this particular outcome, the rapid growth and expansion of the small firm, despite its important place in the social mythology of our society, is likely to be less frequent than many expect. The small entrepreneur may well make an assessment of the results of certain courses of action, and decide that, on balance the 'costs' (in social and psychological terms) of some of these are too high.

Adopting a conscious no-growth stance in our society is not easy. We live in a society with a strong growth ideology. Growth is 'progress' and businessmen are often judged by this criterion. It is not therefore surprising that small firm entrepreneurs are rather circumspect, even to the extent of self-deception, in not striving too hard for growth. One study of small firms in Britain summed up the atittudes among their sample as being

> roughly divided on this question [the amount of growth thought desirable]. Rather more agreed that expansion was desirable than backed the maintenance of the status quo. But it was noticeable that they often tended to express their views in a somewhat generalized way, as if they were paying lip service to an absolute abstract ideal of growth.[26]

The reasons given for not growing were often difficult to accept at face value. Relatively minor administrative chores such as collecting insurance contributions and PAYE were offered as 'barriers' to growth. Our view is that reluctance to grow has, in fact, much more to do with the consequences, in social terms, of growth than these vocalised reasons.

If this alternative view of the small firm growth patterns is accepted, a number of issues, not adequately covered by previous theories, are resolved. For instance, a social action view of the small firm and growth offers reasons as to why growth is, on the whole, much less common than the prevalent growth ideology would indicate. It explains why, given the data on the low level of rewards[27] (in material terms) of small businessmen the popularity of self-employment remains. It explains why the attractions of working for a large firm, with all that this implies in terms of security and material rewards, are rejected by certain people in our society. Also, it explains part of the highly skewed size distribution of firms in advanced industrial societies; it is not simply economic but social and psychological factors which also influences this distribution. Finally, this analysis also tells us something about the growth processes of those small firms who do join the 6 per cent of large firms in our economy.

Earlier theories of small firm growth, such as those discussed above, had, as one of their objectives, that of helping the owner-manager to understand better the growth process of his firm. Few theories in the social sciences would claim not to have practical implications, and ours is no exception. Our alternative approach to understanding the small firm has policy implications for small firm decision-makers, for government attempts to aid the small firm, and for consultants and others who seek to provide expert guidance. By taking a new starting point for analysis and a new theoretical stance, we see that much of the available effort here is likely to be ineffectual. In particular, our analysis and findings point up the fatuity of policies or advice uncritically taken from the experience or techniques of large firms.

Change and the small business

One of the main strengths of the model presented here is its dynamic nature, that is, its ability to explain changes which occur over time within small businesses. A close examination of businesses in the research sample over an extended period, backed up by retrospective data, gave the project a longitudinal character. A strategy of data–theory interaction pursued throughout the research ensured a close cohesion between research observations and explanatory theories.[28] The result of this overall approach has been success in understanding changes in entrepreneurial goals and other aspects of the social dynamics of small businesses over time.

The benefits of a dynamic theory can perhaps be usefully illustrated by comparison with the results of other studies. Research on small businesses carried out by the Bolton Committee in Britain and Collins and associates in America, presented a useful and interesting collection of statistics and opinions but provided little theoretical insight into the social dynamics of small businesses. Instead, they tend to leave the reader with a static or 'snapshot' picture of the 'average' small businessman at one point in time.

N.R. Smith went a stage further than this and attempted to develop a typology of entrepreneurs[29] in his reanalysis of data collected by Collins and associates.[30] Smith examined data on 52 entrepreneurs in businesses established after 1945 and which had been in existence at least five years. Using the theoretical strategy of the 'constructed type',[31] he analysed the data to set up two polar types of entrepreneur and labelled these 'craftsman-entrepreneur' and 'opportunistic-entrepreneur'.

The craftsman-entrepreneur tended to come from a working-class background and to have had a limited education usually restricted to technical subjects. Socially, he is detached from his environment, a 'loner' who finds it difficult to relate socially to others. As an employee he is rated outstanding at his job and builds up a big fund of technical expertise. Going into business for himself represents a way of making life easier for a loner and allows him to attain his ambition of producing a technically outstanding product. Working for other people is often frustrating because they are easily satisfied with a technically mediocre product in the interests of profit maximisation. The craftsman-entrepreneur believes people will always want the best.

This type of entrepreneur runs his business autocratically, refusing to delegate authority, and holds strong, paternalistic attitudes towards his workers. He rejects unionism as a threat to his independence. For the same reason he rejects outside sources of capital. He tries to build up highly personal relationships with customers and stakes his personal reputation on quality and delivery. He does not plan very far into the future.

The opportunistic-entrepreneur tends to come from a middle-class background and to have had a wide education covering both technical and non-technical subjects. Socially he integrates well into any social setting in which he participates. As a student at college, he is often involved in student affairs and as an employee he tends to have a wide variety of jobs, many of them needing verbal and social skills. He goes into business for himself when he considers he has the necessary skills, knowledge and opportunity. Entrepreneurship is the result of a plan sometimes taking several years to mature. This long-term attitude to planning is retained throughout his time as an entrepreneur.

As an employer, he finds it easy to delegate authority and hires employees on a universalistic basis. His ambition is to build up a large organisation. He is not afraid of using outside capital and is confident of his ability to 'win out', whatever the future offers.

Smith related these entrepreneurial types to the businesses in his sample and found that the businesses which appeared to be growing faster, as measured by sales turnover, were generally those with an owner-manager who approximated to the opportunistic-entrepreneur type.

It can be seen that many of Smith's ideas echo aspects of the theory presented earlier. His craftsman-entrepreneur type, for example, has many similarities with the artisan entrepreneurial identity outlined above while his opportunistic-entrepreneur type has similarities with the manager or entrepreneurial identities. However, a theoretical difference occurs with his use of the static constructed type to suggest mutually exclusive descriptions of entrepreneurial-role performances. One result of the use of this theoretical strategy is the suggestion that the role performance of the owner-manager remains essentially constant through time. For Smith, growth in the small business is only likely to go with a certain type of entrepreneur — the opportunistic-entrepreneur.

The theory presented in this paper, in contrast, harnesses the concept of role identity to analyse entrepreneurial-role performance. This implies a rejection of the idea of a static personality. Human beings adapt to the social situations in which they find themselves and major changes in the life situation, such as the shift from employee to employer status, can be expected to bring about corresponding changes in attitudes and behaviour.

The concept of role identity attempts to capture these variations over time. Accordingly, the role performance of the small entrepreneur is seen as being in a dynamic relation with business culture, the internal changes in the business's economic and social patterns and the wider society, as well as elements in the life history of the individual entrepreneur. Therefore growth is connected with the whole complex of factors which form the dynamic relations mentioned above rather than only with the personality of the owner-manager at the time of entry into entrepreneurship.

Another interesting echo of the model presented here is Smith's characterisation of the craftsman-entrepreneur as 'marginal'. However, Smith's treatment of the notion of marginality is a narrow one, restricted in its application strictly to the craftsman-entrepreneur prior to entry into business. This person is considered marginal whilst he is employed by others where, because of his 'loner' nature, he fails to identify with, or gain acceptance from, either fellow workers or management.

Smith, like most writers on the small businessman, fails to examine the entrepreneur's relationships with the wider social structure. Why is it that the craftsman-entrepreneur does not identify with other people when he is an employee? What is the impetus toward entrepreneurship for the opportunistic-entrepreneur? Vague assertions of 'a desire for independence' or 'an ambition to get ahead' fail to provide an adequate explanation at the sociological level for entry into entrepreneurship. Smith comes close to pinpointing the social basis of the motivation toward entrepreneurship in the case of the craftsman-entrepreneur but fails to see the central significance of social marginality in this process. It is not that he is merely marginal to his fellow workers and employers but marginal to his broader social milieu.

In the case of the opportunistic-entrepreneur, we are given no social indicators which would distinguish him from many thousands of other people from similar social and educational backgrounds. It may have been that some of the opportunistic-entrepreneurs were socially marginal but Smith's treatment of the data makes it impossible to answer this question.

Conclusion

Given a knowledge of the way the entrepreneur defines his role in relation to his self-identity, and accepting his decisive position in the firm, we can say quite a lot about how the firm is likely to operate in a wide variety of situations. Thus, the owner-manager with an 'artisan' identity places a high value on independence. This leads to an organisational climate founded on an autocratic leadership style, combined with a strong element of paternalism, which minimises dependence on others whether they be inside or outside the firm.[32] He is likely to perceive the firm as a 'contented team', underutilise the skills of subordinates and be blind to certain kinds of industrial relations problems. Awareness on the part of the entrepreneur of these possible results of a particular managerial style can help reduce unwanted side-effects. Outsiders, wishing to aid the small firm, will be able to evaluate the likelihood of success of proposed strategies against their knowledge of social relation patterns within the firm dictated largely by the entrepreneurial self-identity.

Probably the most problematic situation identified by our research is that where the owner-manager attempts to make the transition from an 'artisan' to a 'classical entrepreneur' identity. Growth is a strategy normally associated with this transition and the anticipated consequences of this, we argue, are often instrumental in the transition not being made. Even where it is made, the full consequences are often not fully realised, and this results in problems and conflicts — both identity conflicts for the entrepreneur and structural conflicts within the firm.

The administrative necessity to use a more consultative leadership style, to delegate and 'negotiate' with professionally trained managers brought in from outside, is not easily reconciled with the owner-manager's desire for independence. To this extent, he is a captive of the new situation he has himself brought about to meet his changing goals. Problems of a similar nature are likely to arise out of the increasing likelihood of unionisation. Entrepreneurs in our study were mostly aware of the positive correlation between organisational size and degree of unionisation. However, it was not often that unionisation was seen as an extension of the new order of things in a larger firm presenting management with benefits as well as problems. More commonly, a 'communications breakdown' or the actions of 'militants' among new workers were held responsible.

We are not arguing that all those who take on the owner-manager role are socially marginal. In some cases there are exceptional environmental circumstances which make entry into business comparatively easy. For example, an 'open' social and economic environment for entrepreneurship has apparently occurred in many of the developing countries.[33] Similarly, within advanced industrial societies some areas of economic activity may also become highly favourable to entrepreneurship, as seems to have happened in the US defence and space industries in the 1960s.[34] In these circumstances, many people without feelings of high marginality will found firms, and may quite deliberately aim for high growth.

Finally, it must be remembered that much small firm growth results from the management of second- and third-generation owner-managers. Whether first-generation owner-managed firms have lower rates of growth than their second- and subsequent-generation counterparts is unclear, as they start from different base lines making strict comparisons difficult. The Bolton Report suggested that first-generation owner-managed firms grew rather faster than those managed by subsequent generations, but this was based on a very small sample.[35] This was countered to some extent also by the further finding that fast growing firms relied to a great extent on borrowed funds. Our own research, and that of Collins *et al.,* noted earlier, found that highly socially marginal owner-managers, who are, as we have argued, more likely to be first-generation, were strongly opposed to external borrowing because of the threat posed to their personal autonomy.

We feel that second- or third-generation owner-managers, because they are more likely to have a conventional middle-class background and education, are more likely to have a conventional 'managerial' view of economic activity. Their personal life situation is less likely to be one of strong discrepancy between personal attributes and social role, and their socialisation will be toward the acceptance of the dominant business ideology of our society with its stress on growth and efficiency achieved through economies of scale. They will, therefore, be more receptive to ideas of expansion, merger and the professionally managed business.

References

1. See M.J.K. Stanworth and J. Curran, *Management Motivation in the Smaller Business,* Gower Press, Epping 1973.

2. Readers will, of course, be aware of the caution required in applying US data to the UK — see below our references to Mayer, Goldthorpe *et al.,* Roberts and Warner, and Cooper.

3. Among the best known are J.A. Schumpeter, *The Theory of Economic Development,* Cambridge, Mass., Harvard University Press, 1934; L. Urwick, 'Problems of Growth in Industrial Undertakings', *Winter Proceedings of the British of Management,* no. 2, 1948–9; E. Penrose, *The Theory of the Growth of the Firm,* Oxford, Basil Blackwell, 1957; O.F. Collins and D.G. Moore with D.B. Unwalla, *The Enterprising Man,* East Lansing, Michigan State University Press, 1964; G.F. Thomason and A.J. Mills, 'Management Decision-taking in Small Firms', *European Business,* no. 14, October 1976, pp. 29–41; T. Lupton, 'Small New Firms & Their Significance', *New Society,* 21 December 1967, pp. 890–2; T. Matthews and C. Mayers, *Developing A Small Firm,* London, BBC Publications, 1968; L.L. Steinmetz, 'Critical Stages of Small Business Growth', *Business Horizons,* vol. XII, no. 1, February 1969, pp. 29–34.

4. As in, for example L. Urwick, 'Problems of Growth'.

5. Often the discussion appears to be entirely speculative but even where it has empirical backing the samples are frequently very small. For example, the theory offered by Thomason and Mills is apparently based on a sample of four firms.

6. Urwick, 'Problems of Growth' and Thomason and Mills, 'Management Decision-taking' provide examples of the division of managerial roles occurring in stage two while Lupton, 'Small New Firms' and Matthews and Mayers, *Developing a Small Firm,* appear to offer an example of this occurring in stage three.

7. Exact data on the death rates of small firms is very difficult to come by but see the discussions in Deeks J, 'The Small Firm – Asset or Liability?', *Journal of Management Studies,* vol. 10, no. 1, Feb 1973, and J.E. Bolton, *Report of the Committee of Inquiry on Small Firms* (Bolton Report), Cmnd. 4811, London, HMSO, 1971.

8. A review of the literature on this view of growth in the small firm is provided in D.C. Mueller, 'A Life Cycle Theory of the Firm', *Journal of Industrial Economics,* vol. XX, no. 2, July 1972, pp. 199–219. See also Steinmetz, 'Critical Stages', for one version.

9. A fairly typical example is provided in Urwick, 'Problems of Growth', p. 9, when he suggests that the limits within which a one-man business can work effectively are approached when the owner-

manager has eight people directly reporting to him. The apparent precision here is not qualified by any reference to the kind of small firm the author has in mind; anyone with even the slightest research knowledge of small firms will know that even within a single branch of an industry small firms can display a considerable variation in management structure while remaining economically effective. Between industries such variations can be even greater.

10. For a discussion particularly relevant to economic organizations see D. Silverman, *The Theory of Organizations*, London, Heinemann, 1970, and more generally, P.S. Cohen, *Modern Social Theory*, London, Heinemann Educational Books, 1968, and P.L. Berger and T. Luckmann, *The Social Construction of Reality*, London, Allen Lane, 1967.

11. By 'external forces' we mean those factors which influence the structure of social relations in the firm but which originate from outside the firm. Actors in the firm may or may not be aware of these forces and their effects may be actual or potential.

12. M. Weber, *The Protestant Ethic and The Spirit of Capitalism*, London, Unwin University Books, 1965.

13. K.B. Mayer, 'Business Enterprise: Traditional Symbol of Opportunity', *British Journal of Sociology*, vol. IV, no. 2 (1953), pp. 160–80.

14. See, for example, J.H. Goldthorpe, D. Lockwood, F. Bechhofer and J. Platt, *The Affluent Worker: Industrial Attitudes and Behaviour*, Cambridge, Cambridge University Press, 1968, pp. 131–6.

15. For instance, a recent survey of material on this topic, W.M. Williams (ed.), *Occupational Choice: A Selection of Papers from the Sociological Review*, London, George Allen & Unwin, 1974, contains no discussion of this occupational alternative.

16. Bolton Report, pp. 8–9.

17. J. Deeks, 'Educational and Occupational Histories of Owner-Managers', *Journal of Management Studies*, vol. 9, no. 2 (May 1972), pp. 127–49.

18. Collins and Moore with Unwalla, *The Enterprising Man*, Chapter 5.

19. E.B. Roberts and H.A. Warner, 'New Enterprises on Route 128', *Science Journal* (December 1968), pp. 78–83; A.C. Cooper, 'Entrepreneurial Environment', *Industrial Research* (September 1970), pp. 74–6; P.R. Miles, 'Who Are the Entrepreneurs?', *MSU Business Topics* (Winter 1974), pp. 5–14. These sources seem, however, to refer to a special variety of entrepreneurship which emerged under conditions of a kind not frequently encountered in private enterprise societies. See the discussion below.

20. Collins and Moore with Unwalla, *The Enterprising Man*, pp. 243–4.

21. For a comprehensive history of the concept of 'social marginality' see H.P. Dickie-Clark, *The Marginal Situation*, London, Routledge and Kegan Paul, 1966.

22. K.B. Mayer and S. Goldstein, *The First Two Years: Problems of Small Firm Growth & Survival*, Small Business Research Series no. 2, Washington DC, Small Business Association, 1961, reported in Deeks J, 1973, op. cit.

23. A.W. Gouldner, 'Cosmopolitans and Locals: An Analysis of Latent Social Roles', *Administrative Science Quarterly*, vol. 2, no. 3 (December 1957), pp. 282–92, and vol. 2, no. 4 (March 1958), pp. 444–80.

24. Some readers will note the similarity between this analysis and that of N.R. Smith, *The Entrepreneur and his Firm: The Relationship Between Type of Man and Type of Company*, East Lansing, Michigan State University Press, 1967. However, there are fundamental differences between our approach and that of Smith. He assumes a fixed and unchanging entrepreneurial personality type pre-dating entry to entrepreneurial role. This denies the interplay between role and social experience and the constant reinterpretation of social reality and self which occurs in any role performance. For a further discussion see Stanworth and Curran, *Management Motivation*, pp. 171–6 and below.

25. For an example of this occurring see Stanworth and Curran, *Management Motivation*, Chapter 7.

26. C.W. Golby and G. Johns, *Attitude and Motivation, Committee of Inquiry on Small Firms, Research Report no. 7*, Cmnd, 4811, London, HMSO, 1971, p. 17.

27. See Merrett Cyriax Associates, *Dynamics of Small Firms, Committee of Inquiry on Small Firms, Research Report no. 12*, Cmnd. 4811, London, HMSO 1971, p. 35, for data for the UK. Collins and Moore with Unwalla, *The Enterprising Man*, suggest that a similar relatively low level of material rewards are received by small firm executives in the US.

28. The justification of this strategy, which is particularly suitable for the study of change in the smaller firm, is elaborated in B.G. Glaser and A. Strauss, *The Discovery of Grounded Theory*, London, Weidenfeld and Nicolson, 1967.

29. N.R. Smith *The Entrepreneur and his Firm*.

30. Collins and Moore with Unwalla, *The Enterprising Man*.

31. As developed by J.C. McKinney. Smith notes the following: J.C. McKinney, 'The Polar Variables of Type Construction', *Social Forces*

(May 1957) and J.C. McKinney and J.C. Kerckhoff, 'Towards a Codification of Typological Procedures', *Sociological Inquiry* (Winter 1962), pp. 128–35.

32. See the Bolton Report, Chapter 2, p. 24, on the attitude of many owner-managers towards sources of outside help and assistance.

33. This inference may be drawn from the data presented in W. Warren, 'Imperialism and Capitalist Industrialization', *New Left Review*, vol. 81 (September–October 1973), pp. 3–44.

34. Roberts and Warner, *Route 128*; Cooper, 'Entrepreneurial Environment' and Miles, 'Who are the entrepreneurs', all provide data on this type of entrepreneurship.

35. The Bolton Report, p. 17.

6 Technical Entrepreneurship: What Do We Know?

ARNOLD C. COOPER

New, technologically-based firms contribute in a variety of ways to the growth and vitality of the economy:

1 They are important sources of innovation, sometimes achieving great success in matching developing technologies and market needs.

2 They add to the vitality of industry, serving as new sources of competition and complementing and spurring the efforts of established firms.

3 They offer alternative career possibilities to those engineers and managers who do not function most effectively in large organisations.

4 From the standpoint of regional economic development, they make pleasant neighbours, producing relatively little noise and pollution, employing highly paid, technically trained people, and broadening the regional economic base, thus lessening reliance upon a few organisations.

Although many such firms have enjoyed only modest success and others have failed, some have become extremely successful businesses.

* From: *R & D Management* vol. 3, no. 2 (February 1973).

Companies such as Metals Research Ltd and Nuclear Instruments Ltd in England, and Digital Equipment and Memorex in America have enjoyed great success. Compared to other kinds of new business, technically oriented firms in America have experienced relatively low failure rates (Draheim *et al.* 1966; Roberts 1972; Cooper 1971). The employment provided by new firms, considered in the aggregate, can be substantial. For example, spin-off firms from the major laboratories affiliated to MIT provided, within a few years of founding, substantially more employment than did the parent laboratories (Roberts 1969).

In America, the birth of these new firms seems to be concentrated in particular places and at particular times. Cities such as Boston, Los Angeles, San Francisco, and Minneapolis have had in recent years large numbers of new firms. There are other regions which, although they employ large numbers of technical personnel, have had relatively few new companies founded. Outside the USA, the study of technical entrepreneurship is in its infancy (Watkins 1973).

Understanding what has been learned to date about technical entrepreneurship should be of interest to a number of groups, including engineers or technical managers who envisage becoming entrepreneurs, those concerned with regional economic development and managers of organisations interested in alternative ways of exploiting technology.

Influences upon entrepreneurship

The founding of a new firm is the result of a decision made by one or several entrepreneurs. The influences upon this decision might be organised under three general headings:

1 *The entrepreneur* himself, including the many aspects of his background that affect his motivations, his perceptions and his skills and knowledge.
2 *The established organisation* for which the founder had previously been working, which might be termed an 'incubator organisation'. Its characteristics influence the location and the nature of new firms, as well as the likelihood of spin-offs.
3 Various *external factors,* many of them regional in nature. These include the availability of capital, collective attitudes and perceptions relating to entrepreneurship, and accessibility to suppliers, personnel and markets.

The various influences on the entrepreneurial decision are shown in Figure 6.1.

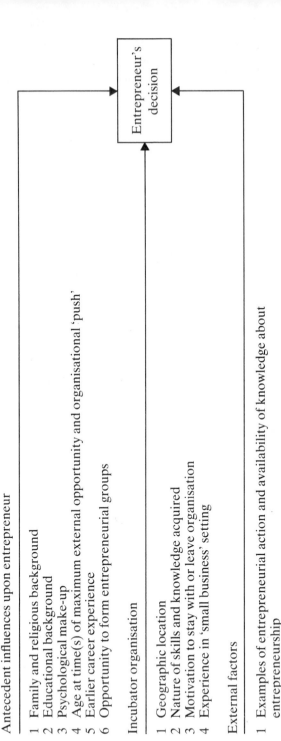

Antecedent influences upon entrepreneur

1 Family and religious background
2 Educational background
3 Psychological make-up
4 Age at time(s) of maximum external opportunity and organisational 'push'
5 Earlier career experience
6 Opportunity to form entrepreneurial groups

Incubator organisation

1 Geographic location
2 Nature of skills and knowledge acquired
3 Motivation to stay with or leave organisation
4 Experience in 'small business' setting

External factors

1 Examples of entrepreneurial action and availability of knowledge about entrepreneurship
2 Societal attitudes toward entrepreneurship
3 Ability to save 'seed capital'
4 Accessibility and availability of venture capital
5 Availability of personnel and supporting services; accessibility to customers; accessibility to university
6 Opportunities for interim consulting
7 Economic conditions

Figure 6.1 Influences upon the entrepreneurial decision

The individual entrepreneur

What are the characteristics of these people who choose to take the unusual step of starting new companies? What prepares and propels them toward this unique activity? The longest history of research in entrepreneurship centres on the individual founder. Although the technical entrepreneur has been studied much less extensively than his non-technical counterpart, the following characteristics emerge:

1   Founders of high-technology companies often form groups to start new companies. The percentage of new firms started by groups of two or more was 48 per cent in Austin, 61 per cent in Palo Alto, and 59 per cent in a study of 955 geographically diversified firms (Susbauer, 1967; Cooper 1971; Shapero 1971). Groups permit a more balanced management team, one less likely to have major areas of weakness. They also provide psychological support at a time when the individual may be wondering whether he is taking the right step.

2   Founders tend to be in their thirties when starting high-technology companies. The average age of founders studied was 34 in Austin, 35 in Philadelphia, and 32 in Boston (Susbauer 1969; Susbauer 1967; Roberts 1969). Apparently, at this time in their careers, they have sufficient experience and financial resources, yet are still willing to incur the necessary sacrifices and risks.

3   The typical American technical entrepreneur had at least a first degree, usually in engineering. In Boston and in Austin the median educational level was a Masters degree (Roberts 1969; Susbauer 1969). Since these new companies' competitive advantages are based upon the founders' knowledge, this is not surprising.

   Earlier studies of non-technical entrepreneurs emphasised that they tended to have modest educational qualifications. Often, they got along poorly with their fathers, their teachers and their employers; they often left school at an early age (Collins and Moore 1964). Available evidence on technical entrepreneurs suggests that they do not fit this mould, at least with respect to their tolerance of formal education.

4   Founders appear to be more single-minded in their devotion to careers than hired executives. Within the semiconductor industry, they had fewer outside civic and sports activities (Howell 1972).

5   Studies involving psychological tests and very limited numbers of

respondents showed that high technology entrepreneurs rated higher than average in aesthetic and theoretical orientations, leadership orientation, and achievement orientation. They rated low in religious orientation, need for support, need for conformity, and practical-mindedness. Interestingly, they did not have high scores in regard to economic values (Komives 1972). The high scores in need for achievement are consistent with a considerable body of research focusing upon the importance of this factor in entrepreneurial activity (McClelland, 1961).

6   A disproportionately high percentage of founders are from homes where the father was in business for himself (Roberts and Wainer 1971; Shapero 1971).

7   In some instances, an unusually high percentage of founders are from particular segments of the population. In Canada, 50 per cent were immigrants; in Boston, 16 per cent were Jewish (Litvak and Maule 1972; Roberts and Wainer 1971).

The incubator organisation

When a founder starts a new company the characteristics of the organisation he leaves, which might be termed the 'incubator', influence the entrepreneurial act in a number of ways:

1   The incubator organisation affects the location of the new firm; although technical founders may have been geographically mobile at earlier stages of their careers, they rarely move at the time they found new firms. The percentage of new companies which involved at least one founder who was already working in the area was 97.5 per cent in Palo Alto and 90 per cent in Austin (Cooper 1971; Susbauer 1972).

2   Established organisations also influence the nature of the new business established. In Palo Alto, 85.5 per cent of the new companies served the same general market or utilised the same general technology as the parent company (Cooper 1971). In Ann Arbor, 83.7 per cent of the new firms had initial products or services which drew 'directly' on the founders' previous technical employment, experience and knowledge (Lamont 1971). The founder typically exploits what he knows best. Thus, families of related companies grow up, such as hearing-aid companies in Minneapolis and chemical firms in Buffalo (Draheim 1972).

One study showed that spin-off firms from universities initially concentrated on providing servies — research and development, testing or consulting. Spin-offs from small firms tended to provide standard products, while those from large firms tended to provide custom products (Lamont 1971).

3   The established organisation also appears to influence strongly the motivations of the entrepreneur. In brief surveys founders tend to report the socially acceptable reasons why they became founders; these include the desire for independence, financial gain, etc. (Howell 1972; Roberts and Wainer 1971). However, depth interviews often disclose that the founder is 'pushed' from the parent organisation by frustration. In one study, 30 per cent of the founders quit their previous jobs with no specific plans for the future; 13 per cent had to leave because of factors such as plant closure and an additional 40 per cent said they would have left their previous positions even if they had not become entrepreneurs (Cooper 1971). Studies of spin-offs from individual organisations also show that internal factors influence spin-off rates. Thus, internal problems at Univac in Minneapolis and Tracor in Austin were both associated with subsequent spin-offs (Draheim 1972; Susbauer 1972).

Spin-off rates

Spin-off rates appear to vary widely, even among firms in the same geographical region. Some organisations function as incubators to a much greater extent than others. In Palo Alto, the range in spin-off rates for firms with more than three spin-offs during the 1960s was about 200 to 1. Many organisations had no spin-offs (Cooper 1972); for others, entrepreneurs were a major product.

In Palo Alto, small firms considered as a class (less than 500 employees) had spin-off rates ten times as high as large firms thus considered (Cooper 1971). Studies of four major MIT laboratories also showed that spin-off rates were inversely associated with laboratory size (Forseth, 1965). Consistent with these findings, another study showed that where a city is dependent upon one large, dominant firm, the development of new firms rarely occurs (Draheim et. al., 1966).

Very limited data suggest that, within large industrial firms, spin-offs occur chiefly from the 'small businesses' within the firm and rarely from the large, dominant divisions (Cooper 1971).

Clearly, incubator organisations influence entrepreneurship in a number of ways and some organisations make better incubators than others.

Some of the major complexes of new firms — such as Boston, Palo Alto and Ann Arbor — have grown up around universities and some observers have concluded that universities play a central role in the development of local entrepreneurship (Deutermann 1966; Allison 1965). But the extent to which universities have functioned as incubators, with students or staff spinning off to start new firms, has varied widely. In Boston, Austin, and Ann Arbor, substantial percentages of the new firms studied were direct spin-offs from a university or one of its laboratories (Roberts 1969; Susbauer 1972; Lamont 1971). Where direct spin-offs from the universities have occurred, they have rarely involved faculty giving up full-time positions to become founders. Although faculty have been involved in a variety of roles, including sometimes being the 'driving force', their commitment has usually been only part-time (Roberts 1972). Many spin-offs have occurred from university contract research laboratories engaged heavily in government research; notable examples are the Instrumentation Laboratory and Lincoln Laboratory at MIT.

However, a variety of other patterns also exists. In Palo Alto, only six of 243 firms founded in the 1960s had one or more full-time founders who came directly from a university (Cooper 1971). In that complex, the role of the university as an incubator appears to have been relatively more important in the earlier years. In both England and the United States, there are universities strong in science and engineering which have been associated with very little entrepreneurship. There are also instances of substantial entrepreneurship without the presence of a strong university. Shapero found that of 22 technical complexes studied, only seven had major universities. Several had no colleges when the technical company formation process was first observable (Shapero 1971).

Universities have undoubtedly played a role in attracting able young men and women to particular regions, and sometimes in giving the firms located there competitive advantages in recruiting and retaining these people. They also provide sources of consulting assistance and opportunities for continuing education for professional employees. However, the degree to which universities play a central or essential role in technical entrepreneurship appears to vary widely.

External factors

A complex of factors external to both the individual and the parent organisation also appears to influence entrepreneurship. Research to date provides us with only a limited understanding of many of these factors. Yet it is clear that they interact to create climates more or less favourable to entrepreneurship. It is also clear that climates can change over time and that, to some extent, past entrepreneurship makes future entrepreneurship more likely.

The decision to found a business is affected by the entrepreneur's perceptions of risks and rewards and his knowledge of sources of venture capital and of individuals and institutions which might provide help and advice. Past entrepreneurship creates what might be termed an 'entrepreneurial environment', in which the prospective founder is surrounded by examples and enveloped in knowledge about the process. A number of researchers report that the credibility of the act of starting a company appears to depend, in part, upon whether the founder knows of others who have taken this step (Shapero 1971; Cooper 1971).

Societal attitudes toward business and entrepreneurship are also undoubtedly important in influencing an individual's decision, with studies in a variety of countries showing that some cultures are more entrepreneurially inclined than others (Hagen 1971; McClelland 1961).

Venture capital

Venture capital is supplied both by the founders themselves and by external individuals and institutions. In one American study, 40 per cent of the technically-oriented firms were started primarily with founders' capital; in a Canadian study, 35 per cent of the firms were initially financed by the founders (Cooper 1971; Litvak and Maule 1972). The extent to which founders can save sufficient capital depends upon salary and taxation levels. Observers believe that entrepreneurship in the United Kingdom and Canada is seriously hampered by the difficulty in saving 'seed capital' (Bolton 1972; Hodgins 1972). In the American electronics industry, stock options, which are often intended to bind executives to firms, sometimes make it financially feasible for them to become entrepreneurs (Cooper 1971).

Institutions and individual investors vary substantially in the extent to which they are willing to invest in new, technologically-based firms. The prospective founder seeking capital must thus try to make contact with the 'right' sources of capital, those whose experience and attitudes make it more likely that they will assist this kind of venture. In areas of active entrepreneurship, well-developed communication channels may have developed, such that it is relatively easy for the prospective founder to make contact with experienced venture capital sources (Baty 1964).

In Palo Alto, externally supplied capital for the new firms of the 1960s often came from the successful entrepreneurs of the 1950s. Some of them had become venture capitalists after selling their businesses; others still active in their businesses advised both entrepreneurs and venture capitalists and served as vital communication links (Cooper 1971).

Attitudes toward investing in new, technically-based firms can change substantially over time. The success of Control Data in Minneapolis and Tracor in Austin apparently helped to change the local investment climate and made the raising of capital by subsequent waves of entrepreneurs much easier (Draheim 1972; Susbauer 1972).

Living conditions

To what extent are attractive living conditions essential if a complex of new firms is to develop? Clearly, established organisations consider whether they will be able to attract and keep highly trained, mobile, scientific personnel in deciding where to locate branch plants and laboratories. These organisations, in turn, can become the incubators which bring potential entrepreneurs to a region. However, available evidence suggests that, although attractive living conditions may attract technical people to an area as employees, they rarely attract men who are in the act of founding companies (Cooper 1971). Furthermore, one study of 22 areas of active entrepreneurship showed that only eight had unusually attractive living conditions (Shapero 1971). Some men leave parent organisations and become founders because, in part, they do not want to be transferred from a region they like (Susbauer 1972). However, in most instances living conditions do not appear to bear directly upon the decision to found a company.

Economics of location

How important are the economics of location, including transportation costs and the development of complexes of related firms which buy from and sell to each other? The growth of a complex conveys many benefits to new firms. These include pools of trained labour and the development of specialised suppliers. Although transportation costs may not be very important with many high-technology products, the ability to work closely with customers is sometimes essential. Location in a complex may be particularly important for those new firms which provide custom manufacturing services and which serve as satellite suppliers. An additional benefit is the development of specialised expertise among local accountants, bankers, and lawyers relating to the special needs of small, high-technology firms (Shapero 1971). Location in a complex of related firms also provides opportunities for consulting; these opportunities are particularly important for those founders who quit previous jobs with no specific plans for the future and who need to support themselves while plans are crystallising and capital is being raised (Cooper 1971).

Experienced entrepreneurs and small firms

Past entrepreneurship creates within a particular region many new technologically-based firms which as a class tend to have high spin-off rates and to be almost ideal incubators. In addition, past foundings create experienced entrepreneurs. When the founder sells out (or when disputes cause the founding team to break up) he often starts another firm, drawing upon his prior experience (Cooper 1971). In an area of active entrepreneurship, there may be hundreds of experienced founders whose presence makes future entrepreneurship more likely.

The development of an entrepreneurially active area

If an area is to develop and maintain technical entrepreneurship, organisations which can serve as incubators must be present, be attracted, or be created. Since founders tend to start firms where they are already living and working, there must be organisations which will hire, bring into the area, and train the engineers, scientists and technical managers who may someday become technical entrepreneurs.

However, the nature of these organisations is critical in determining whether spin-offs actually occur. It is certainly not difficult to point to cities where thousands of engineers are employed but where there is little entrepreneurship. Table 6.1 indicates the characteristics of firms and the industries in which they operate which may be associated with high or low birth-rates of new firms.

If the established firms serve markets that are stable or declining, there is little incentive for the prospective entrepreneur to enter the field. If the established firms are in industries which require large capital investments or substantial organisations to compete, it will be difficult to assemble the critical mass needed to get a new firm started.

Table 6.1
Industry and organisational attributes related to the birth-rate of new firms

Characteristics of industry

Low birth-rate	High birth-rate
slow industry growth	rapid industry growth
slow technological change	rapid technological change
heavy capital investment required	low capital investment required
substantial economies of scale	minor economies of scale

Characteristics of established incubator organisations

Low birth-rate	High birth-rate
large number of employees	small number of employees
organised by function	product-centralised organisation
recruit average technical people	recruit very capable people, ambitious people
relatively well managed	afflicted with periodic crises
located in isolated area of little entrepreneurship	located in area of high entrepreneurship

All of the attributes in a given column are not necessarily found together nor are they required to bring about a given spin-off rate. Various combinations may exist.

If the potential incubator firms hire relatively undynamic people, train them narrowly, and organise them along functional lines, it will be difficult to assemble a well-rounded founding team with the requisite knowledge and skills in marketing, engineering, and manufacturing. If the established firms are well managed and avoid periodic crises, there may be little incentive for potential founders to leave comfortable positions.

Under such conditions, a would-be founder will find the going difficult. If he seeks to bolster his confidence or to gain advice, he will find few successful founders who have preceded him. If he seeks to support himself as a consultant while formulating his plans and raising capital, he may find this difficult if there are few dynamic small companies in the region.

Sources of venture capital experienced in investing in new, techno-logically-based firms are probably not available locally and making contact with possible investors may be laborious and time consuming. In such an environment, the prospective founder's personal experience is likely to have been in large, established firms. He is likely to know little about what is involved in starting and managing a new firm.

How does the first new firm become established in such a region? Sometimes it involves those rare instances in which the founder comes from another geographical location or starts a new company not related to the business of the parent firm he has left. Sometimes, it involves a technically trained person who was working in a non-technical organisation (Shapero 1971).

The rate of entrepreneurial activity appears to be accelerated or diminished by a number of factors, one of the most important of which is the rate of development of the markets and technologies on which the area's industry is based. If these rates decline, then technical entrepreneurship will decline, for potential founders will find fewer areas of opportunity. In America, public attitudes relating to new issues of stock from recently formed companies are also important, for they substantially affect the availability of venture capital. However, if these factors are favourable, a self-reinforcing process takes place. Past entrepreneurship makes future entrepreneurship more likely and, in time, a high rate of entrepreneurial activity may develop.

References

Allison, D. (1965). 'The University and Regional Prosperity', *International Science and Technology,* April.

Baty, G. (1964). 'Initial Financing of the New Research-Based Enterprise in New England', Boston, Mass.: The Federal Reserve Bank of Boston.

Bolton, J.E. (1972). 'Small firms', speech to Management Forum, University of Manchester, 26 April.

Collins, D.F. and Moore, D.G. (1964). *The Enterprising Man,* East Lansing, Mich.: MSU Business Studies, Michigan State University Press.

Cooper, A.C. (1971). 'The Founding of Technologically-based Firms', Milwaukee, Wis.; The Center For Venture Management.

Cooper, A.C. (1972). 'Spin-offs and technical entrepreneurship', *I.E.E.E. Transactions on Engineering Management,* vol. EM-18, no. 1.

Deutermann, E. (1966). 'Seeding science-based industry', *New England Business Review,* December.

Draheim, K. (1972). 'Factors Influencing the Rate of Formation of Technical Companies' in A. Cooper and J. Komives (eds), *Technical Entrepreneurship: A Symposium,* Milwaukee, Wis.: The Centre for Venture Management.

Draheim, K., Howell, R.P., and Shapero, A. (1966), 'The Development of a Potential Defense R&D Complex', Menlo Park, Cal.,: Stanford Research Institute.

Forseth, D.A. (1965). 'The Role of Government-sponsored Research Laboratories in the Generation of New Enterprise: A Comparative Analysis', S.M. thesis, Cambridge, Mass.: MIT Sloan School of Management.

Hagen, E.E. (1971). 'How Economic Growth Begins: A Theory of Social Change' in P. Kilby (ed.), *Entrepreneurship and Economic Development,* New York, N.Y.: The Free Press.

Hodgins, J.W. (1972). 'Management Challenges to the Entrepreneur', *The Business Quarterly,* vol. 37, no. 1.

Howell, R.P. (1972). 'Comparative Profiles — Entrepreneurs versus the Hired Executive; San Francisco Peninsula Semiconductor Industry' in Cooper and Komives (eds), *Technical Entrepreneurship; a Symposium.*

Komives, J.L. (1972). 'A Preliminary Study of the Personal Values of High Technology Entrepreneurs' in Cooper and Komives (eds), *Technical Entrepreneurship; A Symposium.*

Lamont, L.M. (1971). 'Technology Transfer, Innovation, and Marketing in Science-Oriented Spin-Off Firms', Ann Arbor, Mich.; Industrial Development Division, Institute of Science and Technology, University of Michigan.

Lamont, L.M. (1972). 'The Role of Marketing in Technical Entrepreneurship' in Cooper and Komives (eds), *Technical Entrepreneurship; A Symposium.*

Litvak, I.A. and Maule, C.J. (1972). 'Managing the Entrepreneurial Enterprise', *The Business Quarterly,* vol. 37, no. 2.

McClelland, D.C. (1961). *The Achieving Society,* Princeton, NJ; D. Van Nostrand, Inc.

Roberts, E.B. (1969). 'Entrepreneurship and Technology' in W. Gruber and D. Marquis (eds), *Factors in the Transfer of Technology,* Cambridge, Mass.: The MIT Press.

Roberts, E.B. (1972). 'Influences upon Performance of New Technical Enterprises' in Cooper and Komives (eds), *Technical Entrepreneurship; A symposium.*

Roberts, E.B. and Wainer, H.A. (1971). 'Some Characteristics of Technical Entrepreneurs', *I.E.E.E. Transactions on Engineering Management,* vol. EM-18, no. 3.

Shapero, A. (1971). *An Action Program for Entrepreneurship,* Austin, Texas: Multi-Disciplinary Research Inc.

Susbauer, J.C. (1967). 'The Science Entrepreneur', *Industrial Research,* February.

Susbauer, J.C. (1969). 'The Technical Company Formation Process: A Particular Aspect of Entrepreneurship', PhD dissertation, Austin, Texas: University of Texas.

Susbauer, J.C. (1972). 'The Technical Entrepreneurship Process in Austin, Texas' in Cooper and Komives (eds), *Technical Entrepreneurship: A Symposium.*

Watkins, D.S. (1973). 'Technical Entrepreneurship; A Cis-Atlantic View, *R & D Management,* vol. 3, no. 2.

7 The Role of Small Firms in Technological Innovation*

ROY ROTHWELL

Introduction

The debate concerning the relative contribution of firms of different sizes to industrial technological innovation has continued for many years. It has on the one hand been argued that large size and monopoly power are prerequisites for economic growth via technological change because of the high costs and the technical and economic uncertainties involved in innovating (Galbraith 1957); on the other hand it has been argued that the smaller firm is inherently more efficient at performing innovation activities and hence that smaller firms are a major source of innovations (Prakke 1974).

During the 1960s in most countries in Europe government policies favoured the large firm, and company mergers were encouraged and facilitated in order to create major national corporations capable of competing in world markets. During this period the dominant ethos could be said to be 'big is beautiful'. From the mid-1970s onwards, in contrast, government policies towards technological and economic

* The author wishes to acknowledge the financial support of the Leverhulme Trust Fund during the preparation of this paper. He would also like to express his thanks to Mike Robson, Joe Townsend and Sally Wyatt of the Science Policy Research Unit for their data contributions.

development began increasingly to favour the smaller firm (Rothwell and Zegveld 1981). This appears to be based on the belief that small and medium-sized enterprises (SMEs), which, for present purposes, are taken to be firms with less than 500 employees, are a potent vehicle for the creation of new jobs, for regional economic renewal and for enhancing national rates of technological innovation (Rothwell and Zegveld 1982). In Europe, and perhaps especially in the United Kingdom, the dominant ethos today can be said to be 'small is beautiful'.

In a number of respects a debate that argues for large firms *or* for small firms, and which does so in a largely static context, fails to grasp both the complexity and the dynamics of industrial technological change. In the first place, small and large firms do not exist in separate worlds, and large modern corporations cannot exist without an appropriate 'hinterland' of small subcontractors and suppliers. Sometimes the small supplier will 'push' innovative components and sub-assemblies into its large customer; in other instances the large user will establish stringent performance specifications designed to 'pull' innovations out from the small supplier. Small firms can also innovate to fill narrow market niches considered as too small by their larger counterparts or can develop innovative customer-specific 'add-ons' to large firm products.

A second crucial point is that the relative importance of firms of different sizes to innovation in a particular industry might depend on the *age* of that industry. The *type* of innovation typically produced by large and small firms at different stages of the industry cycle might also vary between product and process innovation. This suggests the necessity for adopting a dynamic or 'Schumpeterian' view of the roles of different-sized firms in innovation. Schumpeter (1939) emphasised that while entrepreneurs play a significant part in the establishment of new branches of industry, during the latter phases of industrial development innovation requires large firms because of the high costs involved, and considerable market power if innovation is to be worthwhile.

Finally, it should be acknowledged that at any given time the relative innovatory contributions of small and large firms might vary greatly from sector to sector, depending on such factors as capital costs, research and development requirements and optimal scale of manufacturing. Several of these issues will be dealt with below, but firstly we shall briefly discuss a number of advantages and disadvantages variously ascribed to small and large firms in innovation; these are listed in Table 7.1.

Table 7.1

Advantages and disadvantages* of small and large firms in innovation

	Small firms	Large firms
Marketing	Ability to react quickly to keep abreast of fast changing market requirements. (Market start-up abroad can be prohibitively costly.)	Comprehensive distribution and servicing facilities. High degree of market power with existing products.
Management	Lack of bureaucracy. Dynamic, entrepreneurial managers react quickly to take advantage of new opportunities and are willing to accept risk.	Professional managers able to control complex organisations and establish corporate strategies. (Can suffer an excess of bureaucracy. Often controlled by accountants who can be risk-averse. Managers can become mere 'administrators' who lack dynamism with respect to new long-term opportunities.)
Internal communication	Efficient and informal internal communication networks. Affords a fast response to internal problem solving; provides ability to reorganise rapidly to adapt to change in the external environment.	(Internal communications often cumbersome; this can lead to slow reaction to external threats and opportunities.)
Qualified technical manpower	(Often lack suitably qualified technical specialists. Often unable to support a formal R&D effort on an appreciable scale.)	Ability to attract highly skilled technical specialists. Can support the establishment of a large R&D laboratory.
External communications	(Often lack the time or resources to identify and use important external sources of scientific and technological expertise.)	Able to 'plug-in' to external sources of scientific and technological expertise. Can afford library and information services. Can subcontract R&D to specialist centres of expertise. Can buy crucial technical

116

Area	Small firm (disadvantage)	Large firm (advantage)
	can represent a disproportionately large financial risk. Inability to spread risk over a portfolio of projects.)	Better able to fund diversification into new technologies and new markets.
Economics of scale and the systems approach	(In some areas scale economies form a substantial entry barrier to small firms. Inability to offer integrated product lines or systems.)	Ability to gain scale economies in R&D, production and marketing. Ability to offer a range of complementary products. Ability to bid for large turnkey projects.
Growth	(Can experience difficulty in acquiring external capital necessary for rapid growth. Entrepreneurial managers sometimes unable to cope with increasingly complex organisations.)	Ability to finance expansion of production base. Ability to fund growth via diversification and acquisition.
Patents	(Can experience problems in coping with the patent system. Cannot afford time or costs involved in patent litigation.)	Ability to employ patent specialists. Can afford to litigate to defend patents against infringement.
Government regulations	(Often cannot cope with complex regulations. Unit costs of compliance for small firms often high.)	Ability to fund legal services to cope with complex regulatory requirements. Can spread regulatory costs. Able to fund R&D necessary for compliance.

Note: The statements in brackets epresent areas of potential *disadvantage*. Abstracted from Rothwell and Zegveld (1982).
Source: Rothwell (1983).

Two points are immediately obvious from Table 7.1: first, innovatory advantage is unequivocally associated with *neither* large *nor* small firms; second, the advantages of large firms are associated with the relatively greater financial and technical resources available to them (with an associated ability to accommodate higher risks) while the advantages of small firms are those of flexibility and adaptability. Thus, in a sense, the advantages of large firms are mainly 'material', while those of small firms are in the main 'behavioural'.

To enable a firm to undertake the rational planning and assessment of both ongoing and potential innovatory endeavours, a great deal of information is needed on a variety of subjects such as the market situation, new technological developments, sources of technical assistance, government promotional measures and so on. Because of their relative lack of in-house resources, SMEs are often at a disadvantage in gathering and analysing such information. One survey in West Germany, for example (a country in which SMEs have performed competitively extremely effectively), showed that few small firms attempted to forecast technological developments, a major reason being that they regarded gathering pertinent information as being too expensive. Further, funds for hiring qualified employees to perform this work were not available (Oppenländer 1976). A second survey in West Germany showed, with respect to information on economic developments, that most small firms were unable to gather and analyse economic and market data useful to their specific needs (Neumann 1973). The availability of venture capital is also often concentrated at the centre, making access difficult for firms in the more peripheral regions (Oakey 1984; Rothwell 1986).

Table 7.2

Sales in the northern region by new local firms and established plants

Sales in northern region as a percentage of total sales	Number of new firms	Number of plants in 'Morley' sample*
0–5	7 (12%)	44 (53%)
6–25	8 (13%)	19 (23%)
26–75	15 (25%)	10 (12%)
76–100	30 (50%)	10 (12%)

* R. Morley, 'Employment, Investment and Regional Policy in the Northern Region', North of England Development Council, Newcastle, 1976.
Source: P. Johnson and G. Cathcart (1980).

It is for the above reasons that the markets of small independent firms (and especially *young* firms) are often geographically constrained, thus making small firm innovation a largely 'local' phenomenon (Thwaites *et al.*, 1981). This is well illustrated for the UK in Table 7.2, taken from Johnson and Cathcart (1980), which compares sales in the northern region of Britain, as a percentage of total sales, of 60 new local small firms and 83 plants belonging mainly to well-established firms (many being 'immigrant' branch plants). Clearly the new small businesses have significantly stronger links with local markets than do the (larger) established plants. Because of their greater resources, large firms can, of course, establish geographically diverse market and technical links, thereby overcoming local resource and demand deficiencies. Thus in those regions that are deficient in innovation-demanding markets (often the case in the development regions) small firms are at a severe disadvantage relative to their larger counterparts (Rothwell 1984a); the same can be said of small firms located in research and development deficient regions (Marquand 1981). Despite their many material disadvantages, small firms, as we shall see below, have in the past played, and continue today to play, an important role in industrial innovation.

The role of small firms in innovation in the UK

Probably the most comprehensive innovation database currently available is that compiled by the Science Policy Research Unit (SPRU) on significant innovations introduced in the United Kingdom since 1945 (Robson and Townsend 1984). Today this includes details on nearly 4400 innovations introduced by British firms since 1945, including information on the size of the innovating firm.

Table 7.3 presents aggregated data showing the percentage of innovations by size of firm for eight time periods between 1945 and 1983. It shows that SMEs' share of total innovations has averaged 26.4 per cent during the 38-year period covered and that it has increased significantly since 1975. Whether or not the dramatic increase during 1980–3 is due to the influence of the plethora of government policy initiatives introduced to assist small firms, and to the greatly increased availability of private sector venture capital for small firms since 1980 (Rothwell 1986), is not known. The marked decrease in share by firms in the size category 1000–9999 appears to be partly the result of structural industrial shifts caused by a series of takeovers and mergers, although as we shall see later shifts in relative innovative efficiency have also played a part.

Table 7.3
Innovation share (per cent) by size of firm in the UK, 1945–83

Time Period	Size of firm							No. of Innovations
	1–199	200–499	500–999	1000–9999	10 000–29 999	30 000–99 999	100 000+	
1945–49	16.8	7.5	5.3	28.3	13.7	18.1	10.2	226
1950–54	14.2	9.5	4.5	32.3	18.4	12.0	9.2	359
1955–59	14.4	10.1	9.1	24.9	16.3	13.2	11.9	514
1960–64	13.6	9.2	6.0	27.8	16.2	14.5	12.7	684
1965–69	15.4	8.2	8.5	24.2	15.6	14.9	13.2	720
1970–74	17.5	9.0	6.3	20.7	17.1	15.4	14.0	656
1975–79	19.6	9.6	7.5	16.2	14.1	18.6	14.5	823
1980–83	26.8	12.1	4.3	14.9	14.6	12.1	15.2	396
Number of innovations	744	411	299	1004	690	660	570	4378
Average percentage	17.0	9.4	6.8	22.9	15.8	15.1	13.0	100

Table 7.4
Innovation share (per cent) by size of innovating unit in the UK, 1945–83

Time Period	Size of innovating unit							No. of Innovations
	1–199	200–499	500–999	1000–9999	10 000–29 999	30 000–99 999	100 000+	
1945–49	18.6	9.3	8.8	48.7	11.5	0.9	2.2	226
1950–54	20.1	13.6	6.1	46.8	9.2	2.8	1.4	359
1955–59	17.9	14.0	11.5	39.7	11.9	2.7	2.3	514
1960–64	17.4	12.7	10.2	41.8	11.7	3.4	2.8	684
1965–69	21.4	14.2	11.4	37.9	9.2	3.3	2.6	720
1970–74	24.5	14.0	12.2	34.0	10.1	2.9	2.3	656
1975–79	31.3	13.6	13.0	29.8	8.3	2.7	1.3	823
1980–83	32.1	17.7	10.1	29.3	6.8	2.8	1.3	396
Number of innovations	1025	605	480	1625	427	125	91	4378
Average percentage	23.4	13.8	11.0	37.1	9.8	2.9	2.1	100

Table 7.4 presents aggregated time series data for innovation share, not by size of innovating firm as in Table 7.3, but by size of innovating *unit,* i.e. subsidiary, division, central laboratory, etc. This shows a marked shift in share of innovations towards small and medium-sized units (SMUs), from 27.9 per cent during 1945–9 to 49.8 per cent during 1980–3. As Figure 7.1 suggests, this is again the result of changing patterns of ownership with an increasing share of innovations being taken by subsidiaries of larger companies. To some extent this pattern might reflect, at least implicitly, attempts on the part of larger companies to marry the resource-related advantages of large-firms to the behavioural advantages enjoyed by smaller firms listed in Table 7.1. What the SPRU data do indicate is that large firms have moved into new areas of activity often through acquisitions.

It was suggested earlier that the innovatory potential of firms of different sizes is likely to vary considerably between sectors, and the disaggregated SPRU data have confirmed this to be the case. In the scientific instruments industry, for example, SMEs have been consistently innovative and have enjoyed an average of 58.5 per cent of total sectoral innovations between 1945 and 1983. This is an area in which entry costs are relatively low and in which there exist many specialist market niches suitable for exploitation by SMEs.

In pharmaceuticals, in contrast, SMEs' share in innovations averaged only 14 per cent over the 38-year period, and it has been zero since 1974. Pharmaceuticals is a research and development intensive area in which development costs are high and in which the introduction of a new ethical drug involves considerable regulatory costs and sometimes uncertainties (Rothwell 1979). In general, the SPRU data confirmed that where entry costs are high, SMEs' share in innovations is relatively small.

The case of electronic computers is interesting since it illustrates clearly the necessity for adopting a dynamic approach to the question of firm size and innovation. For most of the period up to 1970 SMEs' share of innovations in this area was relatively small or zero. Taking the three time periods between 1970 and 1983, however, shows how SMEs' share has increased dramatically, from 36 per cent (1970–4) to 47 per cent (1975–9) to 64 per cent (1980–3). During the 1950s and the 1960s UK production consisted almost entirely of mainframe computers with associated high research and development, manufacturing and servicing costs, which effectively debarred SME participation on an appreciable scale. With the introduction of the integrated circuit and more significantly of the microprocessor, entry by SMEs became entirely possible, and they rapidly became involved in the production of mini-and microcomputers and peripherals to satisfy the many new

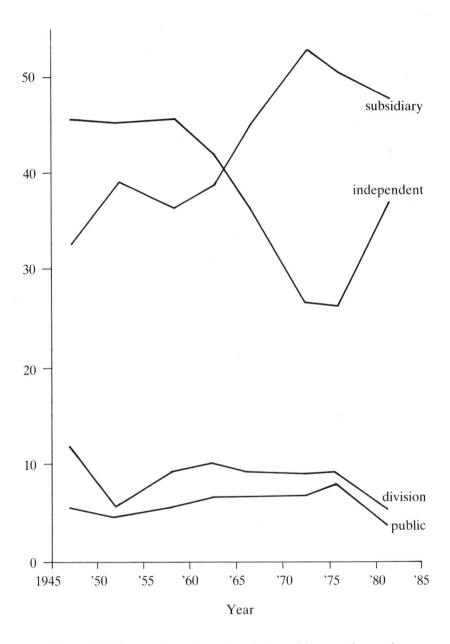

Figure 7.1 Innovation share by status of innovating unit

market segments that emerged. The rapidly developing field of biotechnology might similarly open up niche opportunities for SMEs in pharmaceuticals and related areas. Thus while one type of technology might effectively prevent significant participation by SMEs, another can present them with many new product-market opportunities.

Simply counting innovation shares, of course, tells us nothing about the relative innovative efficiency of firms of different sizes measured as innovations per unit of employment; nor does it provide any indication of relative research and development efficiency measured as innovation per unit of research and development expenditure. This issue has been dealt with in some detail by Wyatt (1984), whose results will be summarised here.

Utilising the SPRU innovation data and employment statistics published by the UK Business Statistics Office, Wyatt has derived time series data on the innovative efficiency (the ratio of innovation share to employment share) for firms in five employment categories. This analysis, using aggregated data, shows:

1   An increase over time in the relative innovative efficiency of firms with between 1 and 199 employees, from 0.46 in 1955–9 to 0.53 in 1975–80.
2   An increase over time in the relative innovative efficiency of firms with between 200 and 499 employees, from 0.66 in 1955–9 to 0.82 in 1975–80.
3   A decrease over time in relative innovative efficiency of firms with between 500 and 999 employees, from 0.76 in 1955–9 to 0.46 in 1975–80.
4   A more marked decrease over time in the relative innovative efficiency of firms with between 1000 and 9999 employees, from 0.83 in 1955–9 to 0.45 in 1975–80.
5   A consistently greater than unity relative innovative efficiency of firms with more than 10 000 employees: for instance, a ratio of 2.02 in 1955–9 and a ratio of 1.91 in 1975–80.

On the basis of these data, Wyatt concludes that the fact that firms with less than 500 employees have maintained their share of British innovations more successfully than those with between 500 and 10 000 employees reflects not only structural industrial shifts, but also changing patterns of innovative efficiency. While the aggregate data indicate that it is firms in the largest size category that have attained the highest levels of relative innovative efficiency, the disaggregated data, as we might expect, indicate considerable variation between sectors, and small firms show relative innovative efficiency levels of greater than

124

unity in plastics, textile machinery, mining machinery, radio, radar and electronics capital goods and scientific instruments.

Turning to relative research and development efficiency of innovation, Wyatt's data paint a rather different picture. In 1975, firms with between 100 and 499 employees made 2 per cent of total national manufacturing research and development expenditure; between 1969 and 1980, they produced 20.6 per cent of total innovations, yielding a relative research and development efficiency ratio of 10.3. The comparable figures for firms in the largest size category (more than 10 000 employees) are 80 per cent and 43.4 per cent respectively, yielding a relative R and D efficiency ratio of 0.54. Thus, on the basis of these data, research and development efficiency is very much higher in the smaller firms. A possible explanation of this, and one favoured by Wyatt, is that there is a lower degree of functional specialisation in small firms with a higher proportion of innovative activities occurring outside of what is formally defined as research and development. This would imply, however, that the informal research and development performed in small firms is very considerable indeed. For example, even if we ascribe a 20 per cent share of total research and development to the smaller firms — a factor of ten increase — their relative research and development efficiency would still be almost double that of the largest firms. Whatever the case, given the overwhelming concentration of research and development resources in the largest-sized firms, it is hardly surprising that they have produced the bulk of British innovations. From the viewpoint of the health of the small firm sector in Britain, perhaps the most promising feature is the increasing innovative efficiency of SMEs; given their relative lack of research and development resources, they have performed remarkably well.

Categories of innovative SME

To talk of the innovatory role of SMEs or of 'the small firm sector', does, in fact, imply a degree of homogeneity amongst small firms that simply does not exist, and it might be useful at this juncture to attempt some form of categorisation. To this end we can identify three basic classes of SME according to the products they manufacture and the markets they serve. These are: SMEs in traditional sectors; 'modern', niche strategy SMEs; new technology-based firms (NTBFs).

The traditional SME operates in long-established areas such as textiles, garments, leatherwear and metalworking. Technical change in such firms has less to do with 'research and development' than with 'design and development'; in other words, with incremental quality and design improvements to well-established product lines. The bulk of the real technological change occurring in traditional SMEs is exogenous: it derives from suppliers of materials, components and capital goods, and it is more often process-oriented technological change. Such firms exist in large numbers in all the advanced market economies, often clustering in the development regions. The various technology transfer schemes being operated by the UK government (and others) are largely designed to assist this class of SME. It is a category of firm which we would not expect to make a significant contribution to national rates of innovation.

Niche strategy SMEs utilise product technology to afford them the ability to compete for specific market segments through the provision of innovative, often custom built, devices. They operate in areas such as scientific instruments and specialist machinery in which, as we have seen, they have made a significant innovatory contribution in the UK. In West Germany small and medium-sized engineering firms have been technologically highly progressive and they have made a significant contribution to German post-war industrial and economic recovery. Because of the nature of the markets in which they operate, many niche strategy firms tend to remain in the SME size range.

NTBFs are a special category of small firm. They tend to operate in newly emerging and fast moving areas of technology, and are highly innovative. Their membership of the SME category is transitory, since it is this type of small firm that has high growth potential and can rapidly develop to attain national and international importance. Many such firms were established in the USA during the early and rapid growth phases of the semiconductor, computer aided design and microcomputer industries. NTBF formation on an appreciable scale appears to be a largely North American phenomenon, and relatively few such firms have emerged in Europe (Little 1977).

In addition to the three categories described above, which are classified largely according to the degree and nature of product technological embodiment, there is a fourth category of SME, that of parts and sub-assembly suppliers. This latter class of SME does not manufacture complete products, but rather supplies inputs to the products produced by firms of all sizes and operating across the technology spectrum. Often they will perform little research and development of their own, but produce to precise user specifications, established on the basis of research and development efforts in the user company. In this respect, their potential for innovation may be determined mainly by the nature of these specifications. In other cases, for example in electronics components and sub-assemblies, supplier firms may be innovative in their own right. In Japan, a system of 'tied subcontractors' has provided the major corporations with considerable production flexibility and other benefits which have made a substantial contribution to post-war Japanese industrial success (Twaalfhoven and Hattori 1982).

Relationships between small and large firms

As we suggested earlier, small and large firms do not exist in separate worlds and there is often a high degree of interrelatedness between them. The most obvious example of this, perhaps, is the supplier–customer relationship, a good illustrative example being the networks of component and sub-assembly suppliers to the automobile sector. But other kinds of relationship also occur which are based on product or technological complementarities. In the United States, for example, a number of large corporations have formed joint technological ventures with innovative small companies in which the small company produces sophisticated products for use by the large firm or which complement the large firm's product range. A number of examples of joint ventures between large and small firms in the United States are given in Table 7.5.

Examples of complementarities between large and small firms also exist in Europe (Rothwell and Zegveld, 1985). A study of new, small, technology-based firms in Sweden, for example, showed that large Swedish firms frequently supported them in a variety of ways, usually through the provision of technology and skilled labour (Utterbach 1982). Moreover, the large firms often acted as early markets for the newcomers, and prepayments were among the most important sources of finances for half the small firms in the sample.

A second study, this time in the Netherlands, looked at the relationship between spin-off firms and their 'parent' company (van der Meer and van Tilburg 1983). It showed that both the parent firm and the spin-off benefited through cooperation, often involving support from the former. An illustrative example is the case of Philips and the spin-off company, B & B Electronics BV, which specialises in the production and installation of electronic scoreboards and related products. These activities were of too small a scale to be of interest to Philips, and B & B were able to produce a qualitatively equivalent product at lower cost. Philips' support consisted of the provision of technical information and appropriate labour to B & B. The most important support, however, consisted of obtaining orders from Philips and assistance with B & B's export activities. Philips included the (complementary) B & B products in quotations to its customers,

Table 7.5
Some large–small US joint ventures

Large company	Small company	Area of joint venture
American Broadcasting Company	Technical Operations Inc.	Black and white film transmitted to colour viewing over TV
American District Telegraph	Solid State Technology	Industrial security systems
Bell & Howell	Microx	Microfilm reader
Bravo Corporation	Anti-Pollution Systems Inc.	Molten salt pollution control systems
Elliot Machine Div. of Carrier Corporation	Mechanical Technology Inc.	High speed centrifugal compressors
Exxon Nuclear Corp.	Avco-Everett Research Laboratory	High-energy laser uranium isotope separation and enrichment
Ford Motor Company	Thermoelectron Corp.	Steam engines for automobiles
General Electric Co.	Bolt Beranek & Newman Inc.	Hospital computer system
Johnson & Johnson Co.	Damon Corporation	Automated clinical laboratory system
Mobil Corporation	Tyco Laboratories Inc.	Long-crystal silicon solar conversion technology
Pitney-Bowes Co.	Alpex Computer Corp.	Electronic 'point of sale' check-out systems
Roche Electronics Division of Hoffman-La Roche	Avco-Everett Reseach Laboratory	Inflation balloon heart assist system
Wyeth laboratories, Division of American Home Products	Survival Technology Inc.	Self-administered heart attack drug and injection system

Source: Professor E. Roberts, Sloan School of Management, MIT.

thus enabling it to offer complete installations for projects such as football stadia.

A second kind of complementarity was the rendering of supplementary services by the spin-off with respect to the products of the parent firm, a good example being in the area of traffic control systems. Philips, a large producer of traffic control systems, considered their installation a necessary but not particularly advantageous undertaking, and a firm spun off from Philips to specialise in installation and related servicing activities. In the first years of its existence, Philips was the new firm's most important customer. The benefit to both companies was clear: the new firm obtained orders for its services and Philips had no further worries about installation activities.

The role of small firms in the emergence of new technologies

Up to this point we have dealt largely with the role of small firms in introducing new product innovations. Below we shall adopt a more dynamic view and describe the role that NTBFs have played in the emergence of new technologies and new industrial sectors based on those technologies. Following the discussion in the last section, it will once again illustrate the importance of interrelationships of large and small firms. (Rothwell and Zegveld, 1985).

The evolution of the US semiconductor industry

An approximate example of Schumpeterian industrial evolution, and one which illustrates the importance of complementarities between large and small firms, can be found in the evolution of the US semiconductor industry. The beginnings of the semiconductor industry can be traced to the invention of the transistor effect in Bell Telephone Laboratories in 1947 by Bardeen and Brattain. Although their findings paved the way for the invention of the bipolar junction transistor, the real breakthrough came in 1952 when Shockley, the research team leader, described a field effect transistor with a central electrode consisting of a reverse-biased junction. Shockley subsequently left Bell Laboratories and several years later he established his own company in his native Palo Alto, backed by finance from the Clevite Corporation. Shockley attracted a number of leading physicists and engineers into his company but, in 1957, eight of his brightest people left to form their own company. This marked the beginning of the rapid growth of new technology-based firms in the Palo Alto area, which subsequently gave it its name of Silicon Valley. While a number of other centres of semiconductor production were emerging concurrently, notably in Dallas, Texas (Texas Instruments) and Phoenix, Arizona (Motorola), nevertheless it is true that Silicon Valley has been the exception in world terms in the amount of semiconductor production and technological innovation that has occurred in such a concentrated area.

The eight ex-Shockley workers succeeded in obtaining backing from the Fairchild Camera Corporation, which had been actively seeking diversification, and, in September 1957, Fairchild Semiconductor was founded in Mountain View, California. In 1959, Fairchild Camera Corporation exercised an option to buy a majority interest in Fairchild Semiconductor. The latter grew rapidly from sales of $0.5 million in 1960, to $27 million in 1967, to $520 million in 1978.

During the next few years there was considerable spin off from Fairchild Semiconductor of both people and technology, and many companies were formed by people formerly with, or associated with, Fairchild. This process has been described by Mason (1979):

> The first spin-off was in 1959, when Baldwin, not from the original Shockley team, left Fairchild to form Rheem Semiconductor, collecting on the way people from Hughes Aircraft. In 1961, four of the originals left to form Amelco and one of these, Hoeni, left in 1964 to form Union Carbide Electronics; moving on in 1967 to form Intersil. Of . . . interest . . . was another event in 1961, when Signetics was formed. This was formed by four people who were a significant part of the Fairchild Semiconductor team. . . . They managed to get venture capital backing from the Dow-Corning group for this move.

At the same time that new technology-based small firms were being spawned in Silicon Valley, Bell Laboratories (a subsidiary of AT & T), continued with its vigorous inventive and innovative activity, although all AT & T's output (via Western Electric) was produced for its own use in order to avoid anti-trust litigation. Bell Laboratories, along with other major companies have, between them, accounted for a high percentage of all major innovations in semiconductor technology: in excess of 60 per cent of all major innovations introduced between 1951 and 1971 (Webbink 1977). Interestingly, since 1976, major Japanese companies have made an increasing contribution to technological advance in semiconductors: Sharp's automatic bonding on 'exotic' subtrates in 1977; Mitsubishi's vertical injection logic and V-MOS in 1978; Fujitsu's 64K bit in 1978 (Dosi 1981).

Despite the initial dominance of large companies in basic invention in the semiconductor field, new technology-based small firms played a key role in commercial exploitation, especially during the earlier stages in the US semiconductor industry's development.

What in fact occurred during the evolution of the US semiconductor industry was a classical example of the dynamic complementarities that can exist between large and small firms. Existing large firms provided much of the basic, state-of-the-art technology, venture capital and technically skilled personnel which were essential to new technology-based firm start-up; the new technology-based firms provided the risk-taking entrepreneurial drive and rapid market exploitation. It was a synergistic relationship.

From the late 1960s onwards the output of the US semiconductor industry began increasingly to be concentrated in the top ten or so companies. Production economies of scale grew in importance (and plant size increased), as did production learning, and firms began actively to seek rapid movement down the production learning curve. The importance of price in competition increased as the unit cost of semiconductor component production decreased. According to Sciberras (1977), the prime motive for rapid cost reductions was to deter new entrants by creating significant scale barriers to entry in addition to technological entry barriers. This might at least partially explain why semiconductor technology was exploited in Europe mainly by large existing electronics companies: Europe entered the race at the late date, by which time existing scale and technological barriers largely precluded entry by new small firms.

Thus, in the development of the US semiconductor industry, we see an example of Schumpeterian industrial evolution from the 'entrepreneurial' model of the newly emerging industry, to the 'managed' model of the mature international oligopoly of today. Nowadays, the main opportunities for new entrants appear to be not in semiconductor production itself, but rather in the application of semiconductor devices to the production of new products, notably in the general area of 'information technology', currently mooted as the 'new' industry of the next decade.

The evolution of the computer aided design industry

A second example of industrial evolution that indicates an important role for NTBFs can be found in the case of the computer aided design (CAD) industry. Kaplinksy (1981, 1982) has identified four main phases in the development of the CAD industry: the period to 1969 (industry origins); 1969–74 (dynamic new firms); 1974–80 (the trend to concentration); the period since 1980 (maturity).

During the first phase development was concentrated in established large companies in the defence, aerospace and aeronautical industries in collaboration with mainframe computer manufacturers, and in the late 1960s General Motors entered the field with the development of its 'Design Augmented by Computers' programme. 'In summary, therefore, during this early period there was hardly any "market" for CAD, with most developments occurring to assist own-use by large, technically advanced engineering corporations in the US and (to a lesser extent) in the UK' (Kaplinsky 1981).

The second phase was characterised by the emergence of new, small, spin-off firms in the US (from both CAD producers and electronics companies) which played the primary role in the rapid diffusion of CAD devices into the electronics industry. Several of these firms grew extremely rapidly to become, along with IBM, today's market leaders. In Europe, in contrast, the major existing electronics firms developed CAD equipment for their own use. 'In summary, therefore, this second period of industry development saw the emergence of new, independent firms and the rapid diffusion of the technology out of the defence, aerospace and automobile sectors to the electronics sectors' (Kaplinsky 1981).

The third phase saw the rapid diffusion in use of CAD across manufacturing, a process in which the 'newcomers' played a key role. During this period of extremely rapid market growth the industry became increasingly concentrated, 93 per cent of US market share in 1980 being held by eight companies (notably Computervision with 33.2 per cent of the total). At the same time patterns of ownership began to change and there were a series of takeovers by major corporations of several of the fast-growing newcomers. 'To summarise, therefore, this third phase of industry development was associated with the growing size of CAD firms, the growing organic trend towards concentration within the sector, and a tendency for formerly independent CAD firms to be swallowed by existing trans-national corporations' (Kaplinsky 1981).

At the beginning of the current phase in development, the market was dominated by turnkey suppliers supplying either mainframe systems (user entry costs of about $500 000) or minicomputer systems (user entry costs of about $200 000). From 1980 onwards, as the user base has broadened, a market niche emerged for dedicated systems. These are based not on a comprehensive and flexible package of software applications, but on limited software packages for specific applications. A number of microcomputer-based companies, founded by spin-offs from existing CAD suppliers, and using 'mature' application programmes developed by these suppliers, have begun to emerge, offering systems for as little as $30,000 each. 'To summarise, therefore, this most recent stage of industry development has seen two divergent trends — a continued tendency to concentration and an opposing tendency for the entry of new small firms selling limited capability dedicated systems' (Kaplinsky 1981).

In the UK, it has been estimated that US firms held a 62 per cent share of all CAD systems installed up to mid-1981 (Arnold, 1982). Of the remaining 38 per cent share of installations, 17 per cent were held by subsidiaries of large electronic companies established in the late 1960s, 12 per cent by spin-off companies, 5 per cent by a public body (essentially a software house) and 4 per cent by other companies.

From the above brief descriptions of the evolution of two high-technology industries we can draw out a number of significant factors:

1   Established large US corporations played a crucial initiating role in invention and innovation both in semiconductors and CAD technology. In both instances the early inventive and innovative activity was geared towards 'own use'.
2   In the case of semiconductors, much of the dynamic growth and market diffusion came about as a result of the formation and rapid expansion of NTBFs.
3   In the CAD industry, NTBFs similarly played the key role in the rapid diffusion of CAD systems to electronics and other areas.
4   In both cases, the technological entrepreneurs often came from established corporations, bringing a great deal of technological and applications know-how with them.
5   In both cases established corporations and venture capital institutions played an important part in funding the start-up and growth of NTBFs.
6   In both cases the industries rather quickly became highly concentrated and subject to external takeover.
7   In both bases, as the industries matured, scale economies became increasingly important in the mainstream activities and strong oligopolies were formed, leaving only specialist market niches for new and small suppliers. In the case of CAD, the most significant scale economy has been accumulated software expertise, i.e. the size of the knowledge base is a very much more significant barrier to entry than manufacturing capacity.

It is clear from the description of the evolution of the semiconductor and CAD industries that it is indeed necessary to consider the interactions between small and large firms if we are fully to understand the evolutionary dynamics of technologies and industrial sectors. In both instances existing large corporations played the major initial role in invention, producing new devices largely for in-house use only. The major role in the initial rapid market diffusion of these new devices, however, was played by new, small but fast growing companies founded by technological entrepreneurs. Moreover, the technical know-how, the venture capital and the entrepreneurs themselves very often derived from the established corporations, as well as, in the case of the latter two, from major companies operating in other areas. A spin-off firm appeared to be the most suitable organisational form for types of innovation where (the application of) new technology was involved. Thus we see a system of dynamic complementarity between the large and the small: both had their unique contribution to make; both were necessary, the former to the initiation of the new technological paradigm, the latter to rapid market diffusion and general commercial exploitation.

What our discussions suggest is that established technology-based large corporations can be extremely effective in creating new technological possibilities; they are highly inventive. While they are adept at utilising the results of their inventiveness in-house (new technology for existing applications), they are less well adapted to the rapid exploitation of their inventions in new markets (new technology for new applications). It appears that new firms, initially, are better adapted to exploit new techno/market regimes, breaking out from existing regimes within which established corporations, for historical cultural and institutional reasons, might be rather strongly bound. Referring back to Table 7.1, it appears that during the early phases in the evolution of a new industry the behavioural advantages of small scale are crucial; as the industry evolves, the technological possibilities become better defined and market needs become increasingly well specified. The advantages of large scale then begin to dominate. Comparative advantage shifts to the larger firms and the industry develops towards a mature oligopoly, a situation characteristic of the semiconductor and CAD industries today.

The question now, of course, is 'what about today?' Can we detect indications of technological entrepreneurship in areas of great growth potential for the coming decades? We have already dealt with CAD and the role of NTBFs in its rapid growth phase, but it is worth adding that markets of up to $12 billion for CAD systems have been predicted for 1990 (Kaplinsky 1982). In the general area of information processing Freeman et al. (1982) have indicated that out of 36 companies that enjoyed an annual growth rate in sales in the US between 1976 and 1980 of greater than 40 per cent, 23 (or 63 per cent) were in the information processing area. Between them these relatively young firms had combined sales in 1980 of approximately $4 billion, no mean feat during a period of deepening world recession.

More recent reports, however, suggest that many of these 'newcomers' in the minicomputer area currently are suffering due to severe price competition from very large corporations that entered the race later, but which enjoy huge advantages of scale in production, distribution and marketing (notably IBM). If this trend continues, then the possibilities for entry by NTBFs might be rapidly diminishing, with only specialist market niches being left open for participation by SMEs. On the other hand, cheap and efficient minicomputers offer many opportunities for existing SMEs to improve their operations through facilitating better purchasing, stock, production and marketing control procedures. The ability increasingly to 'plug in' to large databases should also ease the technical and market information-seeking problems from which many SMEs of all types currently offer.

Turning finally to biotechnology, the economic potential of this infant industry is immense, and many new firms have been established within this area — most notably in the US — during recent years, frequently being closely linked to university-based research (i.e. in this instance the state-of-the-art knowledge is vested in the academic system). It is interesting that, when it became generally realised that biotechnology was still in its research-intensive phase (the commercialisation of biotechnological products on a large scale being a thing of the late 1980s onwards), independent venture capitalists began to have second thoughts concerning their investments in the newcomers. Increasingly, established large corporations have stepped in to fill the venture capital gap. In fact we can today see synergistic interactions occurring between a number of combinations of large and small firms. Dow Chemicals and Monsanto, for example, while pursuing their own research and development programmes, are investing also in smaller companies; Biotechnology General, an entrepreneurial newcomer in the US, is negotiating for venture capital with three large firms to help finance the development of three new agricultural products; Bio Isolates of Swansea is now setting up a joint venture with Dunlop; Grand Metropolitan has invested more than £4 million in Biogen, a new Swiss-based biotechnology company; and so on. The point is, whether or not any of the new small biotechnology firms become the giants of the future, or whether they act as a technical resource for existing large firms is, today, less important than their role in stimulating widespread interest and greatly increased investment in biotechnical research and development, i.e. they have played a crucial *initiating* role.

Summary

This paper has addressed the issue of the role SMEs play in industrial technological innovation. The introductory section listed the advantages and disadvantages generally ascribed to small and to large firms in innovation: small firms' advantages were largely behavioural; large firms' advantages were mainly resource-based. The data presented in the second section on patterns of innovation by firms and units of different sizes in the UK suggested that while large firms (with more than 10 000 employees) had enjoyed the greatest share of total industrial innovations in Britain since 1945, they increasingly have innovated via smaller units. In other words they appear to have succeeded in combining the innovation-related benefits of both small and large size.

The SPRU innovation data also suggested that SMEs and firms employing more than 10 000 had both taken on increasing shares of total manufacturing innovations in Britain with the middle-sized groups of firms losing ground. This was partly the result of industrial structural shifts and partly due to changing patterns of innovative efficiency. The SMEs' position had improved considerably during the past decade in terms of innovative share, and their innovative efficiency had increased during the 38 years covered by the data. Given the relatively limited research and development resources available to SMEs in the UK, their innovation record has been remarkable. Moreover, as expected, the role of SMEs in innovation has varied greatly from sector to sector depending on such factors as technological and market entry costs and scale of production requirements.

In the third section we discussed interrelationships of large and small firms. These can take many forms, including supplier–customer links and the production of complementary products or services. In the United States relationships between large and small firms often take the form of joint technological ventures. The point is that small and large firms operate in the same world and often forge mutually beneficial links. They should thus not be treated as if they operate always in isolation from each other.

Finally, taking a dynamic and rather broad view of innovation, the last section discussed the role of NTBFs in the emergence of new technologies and their associated new industrial sectors. This again highlighted the dynamic complementarities that can exist between small and large firms and it emphasised also their respective advantages and disadvantages in innovation. The large firms enjoyed a marked advantage in radical invention and innovation because of their very considerable in-house research and development resources, but they experienced difficulty in breaking out from existing product/ market paradigms. The small firms enjoyed the advantages of entre- preneurial dynamism and open-mindedness and succeeded in applying the new technologies across a broad range of industries. A different set of complementarities appears to be emerging in the case of the infant biotechnology industry.

It can be concluded that both small and large firms have had, and continue to have, an important role to play in industrial innovation. Their respective roles are sometimes different and they vary across the industry cycle as well as between different sectors of industry. It seems clear, however, that as the world economy moves towards a period of recovery, in which a number of emerging technologies will play a crucial part, there will be many innovatory opportunities for both small and large firms working both separately and together: both are desirable; both are necessary.

References

Arnold, E. (1982). 'Competition and Policy in a Knowledge-intensive Industry: CAD Equipment Supply in the UK', mimeo, Science Policy Research Unit, University of Sussex, July.

Dosi, G. (1981). 'Institutions and Markets in High Technology Industries: An Assessment of Government Intervention in Micro- electronics' in C.F. Carter (ed.), *Industrial Policies and Innovation,* London, Heinemann.

Freeman, C., Soete, L. and Clark, J. (1982). *Unemployment and Technical Innovation,* London, Frances Pinter.

Galbraith, J.K. (1957). *American Capitalism,* London, Hamilton.

Johnson, P. and Cathcart, G. (1980). 'Manufacturing Firms and Regional Development: Some Evidence from the Northern Region' in A. Gibb and T. Webb (eds), *Policy Issues in Small Business Reserch,* Farnborough, Hants, Teakfield Ltd.

Kaplinsky, R. (1981). 'Firm Size and Technical Change in a Dynamic Context', Institute of Development Studies, University of Sussex, August.

Kaplinsky, R. (1982). *The Impact of Technological Change on The International Division of Labour: The Illustrative Case of CAD,* London, Frances Pinter.

Little, A.D. (1977). *New Technology-based Firms in the United Kingdom and the Federal Republic of Germany,* London, Wilton House Publications.

Marquand, J. (1981). 'Regional Innovation Policies in the United Kingdom', Department of Trade and Industry, London.

Mason, D. (1979). 'Factors Affecting the Successful Development and Marketing of Innovative Semiconductor Devices', unpublished PhD thesis, Polytechnic of Central London.

Neumann, F. (1973). *Nutzung von Gesamtwirtshaftlichen Projectionen und Prognozen in der Industrie,* München, IFO Institute.

Oakey, R.P. (1984). *High Technology Small Firms: Innovation and Regional Development in Britain and the United States,* London, Frances Pinter.

Oppenländer, K.H. (ed.) (1976). *Die Gesamtwirtschaftliche Funktion kleiner und mittlerer Unternehmen* München, IFO Institute.

Prakke, F. (1974). 'The Management of the R&D Interface', unpublished PhD thesis, Sloan School of Management, MIT.

Robson, M. and Townsend, J. (1984). 'Trends and Characteristics of Significant Innovations and their Innovators in the UK since 1945', mimeo, Science Policy Research Unit, University of Sussex, August.

Rothwell, R. (1979). *Government Regulations and Industrial Innovation,* report to the Six Countries Programme on Innovation, c/o Policy Studies Group TNO, PO Box 215, 2600 AE Delft, Netherlands.

Rothwell, R. (1983). 'Innovation and Firm Size: A Case of Dynamic Complementarity', *Journal of General Management,* vol. 8, no. 3, Spring.

Rothwell, R. (1984a). 'Technology-based Small Firms and Regional Innovation Potential: The Role of Public Procurement', *Journal of Public Policy,* vol. 4, no. 4.

Rothwell, R. (1984b). 'The Role of Small Firms in the Emergence of New Technologies', *Omega,* vol. 12, no. 1.

Rothwell, R. (1986). 'Venture Finance, Small Firms and Public Policy in the UK', *Research Policy, 14,* pp. 1–13.

Rothwell, R. and Zegveld, W. (1981). *Industrial Innovation and Public Policy,* London, Frances Pinter.

Rothwell, R. and Zegveld, W. (1982). *Innovation and the Small and Medium Sized Firm,* London, Frances Pinter.

Rothwell, R. and Zegveld, W. (1985). *Reindustrialization and Technology,* London, Longman.

Schumpeter, J.A. (1939). *Business Cycle,* New York and London, McGraw-Hill.

Sciberras, E. (1977). *Multinational Electronic Companies and National Economic Policies,* Greenwich, Conn., JAI Press.

Thwaites, A.T., Oakey, R. and Nash, P. (1981). *Industrial Innovation and Regional Development,* Final Report to the Department of the Environment, CURDS, University of Newcastle, October.

Twaalfhoven, F. and Hattori, T. (1982). *The Supporting Role of the Small Japanese Firm,* Indivers Research, Netherlands, October.

Utterbach, J.M. (1982). *Technology and Industrial Innovation in Sweden: A Study of New Technology-based Firms,* Centre for Policy Alternatives, MIT, Cambridge, Mass.

Van der Meer, J.D. and van Tilburg, J.J. (1983). *Spin-offs Uit Technisch Kommerciele Infrastructuren,* van der Meer and von Tilburg, Enschede, Netherlands.

Webbink, D.W. (1977). 'The Semiconductor Industry: Structure, Conduct and Performance', unpublished staff report to the US Federal Trade Commission, January.

Wyatt, S. (1984). 'The Role of Small Firms in Innovative Activity', mimeo, Science Policy Research Unit, University of Sussex (to be published in *Economia and Politica Industriale,* 1985).

PART III
THE STATE, POLITICS
AND
THE SMALL ENTERPRISE

Introduction

The final set of papers in this collection concerns the wider context of the small enterprise. Small firms are not only shaped by the wider society, they also help sustain it. By and large, however, the overwhelming emphasis rests typically upon the small firm as the victim of wider influences emanating from the environment. In discussions of the decline of small enterprise, for example, decline was usually attributed to a variety of these wider influences. Small business owners have often described themselves as being at the mercy of the wider environment in the form of predatory large firms, the state, trade unions and a general fall in status in the eyes of the wider public. However, more recent writings discussing the revival of the small firm have also ascribed much of this revival to changes in the economy and the socio-cultural environment.

In the opening paper S.M. Miller offers a picture of the economy of advanced industrial society. He notes the enormous growth in importance of the large corporation, particularly trans-national enterprises. Their needs are increasingly served by the educational and other major institutions in society and they use their power to try to create a sympathetic, predictable wider environment. But, equally, the picture offered stresses that attention must be given to other parts of the economy which co-exist with these economic giants. There is, in other words, uneven development in these economies as a permanent feature of their operation even in the most advanced examples.

Medium and smaller-sized businesses form a very substantial part of the United States economy, for example, and by clear implication, of other advanced industrial societies. Of course, many are closely linked in one way or another with large enterprises but their managerial styles and organisational structures are quite distinct from those of the giant corporation. Together these form three private economies — big business, medium businesses and small business — which co-exist with the public sector which is also responsible for the provision of goods and especially services. In the United States these four sectors all employ substantial proportions of the labour force.

Miller argues that recent fashionable views have been concerned with the conversion of advanced industrial societies into post-industrial societies based on knowledge in one form or another, but that this trend is easily overstated. There is a failure to recognise the persistence of diversity within modern economies, related to equally persistent cultural differences. Most advanced industrial societies have flourishing black economies anchored in the experiences of various groups which live outside the realm of big business — particularly those who suffer discrimination or who need a counter-culture to maintain their sense of worth. Differences of these kinds within society go with the existence of separate economic sectors which make up advanced industrial societies. Small businesses — legitimate and illegitimate — are important and integral aspects of these processes.

The author of the second paper in this section, John McHugh, offers a historical account of the development in Britain of various pressure groups which purport to represent the small business owner. Such groups seek to promote the values and interests of the small capitalist and to maintain the culture of petty capitalism as an alternative to both big business and the state in the provision of goods and services. The starting point for this account is 1971, the year the highly influential government-sponsored Bolton Report on the small firm was published. This marked an upturn in the willingness of the self-employed to indulge in promoting their interests. Prior to this they had been almost totally quiescent, reflecting perhaps the decline in the small business sector just as their new interest in achieving political influence reflects the revival of the small enterprise.

There were existing pressure groups who claimed to represent the interests of small business but their representation of the small business owner was only part of their wider role. The Confederation of British Industry, for example, claimed to look after the interests of small firms but as part of its representation of firms of all sizes in both the private and public sectors. Many small business owners obviously felt this produced an inevitable conflict of interest.

From 1974 onwards a number of new groups set up exclusively to help the small business owner came into being, often achieving spectacular growth in the short term. They seized on issues, such as taxes on small businesses or the introduction of VAT, to win members and mobilise support. However, some of these pressure groups experienced problems in maintaining their membership and in preventing breakaway groups from undermining their effectiveness. McHugh shows in detail how these processes occurred and how, despite these internal weaknesses, the new small business pressure groups achieved some remarkable successes, particularly in galvanising the CBI and the Conservative Party into rediscovering the small business owner as a potential supporter and putting more energy into serving their interests.

However, membership of these pressure groups has never included more than a small fraction of the total small business-owning population — most small business owners are simply not joiners, partly because they are often too involved in their enterprises but perhaps mostly because they find collectivism in any of its forms distasteful. Further, there has been a tendency for some of these pressure groups to be run by people who have distinct political views and who try to harness small business owners' support to the service of these views. While small business owners as a group probably have some sympathy for these views, they are very unlikely to be as strongly committed to them as the leaders of the pressure groups and are probably interested in more immediate and pragmatic issues.

McHugh feels that fragmentation within the small business-owner stratum is inevitable because of the diversity within its ranks. For instance, some small business owners have complained bitterly about the impact of employment legislation on their freedom to recruit and discharge employees and small business pressure groups have made much of this issue. However, many of the self-employed either have no employees or have never encountered any such problems directly and feel that the legislation is unlikely ever to seriously affect them. Similar wide differences arise in relation to the effects of various kinds of taxation on the small business community.

The wider social and political climate in Britain has undoubtedly become much more sympathetic to the small business owner in Britain over the last ten years. The extent to which this is due to the efforts of small business pressure groups is debatable since, clearly, many other factors may be involved. The groups themselves may have reached a limit in their growth and yet remain still very small in relation to their potential membership. They still have a long way to go to reach the position of influence of similar groupings in some other advanced industrial societies or to achieve the links with political parties which would make them more than merely one, rather minor, client group of even the party most sympathetic to their cause.

Westrip's paper on employment legislation and the small firm is an excellent case study of the relationship between researchers and the policy-makers and politicians. It illustrates the point that, while researchers may strive objectively and accurately to describe the position of the small firm, policy-makers may simply choose to ignore their work and listen rather to the special pleading of interest groups or their own inner political voices. Like Storey's contribution earlier in this volume, this paper concerns the job-creation potential of the small firm, but Westrip is interested in the evidence on whether employment legislation inhibits small business owners from efficiently managing their work-forces and especially from taking on more employees. The latter is an important issue since, clearly, if this legislation did have such an effect, removing the inhibiting elements could have a dramatic impact on unemployment.

The paper discusses in detail the period from the introduction of specific unfair dismissal legislation in Britain in 1971 through to 1980, a period which saw first of all a rapid increase in such legislation and then, later, under the 1979 Conservative government, a reversal of several important provisions in the legislation. This was accompanied by a sustained campaign against the legislation by those claiming to represent the small enterprise. Indeed, several of the small business pressure groups examined by McHugh in the previous paper in this section used their campaigns against this legislation as a major means of obtaining publicity for their activities. But, somewhat unusually, the impact of legislation on the small business was also being investigated carefully by two highly experienced, independent research groups on behalf of government departments. The results of the two studies showed that, while employment protection legislation was unpopular with small employers, its real impact on their activities was very limited. Most small employers indicated that, in practice, the legislation did not hinder their freedom to hire and dismiss employees. In both studies only a minority of small business owners reported feeling that the legislation inhibited them from taking on more employees.

But policy-makers chose to ignore these findings and give much more credence to the representations of small business pressure groups who claimed that research amongst their members demonstrated not only the legislation's unpopularity but that it had damaged the majority of members' businesses as well as preventing them from taking on more employees. As Westrip argues, the research strategies,

146

sampling, response rates and methods of reporting the findings of the research conducted by the pressure groups left a great deal to be desired and could not be taken as comparable to those of the two independent studies.

Since the period covered by Westrip's paper, no evidence from independent researchers has substantially altered the conclusions reached by the two independent studies although both pressure groups and policy-makers have continued to suggest that, despite substantial relaxations in the provisions of the legislation, the remaining provisions continue to inhibit the job-creating potential of the small enterprise. Westrip's paper offers an important object lesson in researcher–policy-maker relations but it is a lesson whose message seems difficult to get across to those who have the ability and responsibility to shape the small enterprise environment.

The final paper in this collection is devoted to an examination of the forces involved in the production of the small business-owner stratum in advanced industrial societies. Only a few years ago the consensus among social scientists was that small business owners were facing inevitable decline as new, more efficient, large-scale economic enterprises squeezed the small firm out of all but the least profitable and backward areas of economic activity. More recently, the persistence and even revival of the small enterprise has suggested that previously accepted views required questioning and alternative interpretation. Small-scale enterprise is far from confined to the least profitable or traditional sectors of the economy as the recent history of the information technology industries shows. Even in manufacturing generally, numbers of small firms have been increasing sharply and they are strongly represented in most varieties of services.

Before an economic enterprise comes into being it requires a motivational impulse on the part of those involved in setting it up — what is distinctive about such people and what influences in the wider social environment predisposes these people to embark upon enterprise ownership? After discussing some of the recent theoretical treatments of the *petite bourgeoisie*, Curran concentrates on the much less-discussed forces which exist in the wider society and ensure a constant and even increasing supply of people willing to enter this form of involvement in the economy. He divides these forces into the economic, political and social-cultural and goes on to analyse each variety to show not only that previous influences pushing people towards self-employment and small enterprise ownership persist in modern society but that new influences are also emerging.

In other words, advanced industrial society contains within its core essential influences for the reproduction and sustaining of the small business-owning stratum. For instance, the increasing size of large firms in advanced economies also paradoxically promotes opportunities for small-scale enterprise since large firms are less able to cope with small, specialised markets, or in coping with their own market and other uncertainties large firms find it convenient to create special relations with small firm suppliers in order to ensure their own survival.

In the political sphere the taxation systems of modern societies have gradually changed to respond to the ability of large firms to shift the tax burden on to other groupings in society, notably those in the lower middle levels of the social class hierarchy who are most likely to be tempted by self-employment, particularly because of its opportunities for tax avoidance and evasion.

In the socio-cultural sphere the paper brings out a wide variety of persisting and new influences working towards the survival of the *petite bourgeoisie*. These include social marginality — the frequent placing of people into social positions discrepant with their abilities, potential and self-image — the persistent failure of education systems to allow all children to realise their potential, and deskilling resulting from the increasing rationalisation of work roles through the introduction of new technology.

But perhaps the least emphasised element in the influences working towards the reproduction of the small business-owning stratum is its cultural significance. As a stratum it embodies the key values of free enterprise society. In this sense the survival of this stratum is closely bound up with the survival of society itself. But, equally, for the small business-owning class, being the embodiment of core values is a resource to be exploited in their relations with other groups in society — political parties, the state and large enterprise — to ensure their own survival.

In this final paper of the two volumes, Curran is clearly optimistic about the survival of the small business-owning stratum and uses it to sum up the major theme linking the 24 papers in the whole collection — the survival of the small firm itself. Where some of the papers have been critical or questioning, it has not been to question this optimism but to attack misconceptions which, despite any superficial appearance to the contrary, have frequently been the enemies of small enterprise. To misunderstand the role of the small firm in our economy and society is often to undermine its survival, for consultants, policy-makers and others can do untold damage through misguided attempts to help. The need for the clear critical thinking and high-quality research embodied in this collection of papers has never been greater in ensuring not just the survival of the small firm but the fullest exploitation of its potential.

8 Notes on Neo-Capitalism*

S.M. MILLER

A land that is now unknown is most disturbing when we felt that we once knew it and were comfortable in it. The sense of security and understanding is ebbing among citizens of advanced industrial capitalist nations. Short-run events disturb, partly because of their unpredictability. More important, intimations of deeper changes, indeed transformations, jar one into doubting the traditional, comforting wisdoms. In such circumstances, social analysis is needed, emerges, and plays a key political as well as intellectual role. Social analysts are now shaping the perceptions of the profound changes sweeping through industrial societies. Some analysts, like economist John Kenneth Galbraith,[1] perceive a 'new industrial state' with dominating giant corporations; sociologists Daniel Bell[2] and Alain Touraine[3] write of a 'post-industrial society' in which knowledge and organisation rather than physical capital are the motors of change; economist Victor Fuchs[4] and policy analysts Alan Gartner and Frank Riessman[5] focus on the emerging service economy or 'service society' in which health, education and welfare are becoming the main elements of economic and social action.

---

* From: *Theory and Society,* vol. 2 (1975), pp. 1–35.

I find these analyses partial and am groping for a more comprehensive approach. The term 'post-industrial society' has been widely adopted as the description of the changes taking place. Since I believe that the mode of social organisation, capitalism, is still the main element in what is taking place, I prefer the term 'neo-capitalism'. What seems to be happening is not a simple unimodal unfolding. Three sets of forces are simultaneously interdependent, independent, and in struggle. The large oligopoly firms are expanding in scope and economic importance in the form of multinational corporations and conglomerates. A secondary set of industrial and service activities taking in a wide variety of enterprises exists; some are large, some very small, some in close contact with the oligopolist sectors, others not. Finally, the public sector has grown in importance as an economic regulator affecting the oligopolistic and secondary sectors and their workers as a taxer and service provider and as an employer of millions.

In this paper, I have followed this division with the exception of breaking down the secondary sector into two: medium enterprises and small enterprises. After discussing the four sectors and uneven development, I then take up the post-industrial society image which somewhat criss-crosses these sectors.

The domination of the oligopolistic corporation

The great value of Galbraith's work has been his insistence on the towering domination of the large corporation in economic life; it, rather than the university, is the key institution of high-income capitalist societies. In the case of the United States, perhaps 1000 multinational corporations and conglomerates affect what is produced, effectively elicit and manipulate demand for their products and have a major impact on governmental policy. Together with the large banks whose control of credit Galbraith largely ignores, they appear as the American economy to the rest of the world. As we shall shortly see, they are not all of the economy for Americans.

The conglomerate and multinational developments are enormously important. The big enterprises have become even larger, and employment is more concentrated than before. Financial houses and banks have become more significant with the reliance of many large enterprises on banks for loans after the cash liquidity crisis of the late 1960s and with financial manipulation to raise stock values. The stock market has become a major way of achieving wealth (or losing it).

The economic significance of big business is shown in its concentration of assets, profits and employment. The 500 largest corporations, as tabulated by *Fortune* magazine in 1973, accounted for 65 per cent of the sales of all American industrial corporations and 79 per cent of the profits in the industrial sectors.[6] If all corporations, not just those in the industrial sphere, are included, then the 1200 corporations with assets of at least $250 million in 1970 had 57.4 per cent of all profits.[7] One of every five persons in the employed, non-agricultural labour force in 1973 worked in the 500 largest industries named by *Fortune*. (The 500 would have a somewhat smaller percentage of employment if all members of the labour force are taken as the base, which we do in the later calculations for other sectors.) This degree of concentration is not unique to the United States. Sweden and Japan are probably more concentrated in each of these regards.

The oligopolistic or planned private enterprise sector depends upon a stable and expanding economic environment. It needs stability in order to be able to predict what will happen; that is, it has to be certain that things will move in predictable ways. And it needs expansion in order to be able to realise its profits, to increase its growth which — as Galbraith explained — is basic to the perspective of its managers. To some extent stability and expansion are in conflict with each other. While it is possible to have a stable predictable environment that is expanding, growth situations are likely to have loose, somewhat uncertain edges to them. The absence of a stable equilibrium in which predictability is high and knowledge is widespread means that the oligopolistic corporation is involved in highly complex and perplexing situations.

In terms of its internal operation, big business needs a skilled labour force. At the executive level, it needs people with technical and administrative capacities. Effective management is not very easy to accomplish when an enterprise is sprawled over many nations and is involved in a diversity of activities. Loyalty to the organisation is important. This loyalty sometimes collides with the organisational emphasis upon competence. The notion of a careful and rigorous selection process can mean that many employees are shunted aside. In addition, a large corporation is filled with factionalism, even though this is not what the organisational chart says. Individual ambition and corporate objectives cannot always converge.

At the plant level, big business needs a labour force that is able to perform the various tasks which the industrial technology requires. Thus, there must be an educational system which facilitates the kinds of operation which a large corporation needs. But to a major extent, these large corporations depend upon their internal training structures to hone the labour power that they seek. Loyalty to the corporation is increasingly difficult to maintain, and commitment to high productivity must be pursued through inside-the-plant pressure.

Wall Street is becoming more critical of conglomerates which proved to be as strong as their weakest rather than their strongest links. Liquid assets, which made conglomerate mergers immediately profitable, are not as available. Recent conglomerate history showed that the belief in great management ability which could turn around any ailing enterprise was based on grandiosity, not performance.

Multinational or trans-national corporations will be expanding with various mixtures of control and employment at international and national headquarters. An increasing need will be to regulate them and to work out balances between the interests of international and national headquarter countries, especially in regard to repatriation of profits, taxation, reinvestment and movement of currencies. Also the political role of world conglomerates is important. Of special importance are the trans-national oil corporations whose manipulations of price and supply profoundly affect national economies.

Power in the corporation

Discussions of the relative importance of managers and core stock-holders in the large corporations frequently misses the crucial point:[8] which is that the corporation is *institutionalised property*. The great wealth of society is in this institutionalised form, particularly when insurance companies and other institutionalised investors who now provide a large part of funds in the stock market are included in the analyses.

From a longer-term viewpoint, or at least from a different perspective, the question of control is less significant than the sheer dramatic impact of these enormous aggregations and the economic and political power (and social standing) of those in key roles in relationship to them. The top executives of large enterprises do not stay at the very top for long; they may shift from one company to another or are close to retirement when they reach the top, so that they have a short reign. While at the top they have enormous power.

These institutionalised properties have been and are continuing to be central to the operation of the economy and polity. Galbraith's concept of the 'technostructure' emphasises the manager (the administrator with some technical competence and financial abilities) and the expert, in contrast to Bell, who stresses the expert-scientist who provides the codified knowledge, but has neither administrative nor financial roles nor perhaps even technological (as contrasted to scientific) knowledge. Galbraith seems much closer to what goes on in the corporation.

Galbraith and Bell believe, as do many others, that high efficiency and rationality exist in the large economic institutions. One can criticise such a conclusion on the basis that it employs narrow criteria of efficiency and rationality. If 'external diseconomies' — the economist's phrase for the sociologist's looser term of 'unanticipated consequences' — were included in the evaluation, efficiency and rationality would not be so obvious. But even on narrower grounds where the corporation's goals are accepted and the only question is the efficaciousness and productivity of the means deployed to achieve the goals, one can question the success of the modern large-scale corporation. Some sources of incompetence are: corporate in-fighting among departmental interest groups, personal competitiveness, occupational and class blindness, bureaucratisation, faddism, cronyism, insensitivity, particularism, and stubbornness in the face of changing situations.

The general point is not to assume with Galbraith, and to a lesser extent with Bell, that largeness means efficiency, that experts mean effectiveness and scientific impartiality, that high technology is wisely used, that financial success results only from efficient management rather than from luck or being able to force out competitors, and that time will eliminate inefficiency and incompetence.

I do not mean to foreclose on the issue of corporate rationality or efficiency, but to encourage a great scepticism about the likely degree of their achievement. We have learned a good deal about organisations and bureaucracies, perhaps the first lesson of which is not to accept their view of themselves as rational, efficient, single-goal-oriented enterprises.

Uneven development

Despite the importance of the big business and finance sectors in many nations, it is misleading to think that they are everything. 'Uneven development' is a central issue and antagonism within all societies. The emergence of a dominant economic form, the factory or the 'post-industrial' organisation, does not mean that pre-industrial or industrial forms vanish. Thus, attention must be paid to the other parts of the economy which lie in the shadow of the dominating industrial organisations. The dominants do not fill every nook and cranny of the economy. Far from it. Indeed, an important issue is the extent to which the dominants affect other economic organisations.

Galbraith alone among recent authors stresses uneven development and recognises the extent to which the United States is a split society.

(Bell notes how varied organisations are, but does not explore the implications of these differentiations.) The new Galbraithian analysis still does not have a sufficiently refined analysis of the non-big business parts of the economy. He lumps together all of the non-big firms, declaring that they are within the 'market sector' in contrast to the 'planning sector' of big business. Not only does he fail to differentiate within the market sector, but some firms in this sector are local monopolies as entrenched as any big oligopoly. Nor does he discuss in this context the role of the government.

On the other hand, he has been criticised for taking up the dual labour market analysis without giving credit to the young political economists who have made the analysis well-known. In fairness to Galbraith, it should be noted that he has not restricted his analysis of uneven development to the labour market and employment conditions, as have the political economists, but has taken the bolder and significant step of looking at these secondary enterprises in terms of their role within the total economy. That is an important step even if his classification of the non-dominants is weak.

Medium business and finance

Many sizeable enterprises are not large or significant enough to be regarded as part of the big, oligopolistic sector. Since little is known about the firms below the big business level, it is hard to know how to classify them. Because of the availability of data, I am applying the term 'medium-size' to all American corporations with assets between $1 million and $250 million. Obviously, that term covers an enormous range of situations.

Perhaps 30 million persons are employed in medium-size business and finance.[9] If this guess is fairly accurate, it would mean that two of every five members of the civilian labour force are in the medium business sector.

While recognising the importance of the big business sector, one should not underestimate the smaller business enterprises. While the 1200 active corporations in the United States in 1970 with assets of over $250 million had 57.4 per cent of all corporate net income (before taxes), the 164 200 corporations with assets between $1 million and $250 million produced 30.9 per cent of corporate net income.

Many of the 3500 firms with assets between $50 million and $250 million (the large mediums) may be closely intermeshed economically with big business. They may be in the same economic sectors as big business, although smaller in size. Many of them engage in activities which are ancillary to big business and finance, as in the case of enterprises which provide parts or services (for example, advertising, locally important banks and law firms) for big businesses. They are probably dominated by big business. Others are minor or specialised competitors of big business, smaller-scale firms in the same activities as big business, for example, the smaller hotel firms. While their size might be considered substantial in other fields, in their own fields they are dwarfed by the big firms. Some are large firms in their industries (for example, chain department stores) but not by the standards of big business. Others are locally or regionally important, influencing not only economic but political events as well in their particular areas: kings in Middle America, if only knights in Washington and Wall Street.

The smaller mediums (these with assets under $50 million) are also very varied. Some are locally important or even important in their industrial sector; others are enlarged small businesses in outlook and situation.

To what extent are these medium firms qualitatively as well as quantitatively different from big business? The larger medium firms probably are much like big business in operation, prospect and (regional) influence. There is turnover in the *Fortune* 500 largest corporations: every year some drop off the list, others grow into it. Over a larger time period, as Robert Heilbroner has shown, considerable change takes place. The smaller firms do not have the same organisational structure, are less managerially dominated. They have less research and development expenditure, less effective planning, less expertise.

When a medium-size firm is concentrated in particular products and service in which few oligopolistic firms operate or are only marginally important, its interests may diverge from those of big business. What's good for General Motors may not always be good for the Sacks Brothers furniture chains on the East Coast. They differ, too, from big business in that they cannot absorb big losses as easily; one bad season can be disastrous.

These enterprises are likely to be more owner-operated than manager-operated. Probably there is a strong relationship between size and owner-operation: the smaller the firm, the less reliance at the top on non-owner, manager expertise.

Small business

If those corporations with less than $1 million in assets were considered as small business, then small business had only 11 per cent of all net income before taxes of corporations in the United States. While that would still not be a force to ignore, since there were 15 million of such enterprises in 1970, the more important fact is that unincorporated enterprises (largely but not exclusively small business) had a larger aggregate income (profits) before taxes than all corporations ($70.7 billion for unincorporated enterprises compared to $65.9 billion for all corporations, including $37.8 billion for corporations with assets above $250 billion). Small businesses are not small in the aggregate. While they obviously do not dominate big business, although they outdraw it in profits, they are not to be casually ignored. I would guess that at least one of every six members of the American labour force is in non-agricultural, non-professional small business as an employer or an employee.[10]

Small business comprises smaller independent stores, including Mom and Pop shops, manufacturing and repair places, gasoline stations, independent motels, and the like. Small agriculture should be included, although it is distinctive in some ways. Some of the manufacturing activities may connect with medium business, and to a much smaller extent, big business. Indeed, small business, as defined here, encompasses an enormous range, from a well-to-do service enterprise (for example, a local chain of dry cleaning stores) to a street peddler hawking his wares.

Small businesses are in the low value-added fields, for example, clothing industries, where there is low capital investment, high competition and considerable chance of bankruptcy. Workers in this sector are the lowest paid. They have little chance of promotion and upgrading, for there is no 'internal labour market' within these enterprises.

The irregular economy[11] of small enterprises with low wages, hustling, job insecurity, which is the setting for the dual labour market, is an important component of the small business sector. The individuals involved in this irregular economy largely comprise the working poor.

Obviously, the small business sector has few of the characteristics of the post-industrial society — its degree of systemisation and organisation is low, organised scientific knowledge plays a very limited role, and so on. It has limited relationship to the large and medium-size sectors, is more involved in services, criss-crosses with the welfare system, involves a low degree of technology and technical skill. Its existence is a response to the limited prospects of large sections of the population (low wages keep down the price of various commodities and services) and is a cause of their limited prospects.

I am not certain to what extent the irregular economy exists in other capitalist nations. Probably not to the extent that it does in the United States, where high consumption expenditures have increased the demand for household services and where large populations are discriminated against. But my guess is that what Bennett Harrison calls 'casually organized production activities' exists in all nations to some extent, especially where ethnic differentiation is important. In Western Europe, where much of the manual work is done by foreign workers, the potential for an irregular economy may become great if the 'guest workers' develop rights and become less susceptible to being pushed out of the labour market when unemployment occurs.

If we switch back to the small business sector as a whole, it is large and strong in most capitalist nations, as manifested in the power of small farmers in the Common Market and the ability of the shop-keeper to push the French government to slow the spread of super-markets. The small business sector should not be regarded as an anachronism that will surely and swiftly fade away as big enterprises grow. Small business is interstitial, filling in the economic nooks and crannies not profitable for large enterprises; it is also increasingly oriented toward local service, and takes up a major slice of consumer expenditures. Small business may not retain its importance or character in any kind of economy, but it is likely to demonstrate its durability and flexibility (as some socialist nations have discovered).

The enlarged public sector

The public sector has different rhythms than the three private economies discussed earlier. Decisions are made on different bases; the nature of work is primarily towards services. It seems appropriate to link private health and education (largely private universities) with the public sector, which includes all governmental activities, not only health education and welfare. What happens in the private health and education sectors increasingly depends on the policies and expenditures of the public sector; they also have different qualities than those of the three private sectors.

This enlarged sector (EPS), which includes what Eli Ginsberg has called the not-for-profit sector, is huge. One of every five civilian members of the labour force is in it; it is as large in terms of employment as the big business and finance sector. If the employment resulting from government contracts (for instance, in defence firms) were included, government would be more significant. In other advanced capitalist nations with big social welfare functions, the employment importance of the public sector is even greater, although defence expenditures are less. Of the incomes received by individuals (personal income), well over a quarter ($245.8 billion)[12] is obtained from government (federal, state and local) in the form of wages and salaries (including those of the military), transfer payments (social security, public assistance and unemployment insurance, which together contribute over a tenth of income) and interest payments. The contribution of employment in the private health and education sectors should be added to these figures. The United States would still be far below the Swedish and Danish situation, where probably as much as half of personal income flows from the public sectors.

Influencing and regulating the economy is now a crucial role of government but not its only activity. Others are: employer; provider of income through transfer payments and diminisher of income through taxation; distributor of largesse in the form of patents, airway and television rights; purchaser and consumer, such as contracts for defence, highway construction; provider of services — medical, sanitation; socialiser and developer — schools; social control — crime, internal defence, police and military, external 'defence'; regulator of behaviour — courts and statutes, police. In a larger sense, governments now cope with some of the social costs of our industrial society and thereby legitimate the pursuit of private profit.

A summary of labour force distribution

A very rough indication of the distribution of the labour force among the four sectors in 1973 is given in Table 8.1. In addition to these, an additional 2.9 million workers were in the agricultural sector; almost all of them would be in small or medium business. The small business sector is also underestimated because many of the uncounted unemployed and irregular workers are involved in this sector. The enlarged public sector also is likely to be undercounted; it omits more than 2 million workers in private employment based on defence contracts. Also omitted are the military force of more than 2 million and a much smaller number of persons in not-for-profit activities. A revised picture, then, would have the enlarged public sector and the small business sector as more important than Table 8.1 indicates.

None the less, medium business would continue to be the largest employer; the enlarged public sector is probably slightly larger than the big business sector and small business is almost as large as big business. Obviously, medium business, powerful especially at local levels, has been neglected by analysts of the American economic, political and social scene.

158

Table 8.1
Distribution of US labour force (civilian, non-agricultural)
by sector, 1973

Sector	Numbers (millions)	%
Big business	17.5	21.7
Medium business	30.0	37.3
Small business	15.4	19.2
Enlarged public sector	17.5	21.7
	80.4	100.0

Will the human services expand?

The expansion of Riessman and Gartner's service society depends on governmental actions to expand health, education and welfare. Some conservative economists of the Institute of Economic Affairs in London argue that decreasing taxes and thereby increasing disposable income would not only provide economic freedom, but might even lead to increased expenditures on services (such as health) as consumers decide that is what they want. This is a dubious argument, as Galbraith effectively argued in *The Affluent Society,* and expenditures on health, education and welfare are likely to increase relatively only if government itself allocates more funds.

Education was the growth industry of the 1960s in the United States, and it clearly is levelling off. Health is likely to be the growth field of the services in the 1970s; how much expansion is clearly a contentious political issue. Day-care could be a growth field later in the 1970s. Welfare, if it continues to expand, will likely be growing as a cash programme rather than as a service programme, providing health and case work to recipients. Expenditures on job training of welfare recipients may partially offset that trend if training continues to be unconnected to direct development of jobs and remains an unsatisfactory preparation for employment without a certainty of a job at the end.

Pension outlays are likely to compete with service expenditures. The slice of wage income going for pensions and savings for old age is increasing and is likely to rise. More people are retiring early or living to long past 65, so that we now have a young-old and old-old (over 75). Higher contributions are therefore needed to Social Security and private (collective bargaining) plans, especially if inflation is to be offset and a sharp post-retirement decline in income is to be prevented. (At present, most of the aged poor were not poor before they were aged.) If we include employers' contributions as part of wages (that is to say, employees could receive those payments in cash rather than as fringe benefits), perhaps a fifth of the wages of many employees goes for old-age protection. If that figure grows, a declining cut of wages is available for other uses.

The human services are battling for expansion. My guess is that health services will be the last big growth area in the United States, although child-care services might expand if the industrial labour force has to grow and more women workers are needed. (This might well happen if the birth-rate continues to remain low). Besides health and perhaps day-care, I do not see any other growth areas, but I do see constant pressure to reduce public expenditures, to make services more 'efficient', to reduce taxes.

People want more cash, not less. They want to buy the things they desire. They want to buy better housing and consumer durables. They want to see their standard of living rising in terms of their direct control over the disposal of income. Tax rises will be resisted. I doubt if public services can withstand this drive for cash in the pocket. Perhaps in the long run, changes in attitude about the basic definitions of productivity, standard of living, and income will occur, and people will realise that their command over resources is increasing even if they do not have much more cash; that there really is a 'new income' which includes a panoply of services as well as cash. But this is no easy shift — to recognise that a rise in real GNP is not best realised in terms of the disposable income of individuals or in better housing.

The post-industrial society

Now we can return to the broader post-industrial society approach. The term is used in a great variety of ways, and even Daniel Bell, who defines it precisely, does not hold to one version, but his main definition centres on the centrality of knowledge and its systematic production. This is Bell's main though not sole emphasis, and he deserves credit for attempting to describe fairly systematically the increased play of codified knowledge today. I shall argue, however, that he exaggerates its significance.

Many who use the concept of a 'post-industrial society' confusedly mix growth of white collar activities with the notion of the growth of the central role of knowledge. The growth of white collar work has taken place in the expansion of white collar industries, such as insurance, as C. Wright Mills pointed out two decades ago, and through the shift within manufacturing from production jobs to white collar ones. But the growth of white collar work does not mean that scientific work has expanded and become 'dominant'.

The post-industrial society thesis does not rest on the figures of occupational distribution. It emphasises changes in the mode of production, the systematic use of knowledge. Here it is crucial to clarify the significance of the 'service economy' theme, a somewhat different than the post-industrial society concept or perhaps one of the variants of it. In turn, Gartner and Riessman's service society with its emphasis on the organisation and delivery of health, education and welfare services is a variant of the service economy approach. Bell seems to grab hold of this variant at some points in his book, but this variant is very different from his notion of a knowledge-oriented society.

Services in the sense of the 'service economy' are activities not related directly to commodity production. An expansion in health services does not directly depend on increased sales of cars. With this restricted definition, we see that commodity production continues to be very important, even though now less manufacturing employment is directly at the production point. Figures on 'white collar employment' are misleading if used uncritically to indicate a trend towards a service or post-industrial society situation.[13] One has to look at why things are done, for what purposes and the sources of remuneration for the work, rather than regarding an occupational category as the sole important perspective. Many service workers are employed in non-service industries; many engaged in service industries are blue-collar workers. For example, 20 per cent of federal employees, and a much higher percentage of state and local employees, are in blue collar jobs although they work in a service industry.

One important implication is that only the growth of *some* services indicates the growth of activities connection with the acquisition of knowledge. A second is that these activities do not cross all sectors; the high-technology science is concentrated in big business and, to a lesser extent, medium-size firms. The small business and enlarged public sectors are much less involved. All four sectors will continue to operate for a long time to come, but the role of 'knowledge' is greatest for the oligopolies and parts of the public sector. The 'post-industrial society' analysis has to move as Galbraith has charged: to recognise that there is more to the economy and society than big business.

In part Bell does this by shifting from an analysis of institutions to a depiction of a cultural split. He perceives an antagonism between the rational social structure and an adversary counter-culture. The social structure is not nearly as rational as he contends. By 'social structure'

Bell is largely referring to the big business sector and neglects the other sectors. These other sectors are in part the impetus or context of many counter-cultural values, as Christopher Lasch suggested.[14] The antagonism against traditional politics and the development of confrontational street politics[15] (for example, demonstrations and sit-ins) partly result from anger about prejudice and discrimination and the inability of the discriminated to escape from the irregular economy. The public sector has encouraged idealism about educating the young and helping the sick, the poorly housed, the poor. The thwarting of this idealism has contributed in part to the spread of counter-cultural values and practices.

At least three major cultural sets compete in the United States: the counter-cultural; the liberal, progressive New Deal ethic, rapidly eroding and, more important, a small town civil service Middle American economic mentality, though battered, proudly beleaguered and durable. Just as Bell exaggerates the role of knowledge in the social structure today, he underestimates the hardiness of rural and urban Middle America in today's culture. He fails to recognise the diversity of American economic life and the impact of this diversity on cultural outlooks.[16]

Nor does he see the economic relationship of the various cultures. Big business, at least that part of it represented by the Committee for Economic Development and big labour, espouse the contemporary version of the New Deal liberal outlook. Medium business and segments of small business and big business have the narrower perspective of Middle America. The counter-culture has had its roots among the offspring of professionals and those in the enlarged public sector. A street culture among low-income blacks and people of Spanish origin is nourished by the irregular economy.

References

1. John Kenneth Galbraith, *Economics and the Public Interest,* Boston: Houghton-Mifflin Company, 1973.
2. Daniel Bell, *The Coming of Post-industrial Society,* New York: Basic Books, 1973.
3. Alain Touraine, *The Post-industrial Society,* New York: Random House, 1971 (translated from the French by F.X. Mayhew).
4. Victor Fuchs, *The Service Economy,* New York: Columbia University Press, 1968.
5. Alan Gartner and Frank Riessman, *The Service Society and the Consumer Vanguard,* New York: Harper and Row, 1974.
6. *Fortune,* May 1974, p. 231.

7. *Statistical Abstract,* 1973, p. 482.

8. Zeitlin argues that the now widely accepted view that managers rather than core stockholders control most large corporations is wrong. See Maurice Zeitlin, 'Corporate Ownership and Control: The Large Corporation and the Capitalist Class', *American Journal of Sociology,* 79, 1974, pp. 1073–1119.

9. This estimate is the residual after adding up the number of individuals in big and small business and the public sector for which direct data are available.

10. The calculation is made in this way: 1.5 million entrepreneurs in corporations with assets under $1 million; of the 10 million unincorporated enterprises, 2.7 million are farmers, 1.5 million independent professional proprietorships and/or large enterprises (a guess). Subtracting farmers, professionals and the well-off enterprises leaves 6.2 million unincorporated proprietors, or a total of 7.7 million small entrepreneurs. If there were one employee on the average in each such firm, the total would be over 15 million or roughly one of every six members of the (82.7 million) civilian labour force in 1970. If small farmers and many agricultural workers are included, the relative size would be greater.

11. S.M. Miller, 'Poverty, Race and Politics' in Irving L. Horowitz, (ed.), *The New Sociology,* New York: Oxford University Press, 1965, pp. 290–312. The concept is further developed in Chapter 3 ('Barriers to Employment') of the *1968 Manpower Report of the President,* which Martin Rein and S.M. Miller prepared. It is reprinted as Chapter 19 in Martin Rein, *Social Policy.*

12. *Statistical Abstract,* 1973, Table 524, L 323.

13. On the other side, some in manufacturing (scientists) would be part of the knowledge society version of the post-industrial society, but not of the service society version.

14. Christopher Lasch, 'Take Me to Your Leader', *New York Review of Books,* 18 October 1973, p. 66.

15. Bell's term is 'mobilization politics', Frances Piven and Richard Cloward use 'dissensus politics'.

16. I think that this judgement is not inaccurate, even though he is aware of the general issue: 'Changes in culture — particularly the emergence of new life styles — are made possible, not only by changes in sensibility but by shifts in the social structure itself' Bell, *Post-industrial Society,* p. 36. He argues (p. 40) that the corporate class failed to articulate a unified value system which could challenge liberation. Middle American values serve as the values of much of corporate capitalism and may be stronger than he believes in combating counter-cultural values.

9 The Self-Employed and the Small Independent Entrepreneur*

JOHN McHUGH

Introduction

Contemporary British politics has been substantially formed by the triumph of collectivism in the post-war period and the parallel development of a formalised and increasingly institutionalised lobby system. The widening role of the state in matters of social and economic policy has been accompanied by the tendency towards the concentration of resources into large units in the private economic sector. This collectivist trend has accelerated in recent years with state involvement in industries such as steel and car manufacturing, aircraft and shipbuilding and the exploration and exploitation of North Sea oil. In an era increasingly dominated by 'big' business, interventionist government and powerful trade unionism, the petite bourgeoisie has become a marginal social and economic category threatened by powerful political and economic forces. The emergence of various groups over the past few years purporting to represent the small entrepreneur and the self-employed in an aggressive, radical fashion can be seen as a reaction to these forces and an attempt to exercise some control over them.

From: Roger King and Neill Nugent (eds), *Respectable Rebels, Middle Class Campaigns in Britain in the 1970s*, London, Hodder and Stoughton, 1979, pp. 46–75.

The background of small business representation before 1974

A useful starting point is the Bolton Committee report[1] on small firms which presented its findings in 1971. Although the Committee was not primarily concerned with the role of small businesses as a pressure group it did observe that the general failure of small businesses to impress their problems on government was 'in large part the fault of small businessmen themselves who, in spite of their numbers, have been extremely ineffective as a pressure group'.[2] This ineffectiveness was explained in terms of the wide diversity of small business organisations representing specific trades or professions which thereby diluted and weakened the impact of small businesses on government policy-making. It was also apparent that large numbers of small entrepreneurs were unwilling or unable to join organisations claiming to represent their interests. This was explained in terms of the lack of time available to the small entrepreneur to join such groups and a general independence of outlook which militated against the ability to conform to a group norm. More interestingly, Bolton felt that the perceived political prejudices of the small business community acted as an obstacle to successful pressure group activity. A generally hostile attitude to the Labour Party and governments as enemies of the independent operator was emphasised by an almost unquestioning loyalty to the Conservative Party. It is significant that the rise of the new groups after 1974 was linked to a change in this situation with sections of the self-employed in particular becoming progressively disenchanted with the Conservative Party.

In most industries a multiplicity of trade associations, employers' organisations or some combination of both exists. In total about 2500 trade associations, employers' organisations or combinations exist in Britain.[3] Almost all trade associations and related bodies are affiliated to the CBI at national level and provide the CBI with a major source of membership. While the CBI is popularly associated with big business it is increasingly at pains to point out that over a third of its membership comes from smaller firms, and when affiliated organisations like trade associations are taken into account, the CBI claims to represent about 200 000 small businessmen. It might appear that the small entrepreneur has an important source of influence on policy-making, given the fact that the CBI is seen by government as the authoritative representative of the industrial, commercial and business interest. Moreover, the CBI has a Small Firms Council composed of 65 members which meets monthly to consider the problems of small businesses. The members of the Council are all required to be the owner-managers of small firms, all of which theoretically strengthens the position of the small entrepreneur.

However, it is commonly argued that the constitutional structure of the CBI weakens the effective role of the Small Firms Council since only the CBI Grand Council is authorised to determine policy and it is held to be dominated by the concerns of big business. Whatever the reality of the situation, the CBI has faced and continues to face the problem of proving its commitment to small business. Indeed one organisation, the Small Businesses Association (SBA), subsequently renamed the Association of Independent Businesses (AIB), came into existence precisely because of small business dissatisfaction over the creation of the CBI. Prior to the creation of the CBI there were two central bodies representing trade associations, one of which, the National Association of British Manufacturers (NABM), was composed largely of smaller businesses. A minority in the NABM remained unconvinced that the CBI would be able to represent adequately the particular problems facing the small business sector, and so set up the Small Businesses Association in 1968. The problem of small business representation is likewise important to the Association of British Chambers of Commerce which derives its membership from approximately 90 affiliated local Chambers. While local Chambers of Commerce retain an important degree of autonomy within the overall ABCC structure, they are increasingly concerned to follow a collective line under the ABCC.[4]

In Britain the main orthodox representative institutions of the small retailer are the local Chamber of Trade and/or the appropriate trade associations. There are more than 830 Chambers of Trade throughout the country and they are represented at the national level by the National Chamber of Trade (NCT) along with more than 30 affiliated trade associations. The NCT claims to speak on behalf of 350 000 businesses, and has a regional structure based on 12 Administrative Area Councils which are proportionally represented on the national Board of Management, as are the trade associations with six seats.[5] The NCT in turn is part of the Retail Consortium, which attempts to act as a general representative organisation for the retail trade by bringing together in a confederal structure bodies like the Co-operative Union, the Retail Distributors Association, the Retail Alliance and other retail bodies.

The emergence of the new groups, 1974–6

This whole system of what might be termed orthodox institutionalised business representation was challenged after 1974 by the newly formed

National Federation of Self-Employed and Small Businesses (NFSE) initiated by Mr Norman Small, one-time Yorkshire regional organiser for the National Union of Shopkeepers. Within six months Small's Federation had recruited more than 30 000 members at £12 per head. It is generally accepted that this phenomenal growth was a consequence of the Social Security Amendment Act 1974 which contained a clause whereby the self-employed would be required to pay a Class 4 graduated National Insurance contribution rate of 8 per cent on gross profits between £1600 and £3600 per annum. The new contribution became the *cause célèbre* for the Federation.[6]

Ironically, the rapid growth of NFSE membership in the first six months of its existence threatened to overwhelm its rather fragile administrative structure. While the Federation was attempting to develop an organisation to handle its growing membership and construct a system of local branches, the newly recruited rank and file were reported to be 'screaming for action'.[7] In March 1975 Small urged the Minister of State for Health and Social Security to back the Federation's plan for the self-employed to receive social security benefits to match the increased levy. It also argued for a separate insurance fund to provide the self-employed with the same pension rights as ordinary employees. According to Small, members of the Federation were so incensed, that it was possible that they might go as far as breaking the law to gain redress.[8] The Department set up a commission to investigate the possibility of constructing a comprehensive system of earnings-related contributions and benefits for the self-employed. However, the result was a ministerial statement that the cost of such a system made it prohibitive.

While the Class 4 levy payment stimulated the initial growth of the NFSE and remained a constant focus for discontent, the issues surrounding value added tax (VAT) probably provoked the most militant rhetoric and most serious threat of direct action. VAT had originally been introduced in 1973 and extolled as a straightforward flat-rate system of tax collection. However, almost immediately following its introduction VAT had operated at different rates. For small entrepreneurs and particularly the self-employed, VAT was a bitter grievance and the NFSE attacked it on the grounds that it placed the businessman in the position of unpaid tax collector and that the VAT system was already 'too complicated and time consuming for the self-employed to be able to contemplate any further changes'.[9] To emphasise its view the Federation sent a memorandum to the Treasury in the hope of influencing the Labour Government's 1975 Budget.

The Federation's memorandum had no discernible impact on the Budget proposals since the 25 per cent levy which had previously operated on petrol was now extended to include a wide range of domestic electrical appliances. The new differential rates were intended to operate from 1 May and their imposition prompted the 32-man National Executive of the NFSE to meet and agree to advise their membership to withhold VAT payments to the Customs and Excise after 1 July.[10] This move was prompted by a groundswell of grass-roots opinion demanding action, and this groundswell was felt by the National Chamber of Trade which faced the possibility of being outflanked by its more aggressive rival. The NCT publicly deplored the Federation's proposal as a threat to democracy and the leadership was relieved when a motion calling for non-cooperation with the government over the proposed VAT changes was overwhelmingly rejected at their annual conference.

While the NCT appeared to agonise over the question of direct action, the NFSE gained much publicity and a certain amount of kudos within the self-employed and small business sector from its more militant stance. Recruitment was claimed to be increasing by several hundred a day and the Federation's growth raised the question of whether it was on the point of leading the loose coalition of self-employed, small entrepreneurs and middle class militants in a British Poujadist-type movement.[11] In fact the threat of militant action over VAT was quickly withdrawn following a promise by the Treasury that the Federation would be able to meet the Financial Secretary to the Treasury and senior officials at the Customs and Excise to explain their grievances. The Federation leaders tended to see this as an important breakthrough in establishing their position with the government as the authoritative body representing the self-employed. At the same time elements within the Federation and even at the leadership level may have seen this development as a government strategy of enveloping it in the Whitehall web of committees.

The Federation's attempts to establish a relationship with a government took place against a background of growing internal unrest which produced a major upheaval in the autumn of 1975. As early as February the Chairman of the Solihull branch issued a statement claiming that members of the National Executive had voted themselves large salary contracts and raised more general doubts about the Federation's financial management.[12] Dissatisfaction with the Federation's leadership was more than an individual gripe since rumours of internal wrangling on the Executive over policy and bitter personality clashes were widespread throughout the Federation.

In October 1975 the new management committee, which had replaced the old executive committee and contained the chairman of each of the 35 regional committees, held a press conference to outline the NFSE's future strategy. They announced the Federation would spend £15 000 on a recruitment drive and find a 'thoroughly professional' chief executive officer who had experience of negotiating with government departments. Along with the intention to strengthen the membership and administrative capacity of the Federation, the management committee advised their members to withhold the additional Class 4 National Insurance levy unless the government agreed to grant tax relief on the payment. David Kelly warned that they would operate a system of 'dirty tricks' short of law-breaking to create bureaucratic confusion and general chaos.[13]

At the end of its first year the NFSE had survived the constant personality clashes and arguments over financial spending, albeit somewhat shakily. It had established its position as the largest of the new groups with a membership of about 43 000 organised in a system of 35 regions and 300 local branches. Despite this large membership, the Federation was not without rivals, although the majority remained small and often localised.

The most significant of the groups that emerged in 1975 was the National Association of the Self-Employed (NASE). The NASE was formed shortly after the Federation as a loosely oranised amalgamation of a host of local groups which had emerged spontaneously in the wake of the Social Security Amendment Act 1974. The actual amalgamation was effected through a newspaper advertisement placed in the *Daily Mail*.[14] At its peak the NASE claimed to speak for an associated membership of 27 000, although this figure may be optimistic. In many ways the NASE represented a reaction against the financial wrangles taking place within the NFSE and more specifically against the Federation's annual subscription of £12. It appears that many self-employed and small entrepreneurs considered this sum excessive, and the NASE never charged more than £3. Moreover, the looser organisation of the NASE allowed more autonomy to local groups and this suited sections of the active self-employed who were suspicious of the more structured, centralised and potentially bureaucratic NFSE.

The other significant self-employed group which emerged out of dissatisfaction with the conduct of the NFSE's affairs and its lack of a firm ideological line was the Association of Self-Employed People (ASP), founded by Mrs Teresa Gorman. Mrs Gorman was an active member of the NFSE and remained so for some time after the formation of ASP. Her dissatisfaction with the NFSE has been directed against the failure of successive leadership groups to grasp firmly and operate the liberal-conservative ideology which Mrs Gorman believes to be the central requirement for a group purporting to represent small independent entrepreneurs and especially the self-employed. She had always been concerned to differentiate between NFSE leaders and the rank-and-file activist whom she believed to be broadly sympathetic to her position but loyal to a leadership which failed to provide the correct ideological direction.

In an important sense, ASP has never been solely concerned to present itself as the champion of the self-employed or even small business, but is engaged in a crusade on behalf of the extreme libertarian ideology espoused by Mrs Gorman and her close associates. This ideology is based on the primacy of market forces in the allocation of resources and envisages a strictly limited role for the state which strongly resembles the classic model of nineteenth-century *laissez-faire* liberalism. ASP draws its historical inspiration from the Manchester School, Cobden and Bright, and the French economist Bastiat. In the contemporary period ASP looks to Milton Friedman and F.A. von Hayek for guidance and inspiration, and, closer at hand, to the Institute of Economic Affairs.[15]

Initially Gorman's press advertisement generated about 4000 replies and produced a membership of 2000 drawn from a wide range of self-employed occupations. Although ASP has never achieved the numerical support enjoyed by the NFSE, it has defined its role less in terms of mass support and more in terms of propagating libertarian values and exposing the alleged ideological shortcomings of the NFSE. For ASP there are two kinds of self-employed, those faithful to the ethic of rugged individualism and those who 'see the salvation of the self-employed as getting into the pork barrel with everyone else'.[16] ASP was determined to remain in the first category and has refused to build up any formalised branch system or make a pretence of internal democratic decision-making.

At the end of 1975 the growth of support for these groups had been so rapid as to create alarm in Conservative Party circles. The traditionally close relationship between the small independent entrepreneur and the Conservative Party appeared to be less secure. The virtues of the independent entrepreneur, individual effort and initiative, have been consistent elements in Conservative propaganda. At the local level the independent entrepreneur has traditionally played an important political role in local Conservative Associations. Yet while the rise of the militant self-employed groups has been widely interpreted as a reaction to a punitive Labour government it is explicable, in part at least, in terms of a growing small business disillusion with the Conservative Party.

While many self-employed members of the NFSE, NASE and ASP might not have been able to catalogue the 'sins' of the Heath government, there can be little doubt that disillusion with the Conservatives as the traditional guardians of the interests of the small entrepreneur was quite widespread. In fact, a small number of Conservative backbenchers had already set up a backbench committee to watch over small business affairs in 1973.[17] In the aftermath of the self-employed revolt in late 1974 and its apparently rapid growth in 1975, the Conservatives set up a Small Business Bureau (SBB). The driving force behind these developments, Paul Dean and David Mitchell, have been anxious to point out that the SBB is not a rival of the existing groups but a complementary organisation.[18]

The NFSE and ASP have often collaborated with the SBB by providing information used in Parliamentary Questions or press statements, but both have been concerned to maintain their independence. While many of the NFSE's leaders might welcome closer relations with the Conservative Party it would almost certainly precipitate a split in the membership. ASP is likewise suspicious of Conservative intentions to reverse the slide to collectivism. The ASP attitude to the SBB is quite instrumental: they have affiliated for access to literature, platforms, and to reach an influential audience which would be otherwise denied them. Although the SBB has not been able to channel the energies and activities of the new self-employed groups into the orbit of the Conservative Party, it has enjoyed significant success. It has established itself as an influential organisation in the field of self-employed and small business representation and enabled the Conservative Party to reach, and possibly gain recruits from, an important section of the electorate.

The realignment of the self-employed groups, 1976–7

While the Conservatives tried to respond to the new groups, a number of important changes were taking place between and within the NFSE, NASE and ASP. In early 1976 the NASE approached the ASP with a proposal for establishing a system of liaison which would enable both to act in concert. Although the NASE had shortly before claimed a membership of about 27 000, subsequent events would seem to show that its position must have waned dramatically and that its overture to ASP was made from a position of weakness rather than strength. It is apparent that the NASE was already on the point of disintegration. At the point of establishing a working relationship with ASP it is probable that NASE membership had fallen from an estimated 27 000 to less than 10 000. Moreover, not all sections of the NASE were content to associate with ASP and the active East Anglia branch was already moving towards affiliation with the NFSE.[19]

The NFSE was itself undergoing internal organisational changes in the light of the September leadership changes but more importantly was becoming more cautious and moderate in its general political approach. One consequence of the changes was an approach to a number of established political leaders for advice about the future role of the NFSE. It appears that the NFSE was told of the importance of establishing a responsible and credible image as the necessary prelude to acceptance by the government for the purposes of negotiation. Certainly it can be argued that the NFSE was much less vociferous in its public outbursts and was moving away from an emphasis on a publicity-conscious propagandist role, towards 'a more conventional pressure group role'.

It is ironic that the NFSE's movement towards a more accommodating position took place at a time when the Labour government implemented a number of important Acts seen to be antagonistic to small employers. Although the legislation was not specifically directed at small business, small entrepreneurs interpreted it as an attack and a further stage in the drift towards full socialism. Most contentious among this legislation were the Trade Union and Labour Relations Act and the Employment Protection Act. The Trade Union and Labour Relations Act extended the opportunities to trade unions for increasing membership through the development of the 100 per cent unionised closed shop. Although the Act did not make the closed shop compulsory on employers, it did require them to consider the imposition of a closed shop when more than half the employees of a firm requested it.

The Employment Protection Act was likewise seen as a threat to the small entrepreneur. Under this Act the Advisory, Conciliation and Arbitration Service (ACAS) was empowered to look at the pay and conditions of individual firms and in effect to force an improvement where they were inferior to those in the trade or industry generally. However, the main target for the self-employed groups was the provision which enabled industrial tribunals to impose fines up to £12 000 on firms held to have dismissed workers unfairly. These two Acts of Parliament, together with redundancy payments, the legislation concerning equal wages for women and the employment rights of expectant and new mothers were consistently attacked as harmful to small employers and to employment in general by dissuading employers from taking on new employees.

The ASP was particularly active in attempting to lead opposition to the Trade Union and Labour Relations and Employment Protection

Acts. Both were seen as a general attack on individual liberty and were opposed for that above all else. At the same time the ASP provided practical guidance to employers on the implications of the Acts and advice on minimising their impact. One of ASP's researchers and lobbyists, published a booklet, *Slow to Hire, Quick to Fire,*[20] which provided a brief but well-informed account of the main obligations of employers in their dealings with employees as imposed by a number of Parliamentary Acts.

The booklet outlined the main legal machinery involved in industrial relations and industrial disputes and the liabilities of employers for breaches of the Acts. *Slow to Hire, Quick to Fire* outlined the main pitfalls for employers to avoid and argued the case for recruiting additional workers on self-employed contracts. In a double irony for the ASP, an NFSE activist, Brian Kelly, uncovered a relatively simple way of avoiding the obligations of the Employment Protection Act. It involved recruiting employees on a fixed-term contract of 25 weeks after which they would sign on as unemployed for two weeks and be subsequently re-engaged by the employer. This device evaded the Employment Protection Act because an employee on a 25-week contract did not count as full-time and the Act covered only full-time employees.

One of the more significant campaigns mounted in 1976 and one which served to illustrate the differences between the Federation and ASP concerned the Constantinescu case. This was seen by the ASP as a glorious opportunity to publicise the powers of the VAT inspectorate to search private premises and homes with a search warrant for suspected VAT evasion. Moreover, it was a means of publicising the fact that similar powers had been given to the Inland Revenue under the 1976 Finance Act. The VAT inspectorate had been under attack from the self-employed for employing 'vindictive' methods and for excessive recourse to search warrants despite the fact that warrants are issued by magistrates only where prima-facie evidence of evasion exists. In July 1976 the General Secretary of the Customs and Excise Group of the Society of Civil and Public Servants, wrote to the *Guardian* defending his members and attacking VAT evasion.[21] He argued that since 1 April 1973 some 343 search warrants had been issued for 152 investigations of suspected tax fraud of which 326 produced evidence of offences leading to the recovery of more than £3 million. He went on to argue that VAT evasion was stealing from the consumer and that exceptional but tightly regulated procedures were necessary to combat that evasion, which he estimated was running at £134 million a year.

Mr Petre Constantinescu committed suicide shortly after a lengthy search of his home by VAT men,[22] and members of the NASE action group in Shropshire demanded some demonstration in protest. As a result the ASP/NASE leadership organised a demonstration which also involved members of the NFSE in South-East England. The demonstration involved about 150 people and was followed by a group proceeding to Parliament to lobby MPs about the proposed extension of the search powers to the Inland Revenue.[23]

Despite the differences between the ASP/NASE block and the Federation over the Constantinescu case and ideological questions, the idea of an amalgamation between all three was informally discussed. The Federation was seeking an amalgamation as part of a 'determined effort to present a united front against the increasing pressures on the self-employed'.[24] The ASP/NASE organisation was prompted towards discussion of amalgamation by the unilateral decision of the East Anglia NASE group to seek an agreement with the NFSE.[25] At the same time the Federation was attempting to initiate an important new development, an Alliance of Independent Workers and Enterprises which would become a 'TUC of the middle class and square the triangle of Government, CBI and TUC'.[26]

The NFSE/ASP/NASE amalgamation failed to materialise because the Federation was not prepared to meet the conditions of the ASP/NASE groups which included a new name, significant representation on a new Executive and the continued existence of the ASP London office with its small but energetic political lobby and research staff. The Federation's counter-offer was rejected by ASP/NASE following a mandate conducted through *Counterattack,* and the terms were described by ASP as derisory; 'the NFSE Executive is not interested in amalgamation but only in total takeover with the obliteration of all other groups.'[27]

In fact ASP/NASE had little to offer the NFSE in return for significant concessions within an amalgamated structure. The ASP was a relatively small organisation in terms of numbers and its penchant for creating occasional publicity owed much to the energy and personality of its driving force, Teresa Gorman. However, it is doubtful whether the Federation's Executive would have looked forward with much sympathy to her inclusion in a position of eminence in a new organisation. The NASE prospects were even poorer than ASP's. The Federation was already assured of absorbing the East Anglia group, with its 3500 members, and the remainder was in a weak financial state. Indeed following the failure of the amalgamation discussions the NASE simply disintegrated.

One of the most interesting relationships highlighted by the Alliance conferences and subsequent events was that between the NFSE and the National Association for Freedom (NAFF). NAFF is an overtly political organisation which opposes the growth of collectivism and espouses the values of individualism and the economics of free competition. For NAFF the self-employed/small business sector was, and is, a natural target and NAFF had already established close relations with ASP with which it shared broadly similar economic views.

In December 1976 the rather cloudy relationship between the NFSE and NAFF erupted into a bitter public controversy. Following a series of articles in the *Guardian,* which indicated that a number of NAFF leaders had at some point been sponsored by the American CIA, the Federation issued a public statement that it had informed NAFF of its desire 'to sever all connections "because of the NAFF's political views"'.[28] The Federation was concerned to emphasise that it was not party-political, had not subscribed to NAFF and provided it with no other form of financial assistance.

Although relations between the leaders of the Federation and ASP were constantly strained, a more workable relationship existed at the grass-roots level. This relationship operated over the issue of the Building Tax Exemption Certificate, the so-called 714, despite the refusal of the Federation's leadership to collaborate with ASP in a 'Fight the 714 Campaign'. The 714 issue was specifically concerned with sub-contract labour in the building industry, associated with the notorious system of tax-evasion known as 'the lump'.

The lump derived from the cash payments made to sub-contractors which they were then required to declare to the Inland Revenue. In fact the system was wide open to abuse and in 1971 an attempt to tighten up the situation was made. Only sub-contractors with an Inland-Revenue-approved form could be paid a gross figure by a contractor which would be subsequently submitted as part of an annual tax declaration to the Inland Revenue. The expectation that this would end the lump by providing a means of tracing payments was not realised because forgery and a black market in real and forged forms flourished. The Labour government replaced the original forms with the 714 certificate which contained a photograph of the sub-contractor and thereby made forgery or duplication almost impossible.

The use of photographs and certificates was opposed as an attempt at a licensing system of employment in the sub-contracting trades but more generally as an infringement of individual liberty.[29] Evidence was brought forward to argue that the 714 certificate was being withheld from certain builders and sole traders because of alleged tax irregularities in the past. As early as June 1976 the Federation had responded to rank-and-file pressure by campaigning against the certificate.[30] The campaign was organised by the Federation's Freedom to Work Group and in November it was joined in the field by the ASP/NASE inspired 'Fight the 714 Campaign'.

The NFSE was careful of its image and therefore cautious of too close an involvement with the 714. In the event the campaign against the 714 was carried on by ASP's 'Fight the 714 Campaign' supported by NFSE activists around London. The most important victory was achieved with the decision of the Conservative Party to devote three hours of its parliamentary allocation to a debate on the 714. Credit for this Conservative move was claimed by both ASP and the NFSE. But nothing was conceded by the Labour government, which remained convinced that only exceptional measures could stamp out tax abuse in the building industry.[31]

The NFSE remained determined to impress itself on public opinion and government as the legitimate and authoritative spokesman for the interests of the self-employed and small enterpreneurs. It can be argued that the more considered and moderate tone and approach of the Federation was part of this more general drive for official recognition. However, the fact that the Federation was easily the best supported of the new groups, with a membership of about 43 000 at the end of 1976, has to be placed against the existence of a potential membership of about 2 million self-employed and a further 80 000 small independent firms. In fact the total membership of the various self-employed groups probably accounted for less than 5 per cent of the total self-employed population.[32]

It has always been the objective of the NFSE to achieve a mass membership, and with more than 40 000 recruits at the end of its first year this objective appeared capable of achievement. Yet at the end of 1976 the membership figure remained around the 43 000 mark despite efforts to increase it. To that end a campaign was mounted to stimulate membership and generally increase public awareness of the Federation's existence and purposes. This campaign was officially launched at the Federation's first annual conference held in 1977, which culminated in a rally and a mass lobby of Parliament. It was the result of months of planning and involved a series of full-page advertisements in the national press and meetings organised and co-ordinated by a London-based campaign headquarters supported by the Federation's Lytham St Annes official base. The results of the campaign were a major disappointment in that membership remained substantially unaffected and the campaign cost the Federation an estimated £100 000. Its failure was to create a further round of tension and internal struggle which produced a major change of leadership and a possible change in the direction of the Federation's strategy.

The Federation's first annual conference was something of a disappointment from the point of view of the turnout. *First Voice* noted the thin attendance but felt it was offset by the standard and vigour of the debates.[33] The major guest speaker was Lord Hesketh who had established a public reputation for his pioneering attempt to break into grand prix motor racing as an independent operator. Hesketh made the keynote speech to the conference and emphasised the absolute importance of acquiring public credibility which would assist the Federation in securing a more powerful bargaining position. This necessitated the removal of unspecified extremists from the organisation and a campaign to increase membership and remove media misconceptions. Hesketh understood that some members were concerned at the proposed expenditure of £100 000 on a recruitment campaign but felt it was a risk well worth taking if they could get the members.

The general mood of the conference was pragmatic and hard-headed. While those present were concerned to point out alleged injestices, they tended to take a more realistic short-term approach to their removal. Certainly there was a tendency to argue against collectivism and in favour of free enterprise, but the main concern was less with ideology than with practical issues. The conference ended with the perennial criticism of the administration which prompted a Federation leader, David Dexter, to appeal for an end to 'this inward criticism. Let the administration have a chance to settle down and work. You get out and fight — outside the Federation, not inside.'[34] Despite this appeal for internal unity, the Federation was soon engaged in a further internal struggle.

It appears that activists and leaders alike had an image of the self-employed as an essentially homogeneous group with common economic interests and broadly similar attitudes and values. Consequently, the problem of recruiting the self-employed appeared to be one of establishing a popular identity and formulating a policy likely to activate the massive but still overwhelmingly passive self-employed population. There is little evidence to suggest that the NFSE ever seriously considered that the differences between the self-employed in terms of occupation, social status and scope of activity required a more sophisticated and varied approach to recruitment. It was apparently assumed that such differences were irrelevant or were offset by the shared experience of self-employment and the common attitudes which it was believed to generate.

The diverse nature of the self-employed population was indicated not only by government statistics but also by the NFSE's own research.[35] In April 1977 the Federation analysed a random sample of

7500 members by occupation and produced an interesting profile of its membership. Perhaps the most surprising information was the prominent contribution made by farmers to the Federation's membership. They provided the largest single occupational block, followed by garage proprietors and general builders. Beyond these three groups no specific occupation comprised more than 3 per cent of the total membership.

The existence of such a variety of occupational groupings, each forming a fractional part of the Federation's total membership, goes some way towards highlighting the difficulty of defining the self-employed as a homogeneous social group. It is just possible to suggest that the nature of self-employment is itself sufficient to offset this apparent diversity, but this argument is not convincing. It is a priori difficult to accept that the self-employed artisan such as a bricklayer, plumber or electrician has a readily available identity of interest with the professional groups such as doctors, dentists or lawyers.

Fragmentation of the self-employed class is not restricted to social class and occupational status but includes the economic differences involved in the relative scale of their activities. It is difficult to construct a detailed breakdown of such differences in capital outlay and the amount of plant utilised, but there is an obvious and important distinction to be made between the self-employed who are employers of labour and those who are not. Some self-employed entrepreneurs employ substantial amounts of labour but government statistics indicate that more than half are sole traders.[36] Clearly legislation dealing with employer–employee relationships governing unfair dismissal, equal opportunities for women, redundancy payments and such like have a differential impact on the self-employed as a whole. Those without employees are not directly, or at least not immediately, affected and will presumably be less moved to protest than those who are affected. In an important sense the issues of the National Insurance levy and VAT regulations are atypical pieces of legislation insofar as they have a more general application to the self-employed population. Most legislation has a differential impact affecting particular self-employed groups such as employers or building workers or farmers.

Whatever the significance of the marked differences within the self-employed sector, there can be no doubt that the failure of the Federation's recruitment campaign in 1977 emphasised that growth was going to be difficult to achieve. Further, that failure may have had a deeper significance when taken in conjunction with a closer evaluation of the Federation's membership returns for 1976. At a superficial level it achieved a marginal increase in membership from about 40 000 in 1975 to around 43 000 in 1976, but the net improvement obscures an interesting trend. Between 1975 and 1976 the Federation experienced a loss of approximately 7000 members which was offset by additional recruitment, most notably the 'windfall' afforded by the adhesion of the 3500 former members of the NASE's East Anglia group.[37] Clearly continued wastage of membership on the scale of 1975–6 required substantial fresh recruitment to compensate, and the evidence of early 1977 appeared to suggest that, notwithstanding a substantial financial outlay and a national advertising campaign, such recruitment was not immediately forthcoming.

The Federation's leadership has always recognised the paramount importance of maintaining and expanding its support. It has therefore developed an elaborate administrative and organisational structure which is financed almost entirely by membership subscriptions. This makes it particularly vulnerable to the effects of any significant erosion of its membership, for this would rapidly produce a financial crisis with implications for the Federation's survival. In this context the failure of the recruitment campaign was particularly damaging since it wasted valuable financial resources without producing the vital new membership.

Conclusions

The idea that the NFSE, NASE and ASP constituted a core element in a wider phenomenon of 'middle class revolt' is now open to serious doubt. In 1974–5 the rapid growth in the numerical support for the Federation and the NASE took place against a background of high inflation, a Labour government and the perceived power of trade unions. This background provided a classic recipe for an emerging middle class discontent to manifest itself in groups such as the NFSE, ratepayers' associations and overtly political organisations like NAFF and the Middle Class Association. The confusion and lack of confidence exhibited by the Conservative Party in the wake of the confrontation with the miners, the three-day week and the electoral defeat of 1974, left the Party ill-equipped to deal with these more radical developments and, indeed, possibly encouraged them. All of this contributed to an atmosphere in which the popular media concentrated considerable attention on the new groups and organisations and put forward the general theme of 'middle class revolt'.

While the initial growth of NFSE membership was quite spectacular, it has not been sustained. It is doubtful whether the organisation has achieved any significant growth in membership since late 1975 despite the expensive recruitment campaign in early 1977. Recent (early 1979) assessments of the Federation's membership place it about 50 000, but there are grounds for believing the true figure to be much smaller. From the earliest days of its most rapid growth the Federation has experienced a relatively high turnover in support — perhaps as much as 25 per cent during 1975–6. This wastage has always been a source of concern, and much time is spent trying to contact members who have failed to renew their subscriptions.

Difficulties over membership are complemented by the related problem of fashioning a strategy for dealing with political questions and government legislation in a way that will maximise rank-and-file support. The Federation remains unable to establish whether it is a conventional pressure group operating in the context of bargains and compromises or a group content to remain outside the lobby system propagating a return to a society based on the private enterprise model and the individualistic ethic. In the event it has operated as a kind of 'marginal', group vacillating between the two positions. Many critics argue that this is a consequence of leadership failure or a failure of vision, but again it may be a constraint imposed by a large, diverse membership subject to widely different pressures and without the necessary political skill or experience to forge a workable internal alliance. The ASP has been able to define and propagate a relatively precise ideological line, but the cost has been a small and reducing membership. In May 1978 the ASP claimed a membership of 5126, drawn from a wide range of occupations, of which one-third had no employees, while the remainder employed an average work-force of 13.9.[38] This contrasts with the position in early 1976 when the ASP claimed a membership of over 12 000, including recruits from the NASE. It clearly appears to have lost members at an alarming rate, which may be significant for its future role.

Although the aspirations of the NFSE and ASP have not been realised they certainly alerted bodies such as the CBI, NCT and Conservative Party to the volatility of small business and self-employed entrepreneurs and they have made efforts to represent these interests in a more vigorous, public fashion. The CBI have made efforts to publicise the activity of the Small Firms Council and their efforts on behalf of the small entrepreneur. In November 1977 the CBI held its first national conference, attended by 1300 members including a significant representation from the small-firm sector. The NCT has recently emphasised its position as the premier organisation representing 'independents', 'family businesses' and the 'self-employed'. It has made much of its role in a somewhat mysterious body called the National Trade and Kindred Organisations Committee for National

Insurance (NATKO). This body, claiming to represent over a million self-employed, is composed of 36 constituent bodies, mostly trade associations, has operated for more than 50 years and is recognised by the Department of Health and Social Security for the purposes of negotiating on specialised National Insurance legislation. It claims to have regular, often weekly, meetings at the Department with reasonable access to Ministers.

In conclusion, it may be that the phenomenon of the self-employed groups was a consequence of the existence of a particular set of socio-economic and political circumstances between 1974 and 1976. Since that point the slowing down in the rate of inflation, the revival of morale within the Conservative Party and the more positive attitude of Labour towards small business may have reduced the radical, aggressive appeal of groups like the NFSE and ASP. At the same time the heterogeneous nature of self-employment in terms of occupation, social status and size of plant utilised limits the opportunities of developing a mass organisation on the basis of the simple appeal of shared self-employment. The CBI and the NCT may still remain the dominant organisations in their field, but they may be increasingly challenged by new groups representing specific interests and viewpoints.

References

1. J.E. Bolton, *Report of the Committee of Inquiry on Small Firms* (Bolton Report), Cmnd 4811, HMSO, 1971.
2. Ibid., p. 93.
3. See the *Report of the Committee of Inquiry into Industrial and Commercial Representation*, Association of British Chambers of Commerce/CBI, November 1972, Appendices VII and IX.
4. See R.T. Hamilton 'Government Decisions and Small Firms', unpublished draft manuscript, 1975, p. 14. This piece provides a useful background to the literature on the relationship between government and small business prior to 1975.
5. For an account of its organisation, structure, membership and activites, see *The 79th Annual Report of the National Chamber of Trade*, 1977.
6. See, for example, the *Sunday Times*, 8 December 1974, and the *Sunday Telegraph*, 19 January 1975, which carry accounts of the impact of the proposed National Insurance payments on the self-employed; also the *Guardian*, 14 November 1974.
7. *Daily Mail*, 28 April 1975.

8. *Daily Mail*, 25 March 1975.

9. P.G. Ruffley, 'A Discussion of Some Aspects of the Self-Employed, Small Business and Government', unpublished dissertation, University of Manchester Institute of Science and Technology, 1976.

10. *Guardian*, 17 April 1975.

11. For an early attempt to locate the self-employed revolt in the wider context of a more general middle class political movement, see the *Guardian*, 26, 27, 28 November 1975.

12. *Guardian*, 22 February 1975.

13. *Daily Mail*, 26 November 1975.

14. The information on the NASE is derived mainly from conversations and written communications with Teresa Gorman, General Secretary of the ASP.

15. This assessment of Gorman's view is drawn from an interview and subsequent communication.

16. *Counterattack*, vol. 1, no. 4 (1976), p. 2.

17. *Guardian*, 19 May 1975. See also the *Guardian*, 7 July 1978, for an account of the Conservative SBB.

18. *Guardian*, 7 July 1978.

19. See the *Daily Mail*, 24 August 1978, for evidence of the often confusing nature of the relationships between the various self-employed groups and the proposed alliance between the NASE and the NFSE. In Gorman's letter of 2 May 1978 she points out that 'sometime in 1976 the NASE group in Norfolk decided unilaterally to join the NFSE'.

20. *Slow to Hire, Quick to Fire*, ASP, 1976.

21. *Guardian*, 15 July 1976.

22. *Daily Mail*, 8 July 1976.

23. For an account of the Constantinescu demonstration, see *Counterattack*, vol. 1 no. 3 (1976).

24. *First Voice*, October 1976, p. 4.

25. An account of these negotiations with photocopies of the crucial letters dealing with the terms of the proposed amalgamation is contained in a handout entitled *Lost Voice*, published by ASP.

26. See *The Observer*, 19 September 1976.

27. *Lost Voice*.

28. *Guardian*, 23 December 1976.

29. Teresa Gorman saw this as the crucial element in the campaign and quoted Labour MPs who proposed to extend the use of certificates to other self-employed professions like law and medicine.

30. See *The Times*, 4 June 1976 and *First Voice*, February 1977 and March 1977.

31. See Alex Lyon's letter reprinted in *First Voice*, June 1978, p. 8, which commented: 'Unfortunately there were so many crooks in the building industry that this was the only way to defeat the lump.'

32. An accurate calculation is impossible to make but it is difficult to find evidence to support the view that the various groups ever accounted for more than 5 per cent of the total self-employed population.

33. *First Voice*, March 1977, p. 3.

34. Ibid, p. 5.

35. NFSE Head Office Communication no. 115, 25 April 1977.

36. See *Department of Employment Gazette*, op cit., p. 1344. In 1971 three-fifths of the self-employed had no employees.

37. NFSE Annual Conference Report, February 1977, p. 15.

38. A letter from Teresa Gorman dated 2 May 1978.

10 Small Firms Policy: The Case of Employment Legislation*

AVA WESTRIP

Introduction

A notable feature of the debate on the job-creation potential of small firms has been its focus on the effects of employment legislation. Central to the discussion was the claim that this legislation had inhibited expansion of employment in the small firm sector. An all-party Parliamentary Select Committee postulated in 1978 that if 'each small business could take on one more employee, the unemployment problem would be solved' and called for continuing research into the extent that the Employment Protection Act (EPA) was a deterrent to 'small businessmen from taking on additional personnel'.[1]

Although a number of bodies devoted resources to studying the problem, research findings appeared to be conflicting. Consequently, public discussion of the issue became (and often remains) confused and fragmented. Considerable controversy was stimulated by the legislative measures, resulting in polarised positions, largely (but not exclusively) on party political lines.

Surveys conducted by employer interest groups seemed strangely at

---

* From: 'Effects of employment legislation on Small Firms', D. Watkins, J. Stanworth and A. Westrip (eds.), *Stimulating Small Firms*, Gower Publishing, 1982.

odds with those conducted by independent research organisations, since the former suggested widespread and debilitating effects not borne out by the latter. Closer inspection reveals that methodological differences provide not only the explanatory key, but indicate which category has the greater validity. To illustrate these points, this paper reviews two independent studies and four employer interest group surveys, and draws on other research to support the tentative conclusions presented.

This current paper attempts a systematic review and analysis of the issues, examining the findings, methodology, sample sizes and sample construction of the surveys in question. This review, coupled with analysis of official statistics, suggests that legislative changes made in recent years[2] may be an inappropriate method of dealing with the perceived problems. It is further argued that these modifications in employment legislation are unlikely in themselves to result in any expansion of employment in the small firm sector, may exacerbate the problems of small firm owner-managers, and are almost certainly detrimental to small firm employees.

Employment legislation: a brief background

At the time of the Donovan Report in 1968,[3] the law regarded employer and employee as free and equal parties to the employment contract. Thus, an employer was legally entitled to dismiss an employee whenever he wished, provided only that he gave due notice. The employer did not have to offer any reasons, let alone justify them. The Donovan Commission argued that this situation was unsatisfactory because in practice there is usually:

> no comparison between the consequences for an employer if an employee terminates his contract of employment and those which will ensue for an employee if he is dismissed. In reality people build much of their lives around their jobs. Their incomes and prospects for the future are inevitably founded in the expectation that their jobs will continue. For workers in many situations dismissal is a disaster.[4]

It was against this background that unfair dismissal provisions were introduced initially in the Industrial Relations Act 1971. Thereafter an increasing number of employees qualified for protection against unfair dismissal, mainly by means of reductions in the original qualifying period of two years.[5] The initial two-year qualification period appears to have been a somewhat arbitrary threshold, apparently adopted for no better reason than to ensure congruence between estimates of likely case-load and the capacity and resources of the industrial tribunal system in the early days.[6] Indeed, the Donovan Commission felt there was 'no justification for limiting protection for unfair dismissal to those with at least two years service', since dismissal after a short period 'could in some circumstances have a serious effect on an employee's future prospects'. The exclusion of small firms from the provisions was similarly rejected by the Commission, since it was considered that tribunals would be able 'to take adequate account of the personal factors that inevitably play a larger part in very small undertakings'.[7]

Thus the right not to be unfairly dismissed was enshrined in British law; or, more correctly, for the first time the law provided machinery whereby a dismissed employee, with grounds for believing that the reason for termination of the employment was unjust, could seek redress. This becomes an important distinction when the statistics relating to unfair dismissal are discussed later. But firstly we look at another major statute, which laid down additional rights for employees, the Employment Protection Act (EPA).[8]

The Employment Protection Act

In September 1974, the then Labour government published its proposals for an extension of individual employment rights. By the end of the consultative period the CBI were reporting widespread employer hostility and the *Daily Telegraph* claimed that the 'heavily biased' bill would 'push up industrial costs and hit small companies particularly hard.'[9] Hence, even before enactment, the scene was set for the substantial criticism that was to ensue.

Indeed, the EPA was a substantial legislative package, with measures relating to guaranteed pay for workers laid off, maternity pay and maternity leave, time off for redundant workers to look for jobs, revised remedies for unfair dismissal, longer minimum periods of notice and payment of insolvent companies' debts to their former employees.[10] Critics of the legislation subsequently suggested that its provisions were inhibiting industrial recovery and thus contributing to the prevailing high levels of unemployment. Employers had become reluctant to engage additional employees, it was claimed, due to the difficulties involved in dismissing them should they prove to be unsuitable or surplus to requirements at a later date. The majority of the individual rights provisions of the EPA came into force on 1 June 1976. Less than one year later, the Policy Studies Institute (PSI) was

commissioned[11] to examine some of the consequences of the legisla-
tion on manufacturers, and by the spring of 1978 the Opinion
Research Centre (ORC) was conducting interviews with small firms.
The major findings of these studies are detailed below.

The Policy Studies Institute survey

The PSI examined the practices and policies of a representative sample
of 301 private sector manufacturing firms employing between 50 and
5000 employees. The first phase, structured telephone interviews, was
followed by more detailed personal interviews with a sub-sample of 36
plants that had experienced a fall in demand but were enjoying a
revival at the time of interview. The researchers felt that if employment legislation was having detrimental effects, then it would be most
apparent in firms that had experienced fluctuating demand.

In fact, PSI found 'very little sign . . . that employment protection
legislation was inhibiting industrial recovery or contributing to the
high level of unemployment by discouraging employers from taking on
new people'.[12] Where firms with increasing demand for their products
were not recruiting, or were recruiting smaller numbers than previously, respondents rarely cited employment legislation as the reason
for not increasing their work-force. Increased labour productivity or
spare capacity were by far the major reasons spontaneously cited by
managers.[13]

When subsequently asked directly about the effect of four specific
aspects of employment legislation, the unfair dismissal provisions
clearly emerged as the most significant in the mind of the respondents
(in comparison with redundancy procedures, redundancy pay and
guaranteed payments for workers on short time or temporarily laid
off).

Two important issues arise from these responses. First, as the
researchers commented, it was 'striking . . . that few managers
attributed a major impact to any of the items'.[14] Secondly, whilst 17
per cent of the respondents considered that unfair dismissal legislation
had 'a good deal of effect' on their manpower policies, it should not
necessarily be inferred from this that the effects were detrimental.
Replying to the interviewers' enquiries on the nature of these effects,
the most common response was that it had led to the reform of
procedures relating to disciplinary action and dismissals, selection and
recruitment, induction and training. More attention was paid to
recruitment, to ensure that new employees were competent to undertake the job.

At the close of the discussion with the sub-sample respondents, the interviewers posed the question: 'Some people argue that the package of employment protection laws has made employers reluctant to recruit because of the increased difficulty of getting rid of people. Would you say that argument makes any sense as far as you are concerned here?'[15] Whilst the question clearly invited agreement, nevertheless two-thirds of the respondents said that employment legislation had not inhibited recruitment. The minority who agreed with the proposition generally indicated that the impact was in the direction of additional care in the types of person employed, rather than a reduction in overall numbers.

In their careful analysis of the response, the authors of the report addressed their attention to the particular effects of the legislation on smaller plants. Fifty-four employed less than 200, of which 18 were independent enterprises. Despite the reservations that must be attached to a sub-sample of this size, the report nevertheless shows some interesting results, which are pertinent to the wider debate on the impact of the measures on small firms.

It was found that managers at the smallest plants attributed the *least* impact to unfair dismissal, whether they were independent or part of a larger organisation.[16] Marked differences emerged when dismissal rates were considered: the chances of dismissal appeared to be nearly four times greater in small establishments than in larger organisations. That is, whilst plants employing 1–5000 dismissed one in every 200, smaller plants had dismissed one in every 58 employees during 1977 (only minor differences were noted between independent firms and subsidiaries of larger companies).[17] However, complaints of unfair dismissal showed an opposite trend: the independent small firms employing between 50 and 199 received no complaints. Subsidiary plants of the same size received one complaint for every 25 dismissed; the level of complaint for firms employing between 1000 and 5000 represented one in 10 of those dismissed.

Therefore, where this study isolated the effects of the legislation on small firms, it suggests that generally they fared better than their larger counterparts. The researchers did, however, suggest that the legislation was more *unpopular* in small firms, whilst having had substantially more influence upon practices of larger firms. Indeed, the researchers, whilst being sympathetic generally to the types of problem that such legislation could create, 'unequivocally' rejected 'the crude form of criticism' levelled principally by employer interest groups.[18]

Opinion Research Centre survey

Before the findings of the PSI research had been published, the ORC conducted an interview programme on behalf of the Department of Employment (DE) for a complementary study on the effects of the legislation on small firms. The randomly selected sample of 301 independent businesses, in five different sectors of industry and commerce, all employed less than 50 employees. Nearly two-thirds of the respondents had work-forces of 10 or less; these are referred to below as 'smaller firms'.

The interview schedule, containing over 50 questions, commenced with open questions designed to ascertain whether respondents spontaneously cited employment legislation as a problem. Interviewees were asked whether the size and structure of their labour force had changed and whether business was expanding or contracting. The interviewers then posed increasingly specific questions on the impact of various aspects of employment law. The issue of whether employers had become reluctant to engage additional personnel was raised, both directly and indirectly, at various points during interviews.[19]

Respondents attributed little effect to employment law when asked to list the main difficulties experienced in running their business: only 6 per cent mentioned any aspect of the legislation. Issues of much greater concern included financial problems (44 per cent), staff shortages and related problems (35 per cent) and VAT (16 per cent). Smaller firms were *less* likely to cite legislation as a difficulty.[20]

In a general question on the effect of employment legislation, 7 per cent indicated some reluctance to take on more staff, without prompting. Table 10.1 summarises the general direction of the responses.

Table 10.1
ORC survey: the principal findings

7	(2%)	said employment legislation was the main difficulty in running their business
22	(7%)	referred to employment legislation when asked if any government measures had caused difficulties
24	(8%)	volunteered that they were less likely to take on more staff when asked what effect unfair dismissal legislation had on recruitment

Base 301
Source: DE[21]

However, when asked directly, 24 per cent (71 respondents) said they would have taken on more employees but for the legislation. In view of the apparent discrepancy, the responses given to previous questions by these employers were examined. It seems that the form of the question suggested to respondents an effect that they would *not* have raised spontaneously. The analysis of responses to earlier questions is shown in Table 10.2.

Table 10.2
ORC survey: analysis of previous responses

13	had mentioned employment legislation among their main difficulties
14	had said that no particular government measures caused them difficulty
51	indicated that no government measures related to employment legislation caused them difficulties
29	had indicated that no employment legislation provisions were affecting their business
56	did not find any particular piece of legislation troublesome when confronted with a specific list

Base 71
Source: DE, Research Paper no. 6[22]

Indeed, the researchers caution against viewing the response to the prompted question in isolation. It is notable, though, that it is this type of question that has generally been used in the surveys conducted by employer interest groups.

Although unfair dismissal again emerged as the aspect of employment legislation to have had the greatest impact, this resulted in more care in recruitment. In view of the level of criticism directed against the legislation, it is perhaps remarkable that over half the sample (54 per cent) had no direct experience of any aspect of the legislation. Only 12 per cent said they had experienced and found troublesome at least one item when given a detailed list of current provisions. Although some respondents did feel that employment law created difficulties for firms wishing to reduce their labour force, 63 per cent said it made no difference. The researchers expressed surprise, commenting that the legislation should have made it 'at least *slightly* more difficult to dismiss people'.[23]

The study provides evidence that the policies and practices, attitudes and opinions of owner-managers in the sample had been formulated in the light of somewhat imperfect knowledge on employment legislation. No single respondent could correctly answer six straightforward factual qestions, only 24 per cent were able to answer correctly a question on the statutory unfair dismissal qualification period, and 21 per cent thought the period was *less* than the prevailing six months. Moreover, '55 per cent were making no effort to keep up to date' with changes in employment law. This proportion rose to 64 per cent for the smallest firms (employing ten or less). In the light of this it is indeed highly questionable whether extension of the unfair dismissal qualification period will have the desired effect of increasing the number of jobs available in the small firm sector.

The researchers concluded that the 'results counter the suggestion that the legislation had some massive and widespread effect on small firms'.[24] It is therefore somewhat surprising that one year after the preliminary results of this survey were made available by the DE, the Under-Secretary of State for Employment was able to proclaim 'overwhelming evidence that the present provisions frustrate and unreasonably curtail the creation of jobs'.[25]

Further, it was claimed that surveys 'undertaken by employers' organisations' apparently showed 'convincingly the deterrent effect on employment' arising from the prevailing qualification period.[26] Our attention therefore now turns to an examination of the surveys that apparently influenced government thinking on the issue.

Pressure for change

Employer interest groups had indeed presented a remarkably different picture. Some claimed that 70 per cent or more of small firms had been adversely affected by the legislation.[27]

We focus here on studies quoted in Parliament and look firstly at a survey published in July 1979 by the National Federation of Self-Employed and Small Businesses (NFSE), following a request by a Minister for this organisation's views on changes to the legislation. Its lengthy submission proposed wide-ranging reforms.

Over 70 per cent of NFSE survey respondents claimed that legislation over the last five years had damaged their businesses. Over half those who felt this way (about one-third of all those who replied) identified employment protection. Since there was no further examination of the nature of the effects experienced, it does not seem a particularly sound basis for the organisation to claim that 'it deters a number of people from taking on employees; it introduces an artificial and unhappy note into relations between small employers and their workers'.[28]

The level of impact attributed to legislation generally in this survey was in some ways unsurprising. Given that this organisation, together with a number of others that pressed for reform in this area, have a declared aim to reduce legislative provisions that impinge on the business community, it follows that their membership will consist mainly of those small businessmen who feel most strongly that government action reduces their freedom. This argument must apply with even more force to those members who take the time and trouble actually to complete a questionnaire.

It was, in fact, suggested in a House of Lords debate that this survey had more validity than the PSI and ORC studies, simply because it involved more respondents (1000).[29] However, this ignores the important factor that the PSI and ORC samples were constructed on rigorous research principles to be representative of the industries and size categories under study. It is perhaps more salient to point out in relation to the NFSE survey that since 98 per cent of the membership failed to respond, it was probably not even representative of this organisation's subscribers, let alone small firms in general.

Moreover, examination of a number of questionnaires shows a tendency for certain interest groups to utilise somewhat leading questions, and thereby perhaps suggest to recipients issues which they would not otherwise have considered.

For example, one questionnaire entitled 'Employment Protection or Prevention', requested 'ammunition' for their spokesmen. Respondents were informed that the 'provisions of the Employment Protection Act have been mentioned as an important reason why small firms do not take on more workers. Please tell us how significant it is to *your* business in terms of jobs now and your plans for the next couple of years'. Over 800 people responded; 80 per cent agreed with the implicit suggestion.[30] This organisation has a strong political base; it therefore seems possible that respondents were expressing general antipathy towards the policies of the incumbent Labour government.

Although the response rate to this survey was probably higher than some others, it was not possible to clearly define the total survey population with any certainty. Nor is any information available on the types or size of participating firms. In view of these reservations, it is difficult to regard the results as a sufficiently firm basis for legislative change.

Both the PSI and ORC studies showed that objective assessment of the responses was facilitated by additional information, such as the level of product demand, changes in the structure of the firm's labour force, or whether the respondents understood the legislation. Employers' associations have generally relied on self-administered questionnaires, in which there is obviously less scope for examining issues in the same depth. In the event, it was found that little attempt was made to endeavour to examine any other factor than whether the respondent was prepared to say that the legislation was detrimental. A report by the Labour Relations Agency (Northern Ireland's equivalent of the Advisory, Conciliation and Arbitration Service) on the employment problems of small manufacturing firms pointed to a dichotomy:

> Several of the owner/managers interviewed expressed strong views about new employment legislation and argued that it acted as a constraint upon employment . . . it is significant to note that some of those who argued this point had in fact increased their workforce during the period employment legislation has been in force.[31]

One survey which did collect some information on other constraints failed to link the various factors in its analysis. The primary aim of the Engineering Employers' Federation survey seems to have been to collect evidence that the legislation *had* inhibited employment. The questionnaire entitled 'Impact on Labour Market of Recent Employment Legislation' asked whether expansion of employment had been restricted:

> If, in the period since the beginning of 1975, general economic and business conditions had been more favourable and/or taxation lighter and/or employment legislation less burdensome, do you consider that your company would now be employing a larger number of employees? YES/NO.

Respondents answering 'no' were instructed to turn to the end of the document to answer a question on Temporary Employment Subsidies; thus no attempt was made to elicit views from these companies. Only affirmative responses were included in the analysis, thereby excluding the 20 per cent or so respondents that were unable to agree with the above statement. Difficult economic conditions were by far the most important factor limiting expansion; lack of orders, shortage of skilled labour and inflation featured most prominently (categories which were, predictably, prompted).

Although some surveys asked respondents to estimate the number of people they would have taken on but for the legislation, it seems to produce a rather meaningless figure, unless respondents are able to demonstrate sufficient demand for their goods or services, that the required labour would actually have been available or that they had sufficient working capital to sustain such expansion. A postal survey, conducted by the Birmingham Chamber of Industry and Commerce, did in fact concentrate on this aspect, simply asking its membership to estimate the number of jobs not created or filled during that year 'as a direct result of *the* existing employment legislation'. The survey report makes the somewhat dramatic claim that on average 9.4 job opportunities per firm have been lost as a direct result of the legislation. But only 5 per cent of the membership responded; and nearly half of those that produced estimates of 'lost' jobs said that 'in effect, *the* employment legislation had not had such a direct effect on their recruitment/ employment policies'. Respondents were also given a list of employment law provisions and asked to rank these in order of importance. Ministers were subsequently urged to amend the legislation in the light of the evidence presented in this report.

It is an essential part of the function of a pressure group to obtain publicity for its view; but to suppose that the results of such surveys are impartial or comparable with the standards of independent research focusing on randomly selected samples, is clearly unrealistic. The Bolton Committee Report on small firms similarly identified a marked disparity between evidence submitted by employers' associations and the results of independent research commissioned by the Committee. The report pointed to 'a large measure of straightforward political prejudice against the Labour Government at that time'.[32] Indeed, there are indications in the material collected from the organisations that have pressed for reform of employment legislation that the issue has generally been used as a platform for complaint against a government regarded as being unsympathetic to private enterprise. Moreover, it appears that some small business pressure groups may have *stimulated* antagonism towards the measures, by disseminating misleading or inaccurate information[33] both to their members and through the national press. On a similar theme, other researchers commented:

> Much of the press coverage gives the impression that unfair dismissal legislation is very restrictive and it may be that criticism and anxiety expressed by small employers arise from misunderstanding or ignorance of the legislative provisions. If this is the case, changing them . . . will make little difference to the employer while diminishing the rights of employees.[34]

Legislative changes

Extensive changes in employment legislation were enacted in 1979 and 1980, following the publication of the above reports. Firstly, the unfair dismissal qualification period was extended from 26 weeks to 52 weeks. Secondly, the Employment Act 1980 contained changes directed specifically at small firms. Employees within firms of 20 staff or less now no longer have the right to complain of unfair dismissal until they have worked for the firm for a continuous period of *two years*.

Additionally industrial tribunals are specifically required to take into account the size and administrative resources of the employer. Firms with five employees or less finding it 'not reasonably practicable' to reinstate a woman after maternity leave will be relieved of the obligation. Overall the package represents a substantial negative shift in the protection afforded to workers, yet was greeted with little enthusiasm by those who had advocated reform. Nevertheless, throughout the lengthy parliamentary debates, the government stead-fastly maintained that new employment opportunities would result.[35]

Review of the parliamentary debates indicates several other important issues. Firstly, it was noticeable that the government arguments, at least in some respects, appeared to mirror closely the approach of small business pressure groups. Secondly, there was clearly confusion over the apparently conflicting survey findings. Moreover, there were indications that the methodological short-comings of the pressure group surveys were regarded as unimportant.

The wider implications of the ORC study were ignored in favour of a question that reflected pressure group orthodoxy, despite the ambiguity of respondents highlighted in the researchers' careful analysis. To suggest that those who have agreed with a leading question will expand their labour force once changes in employment legislation are enacted seems somewhat naïve, particularly, if, as in the case of the ORC respondents, they perceived financial difficulties and staff shortages as dominant problems.

Since analysis of survey data suggests doubt must attach to the claim that the legislation discouraged recruitment, attention is now turned to unfair dismissal statistics to ascertain whether these support the assertion that the provisions bore 'over-harshly. . .on small businesses'.[36]

Unfair dismissal statistics

The number of registered unfair dismissal complaints rose rapidly as the qualification period was reduced, from under 10 000 in 1973 and stabilising at around 38 000 a year with the qualification period of six months. Given the estimate of at least 1.25 million job terminations each year,[37] the proportion alleging unfair dismissal seems noticeably low. Only a minority of these complaints went forward to a tribunal hearing. Nearly two-thirds were dealt with by conciliation and an increasing proportion (nearly half) were withdrawn by the applicant. In 1978 the tribunals heard less than 12,000 cases and the employer was judged to have acted unfairly in just 28 per cent of these cases.[38]

Almost a quarter of these complaints involved firms employing less than 20 employees.[39] The DE suggested that small establishments were overrepresented in the statistics, by drawing comparisons with Census of Employment data on the number of employees working in smaller workplaces.[40] Certain reservations must attach to this approach since it implies an assumption that dismissal is always employee initiated.

Since the act of dismissal represents the interaction of two distinct forms of behaviour (the behaviour of the employee and an employer's response to that behaviour), it would seem necessary also to consider the *number* of firms. On this basis, and concentrating on firms employing less than 20, it would appear that each year a complaint was made against less than one in every hundred firms. It is also noticeable that during the period 1971–8 the distribution of unfair dismissal complaints between firms of differing sizes altered very little.[41]

However, since it seems to be widely accepted that small firms were overrepresented, two questions need to be asked. Why should this be so and is the system biased against small firms? These issues are considered in turn.

Golby and Johns in their research report for the Bolton Committee[42] suggested that the underlying motivation for many owner-managers was the need to 'attain and preserve independence', with personal satisfaction ranking as a high priority, often at the expense of rationality. Thus where the desire for autonomy and self-esteem are dominant goals, he tends to adopt a highly personalised style of management, sometimes paternalistic, often autocratic. Resistant to delegating decision-making, he is less likely to consult with colleagues or discuss the perceived problems with the employee before taking the decision to dismiss. Since personal characteristics of employees often appear more important to the owner-manager than skill level, previous training or formal qualifications, any perceived deterioration is unlikely to be tolerated. Priding himself on an informal and flexible form of management, the owner-manager may be inconsistent in the standards he applies, not only to different individuals but with the same employee over a period of time. In short, personnel management in the small firm is likely to be very different to the approach adopted in larger concerns, with a far greater likelihood of the owner-manager dismissing at a whim. In fact, there are many reasons to suggest that smaller firms *will* feature more frequently in the statistics than the percentage of people they employ would at first lead one to expect.

Small firms are significantly less likely to have established disciplinary and dismissal procedures, partly due to the belief that these would lead to an excessive formalisation of relationships.[43] Although recent research suggests that as many as 60 per cent of firms employing less than 20 claim to have such procedures[44] it seems that these respondents, having experienced an unfair dismissal complaint, may have overstated the position. The ACAS Code of Practice, which lays down guidelines for the handling of disciplinary and dismissal matters[45] had been obtained by 16 per cent of the ORC respondents, but only 5 per cent claimed to have made use of it. Relatively few had obtained any of the DE's explanatory leaflets.[46] Similarly, many small firms do not issue 'contracts' of employment[47] or keep written records of personnel matters. Hence, many owner-managers do not understand the legislation or how to adapt their management practices to nullify any possible adverse effects. Indeed, there are indications that many simply ignore the implications of the legislation until faced with an unfair dismissal claim.[48]

Critics claim that tribunals deal over-harshly with small firms. However, whilst there seems to be every indication that small firms could well have more problems than the larger firm, tribunals in the past have been sympathetic to the difference between small and large firms[49] and do not impose their own standards, but concentrate on what 'is reasonable in the circumstances'.[50] Despite this, there are marked differences in the success rate of claims. An analysis of a 10 per cent representative sample of 1978 unfair dismissal cases indicated that whilst firms employing over 1000 won over 80 per cent of their cases, firms with less than 50 employees won around 60 per cent.[51] Indeed, perhaps one of the most surprising indications in these figures is how few applicants dismissed from large firms had their cases upheld by a tribunal. Small firms were more likely than large to settle at conciliation. Thus, overall about 54 per cent of applicants from firms employing less than 20 received a remedy from their former employers (whether at conciliation or at a tribunal hearing) compared with the average rate of 45 per cent.[52] Though small firm employees *were* more likely to receive a remedy as a result of a complaint of unfair dismissal, comparisons may be misleading, since many larger firms have relatively sophisticated internal appeals procedures to deal speedily and promptly with any dispute over a dismissal decision. It is difficult to accept on the basis of these figures that there was excessive bias against small firms, unless we concede the implied suggestion that the owner-manager is invariably fair in his behaviour.

Where small firms had reformed their recruitment and disciplinary procedures as a result of the legislation, this generally seems to have been beneficial to both employers and employees. As the Labour Relations Agency pointed out:

> The introduction of adequate procedures assists the firm in controlling absenteeism, lateness and general disciplinary matters and offers benefits to both employer and employee in ensuring fairness and consistency in the application of disciplinary action. The introduction of such procedures need not lead to excessive formalisation of relationships as feared by some owner/managers — those firms which had introduced procedures did not claim any deterioration in relationships.[53]

Thus, the benefits which gradually began to accrue in the small firm sector as a result of the legislation may be lost as a result of recent amendments.

Perhaps more importantly, the Employment Act seems to have made individual rights legislation *more complex*, with greater scope for misunderstanding.[54] Small businessmen already have many misconceptions about employment law, and unless considerable effort is made to communicate the changes effectively, they may present more actual or perceived problems than have previously been experienced.

Summary and conclusions

Modern employment legislation in the UK dates back to the mid-1960s. One of the most important innovations has been the change from the minimal rights allowed under common law concerning dismissal from employment, to the statutory right not to be unfairly dismissed. Thus the duty was imposed upon employers to ensure that there was just cause for any dismissal. Individual rights legislation was further extended by the EPA 1975, a statute which stimulated considerable controversy. Critics claimed that the legislation inhibited expansion of employment in the small firm sector. Yet the aspect which has been the subject of the greatest criticism, the unfair dismissal provisions, in fact was first introduced in the Industrial Relations Act 1971. As a result of the mounting criticism of the measures and pressure for change, the legislation has now been substantially modified and workers in small firms have fewer rights, which represents a move away from the original intention to give all employees equal protection under the law. It has been argued that new employment opportunities will derive from changes in unfair dismissal legislation. However, analysis of the research and statistics which *appear* to have been utilised in formulation of policy leaves some doubt that this end will be achieved.

The surveys conducted by the PSI and the ORC focused on randomly selected samples, designed to be broadly representative of the populations under study. Employers' organisations on the other hand relied mainly on the attitudes and opinions of their own members. The actions of the latter in joining the organisation probably sets them apart from other businessmen, especially where it is an association with a declared hostility towards legislation. As these surveys generally had low response rates, it would appear that the samples were doubly self-selected, thus reflecting the views of those that felt most strongly about the subject.

Yet it is not only the nature of the samples which suggests that extreme caution should be exercised in interpreting the results of these surveys. The ORC survey indicated the importance of the phraseology of questions, finding that little impact was attributed to the legislation until the notion that it might be inhibiting recruitment was prompted. Analysis suggests that to a greater or lesser extent all the employer interest groups used leading questions, seemingly indicating the type of replies that were required. Affirmative answers to a question such as 'would you have employed more people but for the legislation?' provide no guarantee that expansion of employment will automatically ensue when the legislation is reformed. Thus, employer interest group surveys do not appear to provide a sound basis for legislative change. Independent research reveals that the legislation appears to have had a relatively minor impact, although it cannot be denied that many small businessmen express hostility towards it. This antagonism appears to reflect two different aspects of a seemingly single problem. Clear differentiation is needed here since only one of these can be alleviated effectively by policy measures. Firstly, small businessmen appear to have a low level of understanding of the legislation and perceive it as being unnecessarily restrictive. Since in reality all that the legislation requires is a minimum standard of management behaviour towards employees, there is a clear need for an educative programme to reduce this anxiety. Whilst there is a strong case for suggesting that such a programme should have preceded any legislative change, it becomes even more necessary if the recent reforms are to have any effect at all. Secondly, many owner-managers appear to regard the legislation as a challenge to management prerogatives, thus exhibiting an ideological resistance to the principles that underline the legislation. Hence there is a clash between the strong belief of many small businessmen in their right to manage their business free from outside interference, and the demands of a work-force which has expectations beyond being a mere factor of production. Whilst government policy appears to have in large measure reflected an ideological demand, it is questionable whether this will have any significant impact on levels of employment in the individual firm or across the small firm sector as a whole.

References

1. Thirteenth Report from the Expenditure Committee, *People and Work, Prospects for Jobs and Training*, HMSO, 1978, pp. 50 and 80.

2. Unfair Dismissal (Variation of Qualifying Period) Order 1979; Employment Protection (Handling of Redundancies) Variation Order 1979; Employment Act 1980 and Industrial Tribunals (Rules of Procedure) Regulations 1980.

3. *Royal Commission on Trade Unions and Employers' Associations 1965–1968*, Cmd 3623, HMSO, 1968. The Report is usually referred to as the Donovan Report after the name of the Commission's Chairman.

4. Ibid., Chapter IX, 'Safeguards for Employees against Unfair Dismissal', para 526 (see also para 521).

5. Reductions in unfair dismissal qualification period: September 1974: continuous service qualification reduced from 104 to 52 weeks; March 1975: reduced to 26 weeks; October 1976: small firms exclusion removed, i.e. firms with less than 4 workers no longer exempted; February 1977: protection extended to some part-time workers.

6. G. de N. Clark, *Remedies for Unjust Dismissal, Proposals for Legislation*, PEP, June 1970, p. 32, see also R. Lewis P. Davies and B. Wedderburn. *Industrial Relations Law and the Conservative Government*, Fabian Society, 1979, p. 43.

7. Donovan Report, paras 555 and 556.

8. Note: other important aspects of modern employment legislation have been excluded from this brief summary since generally they have attracted less criticism than the Employment Protection Act, e.g. Equal Pay Act 1970; Contracts of Employment Act 1972; Health and Safety at Work Act 1974; Race Relations Act 1976; Trade Union and Labour Relations Act 1974 and Trade Union and Labour Relations Amendment Act 1976.

9. 'CBI ready for clash on "biased" employment Bill' *The Daily Telegraph*, 2 December 1974, p. 14. Also 'Small companies . . . are horrified at the potential cost of the proposed Bill'. *Financial Times*, 19 November 1974.

10. *Department of Employment Gazette*, April 1976, p. 385.

11. Department of Employment and Manpower Services Commission.

12. W.W. Daniel and E. Stilgoe, *The Impact of Employment Protection Laws*, Policy Studies Institute, June 1978, p. 77.
13. Ibid., pp. 64–9.
14. Ibid., p. 43.
15. Ibid., p. 70
16. Ibid., p. 45
17. Ibid., p. 62
18. Ibid., p. 77
19. R. Clifton and C. Tatton-Brown, *Impact of Employment Legislation on Small Firms*, Research Paper no. 6, Department of Employment, 1979. Referred to in the text as the Opinion Research Centre (ORC) Survey.
20. Ibid., pp. 8–11
21. 'Impact of Employment Legislation on Small Firms', Department of Employment Press Notice, August 1978.
22 Clifton and Tatton-Brown, *Impact*, p. 22.
23. Ibid., p. 23.
24. Ibid., p. 33.
25. House of Commons Official Report, Parliamentary Debates, *Hansard*, vol 971, no. 46, 25 July 1979, col. 523 (the Under-Secretary of State for Employment, Mr Patrick Mayhew).
26. Ibid., col. 531.
27. For example, *EEF News*, December 1978; 'Frightening Protection for Workers', *The Guardian*, 21 January 1978, p. 17.
28. *First Voice*, vol. 3, no. 7, July 1979, pp. 6–7. Although the NFSE Small Business Opinion Survey 1979 was not primarily concerned with employment law, it appears to have been offered as evidence, being published with the Federation's proposals for extensive changes in the legislation.
29. House of Lords Official Report, Parliamentary Debates, *Hansard*, vol. 401, no. 33, 25 July 1979, cols. 1962 and 1975 (Lord Spens).
30. Preliminary results of the Small Business Bureau Survey were reported in *The Guardian*, 21 January 1978. A summary of the completed survey was reported in 'Employment Laws Are Preventing Jobs!', *Small Business*, July 1978, p. 12.
31. Labour Relations Agency, *A Report on the Industrial Relations and Employment Problems of Small Manufacturing Firms*, Occasional paper no. 5, December 1979, p. 5 (unfair dismissal legislation did not apply in Northern Ireland until 1976).
32. *Report of the Committee of Inquiry on Small Firms*, Cmnd 4811, HMSO, 1971, Generally known as the Bolton Report, Para 9.3.
33. For example, *Slow to Hire, Quick to Fire: A Warning to Employers about Recent Employment Legislation*, ASP, November 1976. 'Unfair

Dismissal – The ABC of New Employment Awards', *Small Business,* April 1978. National Federation of Self-Employed, *The End of the ACAS Blackmail Gang,* June 1978.

34. L. Dickens, M. Hart, M. Jones and B. Weekes, *A Response to the Government Working Papers on Amendments to Employment Protection Legislation,* Discussion Paper, Industrial Relations Research Unit of the Social Science Research Council, University of Warwick, November 1979, Section 1, p. 3.

35. See for example *House of Commons Official Report, Standing Committee A, Employment Bill,* Eighteenth Sitting, 6 March 1980, col. 954, and Twelfth Sitting, 21 February 1980, col. 634.

36. 'Employment Protection Legislation', Working Paper on Proposed Amendments, *Department of Employment Gazette,* September 1979.

37. *Personnel Management,* August 1978, p. 11. Published estimates of dismissals per annum vary widely and one source suggests a figure of 3 million (see data cited by P. Lewis, 'Employment Protection: A Preliminary Assessment', *Industrial Relations Journal,* vol. 12, no. 2, March/April 1981, pp. 19–29.

38. 'Unfair Dismissal cases in 1978', *Department of Employment Gazette,* September 1979, pp. 866–7. 1979 statistics show a similar pattern, 'Unfair Dismissal Cases in 1979', *Employment Gazette,* February 1981, p. 82.

39. The DE published and unpublished statistics, cited in A. Westrip, 'An Investigation of the Impact of Employment Protection Laws on the Small Firm, with Special Reference to Unfair Dismissal Legislation', Small Business Unit, Polytechnic of Central London, September 1979.

40. *Department of Employment Gazette,* June 1975, p. 532.

41. Westrip, 'Investigation'.

42. C.W. Golby and G. Johns, 'Attitude and Motivation', *Committee of Inquiry on Small Firms, Research Report no 7,* Cmnd. 4811 HMSO, 1971. Golby and John's report can be criticised for presenting a stereotype that does not reflect differences between owner-managers and differences in motivation over time. For a broader analysis see M.J.K. Stanworth and J. Curran, *Management Motivation in the Smaller Business,* Gower, 1973 and Stanworth and Curran, 'Growth and the Small Firm: An Alternative View', *Journal of Management Studies,* vol. 13, no. 2, May 1976, pp. 95–110.

43. Labour Relations Agency, Report, p. 4.

44. Dickens *et al., Response,* p. 6 (IRRU survey of 1013 randomly selected employers who were party to an unfair dismissal application registered between October 1976 and September 1977).

45. Advisory, Conciliation and Arbitration Service, *Code of Practice*

1, *Disciplinary Practice and Procedures in Employment*, HMSO.

46. Clifton and Tatton-Brown, *Impact*, pp. 25–8.

47. Labour Relations Agency, *Report. Employers Monitor*, Eighth Edition (Employers Protection Insurance Service Ltd, June 1979). Employers are required to provide a written statement of the main terms and conditions of employment (within a prescribed period, depending on the number of hours worked per week) which should include a note specifying any disciplinary rules and any procedures that will be followed in the event of the employer taking any disciplinary or dismissal action against the employee. This statement is often referred to as a 'contract' of employment.

48. Labour Relations Agency, *Report*.

49. Dickens *et al.*, *Response*. pp. 17–18.

50. *Croner's Reference Book for Employers*, February 1979, p. 146.

51. Westrip, 'Investigation'.

52. The term 'remedy' means broadly re-engagement or financial compensation.

53. Labour Relations Agency, *Report*, p. 9.

54. For expansion of this point see A. Westrip, 'New Controls Govern "Unfair" Dismissals', *The Guardian*, 16 January 1981, p. 16.

11 The Survival of the Petite Bourgeoisie: Production and Reproduction

JAMES CURRAN

The small business-owning stratum in advanced industrial societies has shown a remarkable capacity for survival and renewal in recent decades, surprising many who had confidently predicted its demise. Economists, sociologists and others have typically either ignored small-scale economic activities and their originators or treated them as remnants of earlier stages of economic and social development. In part, this dismissal was empirically based; in several industrial societies, notably the United Kingdom and the United States, there was a sharp decline in the share of small-scale economic activities throughout the first half of the century (Bolton Report 1971: Chapters 5 and 6). This was less marked in some other countries, but overall the trend seemed well-established and permanent.

More significantly, these observations were underpinned by well-developed theoretical views which explained the inevitable decline of the small business as a result of the development of industrial economies. The economists' view was well exemplified in the Bolton Report's (1971: Chapter 7) explanation which centred on the importance of economies of scale, internal and external. In areas such as optimum plant size, research and development, managerial performance, communications and marketing, the large enterprise was simply seen as more efficient. Externally, the state had not only increasingly intervened in the economy in ways which favoured the large enterprise over the small by, for example, its purchasing policies as a consumer or its promotion of rationalisation into larger units, but had itself become a major provider of goods and services, restricting opportunities for small enterprise.

Sociologists, like economists, also implicitly or explicitly, adopted a dismissive attitude to the small business-owning stratum. Most sociological texts devote considerable attention to the importance of social class as central to the workings of modern society but often ignore the petite bourgeoisie class entirely. These attitudes may simply follow the views of highly influential early theorists such as Weber and Marx who claimed a decreasing significance for the owners of small capital in mature capitalist societies. Marx, for example, in an argument paralleling that of economists, believed that, in the long run, the concentration of capital would result in intermediary classes such as the petite bourgeoisie disappearing as a significant social force in history and society (Urry 1973; Hall 1977; Tomlinson 1980). (However, it has been pointed out recently (Scase and Goffee, 1982: 21) that despite this long-term view, he nevertheless saw the petite bourgeoisie as surviving well into the development of mature capitalism).

Popular psychology has also reinforced views on the decline of small business ownership by arguing that those who might seek this outlet for their energies and talents would increasingly accept the cushion of the Welfare State or safe employment in the large organisation. Such views were sometimes supported by academic writers (Riesman 1950; Whyte 1960) who, in effect, were reflecting the arguments offered by economists and sociologists who saw modern economic and social structures restricting the motivational bases for self-employment.

But the revival of the small enterprise over the last decade or so has clearly called for a re-examination and reformulation of views of the small enterprise owner role. Despite the inadequacies of statistical data, there is wide agreement that there has been a sharp upturn in the numbers and significance of the petite bourgeoisie in Britain and other industrial societies (Binks and Coyne 1983: 22–30; Curran and Stanworth 1984; Boissevain 1984: 26–8). Equally, there has been a revival of academic interest seeking to reassess previous theories and to offer new interpretations of the contemporary position of small firm owner-managers.

In economics, for example, the work of Hayek has enjoyed a revival with its central emphasis on the importance of the entrepreneur in the competitive market process (Binks and Coyne 1983: 11–15). Contemporary Marxist theorising has also sought to offer an alternative view of the place of the petite bourgeoisie in monopoly capitalism which takes into account both the survival of traditional forms of small business ownership and the emergence of other intermediate group-ings which are neither simply wage labour nor members of the bourgeoisie proper, that is, those who own and control large-scale capital. At the psychological level, evidence abounds of the persis-tence of strong motivations towards independence in the form of owning and operating a small business among ordinary wage earners (Curran 1981) as well as among highly qualified professionals as the history of Silicon Valley in the United States (Cooper 1970) and similar phenomena in other countries has shown.

The aim of this paper is to examine recent thinking on the role of the petite bourgeoisie in the class structures of contemporary industrial societies and to delineate the forces, both existent and emerging, which ensure the production and reproduction of this stratum. Where these issues have been examined previously there has frequently been a selective emphasis on particular factors such as the existence of ethnic minorities or the opportunities provided by the emergence of new technology. What this paper offers is a more generalised account of the processes involved in the production and reproduction of the petite bourgeoisie stratum, giving less emphasis to what are, hope-fully, short-term influences such as redundancy resulting from economic recession and more emphasis on long-term, relatively per-manent influences. In other words, the argument to be presented attempts to demonstrate that the notion of the petite bourgeoisie as a peripheral stratum surviving at the edges of a modern industrial economy which has permeated social science thinking for so long is quite simply wrong. Similarly, the view implicit in some recent discussions that the increase in small business owners is temporary is also held to be flawed. Rather, the place and role of the petite bourgeoisie in advanced industrial societies is argued to be permanent so long as free enterprise economies persist.

Conceptualisations of the petite bourgeoisie

Traditional conceptualisations of the petite bourgeoisie as a social class see them as small manufacturers, farmers, shopkeepers, publicans and others whose identifying characteristic is that they combine relatively small amounts of capital with their own labour and perhaps that of a small number of employees. Unfortunately, as with most conceptualisations of social classes, it is difficult to refine this general view into a precise, watertight definition which clearly demarcates this stratum from other strata.

For example, Bechhofer et al. (1976) who have made a distinguished contribution to the study of small shopkeepers in Britain, suggest that three main characteristics identify the petite bourgeoisie as a stratum: a small amount of capital; traditional technology; and a simple organisational framework. They recognise that some small enterprises come into being to exploit recent technological innovations but seem to regard their owners as not really part of the petite bourgeoisie but rather as part of the modern middle class. The implication here is that technological entrepreneurs have more in common with professional, scientifically qualified employees than with small business owners such as the corner shopkeeper.

In a later publication, however (Bechhofer and Elliot 1981:178), they qualify this view but retain the distinction between the 'traditional petit bourgeois' who operates with 'little esoteric knowledge' and those who set up new high-technology enterprises often with the help of external sources of capital. As they admit, this does not resolve the definitional issue, and they appear to wish to continue to see the petite bourgeoisie proper as inextricably linked with older, established forms of simple technology. In this they reflect a widespread view of the technological basis of small-scale economic activities.

The problem with an emphasis on traditional technology as a defining characteristic of the petit-bourgeois-owned enterprise is that, at some time, all technology is new. What is more crucial is whether any technology, regardless of when it was introduced, is appropriate to small-scale economic activity. Some relatively recent technological developments in modern plastics and electronics, for example, have made it possible to establish small enterprises which would have been impossible using the previous equivalent 'traditional' technology (Blair 1972: Chapter 6). Neither, it should be emphasised, does the use of modern high technology for small-scale economic activities depend on any sophisticated understanding of the technology by the entrepreneur.

An additional problem in producing a clear conceptualisation of the petite bourgeoisie is that, as almost all interested commentators stress, it contains a wide mix of subgroupings. For instance, Scase and Goffee (1982) have pointed out that although the relative amount of capital at the disposal of small business owners is slight compared to that utilised in modern large-scale enterprise, there is, nevertheless, considerable variation within the stratum. Equally, the largest subgrouping within the petite bourgeoisie are the self-employed who do not employ anybody. But other small business owners sometimes employ substantial amounts of labour whose management and control form an important part of their responsibilities in running their enterprise. More generally, the sheer range of industries and economic activities in which small business owners are involved, extending to almost every area of the economy, is itself a major source of heterogeneity in the experiences of members of the stratum.

One key weakness of primarily economic approaches to the conceptualisation of the petite bourgeoisie is the neglect of the distinctive cultural features of the stratum. Study after study has shown that both historically and currently, the petite bourgeoisie possesses a well-developed class ideology. The latter refers to the possession of a shared set of values, ideals and opinions which, in combination, set the petite bourgeoisie apart from other social strata (Bechhofer *et al.* 1976; Scase and Goffee 1980; Bechhofer and Elliott 1981). The main values emphasised are autonomy and independence with an extreme dislike of collectivities of all kinds from the state to large-scale business to trade unions and political parties. The economic rationality of the petite bourgeoisie can only be understood by reference to this ideological set which often overrides any simple straightforward commitment to profit maximisation, growth or bureaucratic efficiency.

The most ambitious recent attempt to conceptualise the contemporary petite bourgeoisie has emerged within the Marxist perspective. The writings of Poulantzas (1975, 1977) and Erik Olin Wright (1976, 1978, 1980) are central to this approach and essentially the self-imposed objective of these writers is to accommodate the petite bourgeoisie in the traditional sense, as well as more recently emerging economic groupings such as professional employees, technicians and middle and lower-level administrators and managers, into an overall class analysis. This class analysis, in turn, serves to provide a framework in social and political terms for the interpretation of the development of contemporary capitalism.

Marx himself, as noted above, held the view that the nineteenth-century petite bourgeoisie — small manufacturers, shopkeepers, peasants, and so on — would eventually sink into the proletariat as a result of the concentration of ownership and economic activities. Again, with other nineteenth-century writers, Marx underestimated the rise of what has been termed the 'new' middle class of middle-level, white collar workers. More recent Marxist theorising struggles to repair the deficiencies in Marx's original thinking resulting from the growing significance of non-manual employees in contemporary economies.

Poulantzas (1975), for example, offers a 'new' petite bourgeoisie which is emerging in addition to the traditional one. The new petite bourgeoisie is made up of salaried white collar employees — technicians, civil servants, middle-level managers — who are distinct from the working class proper because, although they are employed by others, they are non-productive labour and have authority over other employees. (By 'productive' labour here is meant labour that produces surplus value through producing material goods.) The traditional petite bourgeoisie continues to survive but only in those areas of the economy where 'simple commodity production' survives while monopoly capitalism dominates the most advanced and important sectors of the economy.

It is not only non-Marxists who find this intermingling of small business owners and white collar employees in larger enterprises into a single petite bourgeoisie class questionable. Wright (1978: 46), for example, makes the obvious point that seeing surplus-value creation as synonymous with the production of material goods is curiously old fashioned: surplus value is increasingly generated in advanced capitalist societies in non-material forms such as services and the manipulation of non-tangibles such as information. The employment of people in these new areas of economic activity does not, of itself, place them in a special class position or make them similar to the traditional petite bourgeoisie.

Poulantzas also stresses the orthodox Marxist view that ideological and power considerations are necessary to the full conceptualisation of any class position under capitalism, a point neglected by many commentators on the position of small business owners in modern society. Members of the 'new' petite bourgeoisie, according to Poulantzas, occupy supervisory roles or are 'experts' of one kind or another and these characteristics separate them ideologically from manual workers, the proletariat proper. This ideological separation, based on the mental character of their work, puts them in a position of superiority over ordinary workers. The traditional and new petite bourgeoisie share a single class position, argues Poulantzas, because, despite any other differences, they are conscious of their distinctiveness in the form of a broad ideological unity emphasising individualism, antipathy to large-scale capitalism and a yearning for its reform as well as a tendency to see the state as, ideally, a neutral arbiter between classes.

Erik Olin Wright's (1978, 1980) critique of Poulantzas includes the questioning noted above of the latter's view of productive labour as well as arguing that Poulantzas overemphasises the political–ideological dimensions of class relations to the extent of seeing them as overriding the great economic similarities between, for example, all paid employees in the enterprise. Wright is also sceptical of the ideological unity Poulantzas sees between the 'traditional' and 'new' petite bourgeoisie. At a simpler, numerical level, Wright calculates that Poulantzas's formulation of the petite bourgeoisie, the supposed intermediary class between the two main classes of capitalism, would constitute 70 per cent of the United States labour force. Such criticisms might be voiced by others who do not otherwise share the Marxist perspective.

Wright himself offers an alternative conceptualisation of the petite bourgeoisie as a part of the wider class relations of contemporary capitalism which turns on the notion of 'control'. The three central processes which underly socio-economic relations in modern free enterprise society are: control over the means of production; control over the labour process; and control over investment and resource allocations. Workers are distinguished by their lack of control over all three, except in a very limited sense, while the dominant bourgeoisie is distinguished by its clear control over all three processes. Conflict arises out of the attempts of workers and capitalists to gain or consolidate control over the three processes and this conflict constitutes a central dynamic of industrial society.

Some of the traditional petite bourgeoisie are anchored in a subordinate economic form — simple commodity production, involving self-employment with no employees — which exists in all capitalist industrial societies alongside modern advanced, complex economic forms based on large-scale enterprises. Others employ a small number of employees and become small capitalists. But there are also, thirdly, semi-autonomous workers who occupy contradictory class positions either between the working class and the petite bourgeoisie or between the petite bourgeoisie and the bourgeoisie proper. Examples would be a franchisee who controls labour and the initial allocation of resources but does not control what is produced, or a university professor who controls how he or she works and what is produced but has little control over overall resource and investment allocation within the organisation.

Wright estimates that in the United States the traditional self-employed petite bourgeoisie comprises about 4.5 per cent of the economically active population, small capitalists a further 6–7 per cent and semi-autonomous workers between 5 and 11 per cent (Wright 1978: 83–5). The proportions would clearly accord more with common-sense views of the numerical significance of petite bourgeoisie groups in industrial society than those derived from Poulantzas's conceptualisation.

Although Wright's formulation is systematic in the sense that great care is taken to relate the petite bourgeoisie to the rest of the class structure, it is static and over-structural: it tells us little of the processes by which the petite bourgeoisie is produced either as a stratum or as individuals and the ideological dimension is glossed over.

Consciousness, particularly its shared aspects, is a distinctive and important characteristic of the petite bourgeoisie and needs to be fully incorporated into any analysis since it is the key to the motivational processes underlying its production and reproduction as a social class. This neglect of the consciousness of the petite bourgeoisie enables the question of whether a university professor and a small shopkeeper really do share a similar class ideology to be sidestepped. There is, finally, a further unsatisfactory feature of the approaches of Poulantzas and Wright. Both write within a shared theoretical tradition and their contributions are as much aimed at solving inherited weaknesses in that tradition, revealed by the actual development of modern industrial societies, as in analysing the contemporary situation of the petite bourgeoisie.

The approach typified by Bechhofer *et al.* discussed above, and the more theoretical and conceptually complex approaches of writers in the Marxist tradition such as Poulantzas and Wright, are representative of the main perspectives in recent conceptualisations of the petite bourgeoisie. As has been shown, none of these approaches provide an adequate conceptualisation. There is agreement on both the need to separate the petite bourgeoisie from other classes and on some of the characteristics which distinguish it economically, socially and ideologically, from other social groupings. There is, however, less agreement as well as less attention given to the connections between the petite bourgeoisie and the rest of the economy and society. Most interpretations emphasise the apartness and vestigial existence of the petite bourgeoisie, particularly in their relationships to mainstream economic activities or the stratum is used as a dumping ground for social groups who do not fit conveniently into other conventional social categories.

Scase (1982) suggests that besides the two above approaches there is also a third. This argues that the petite bourgeoisie is likely to become *more* important in advanced industrial societies. Concern with the 'quality of life' expressed in a demand for specialist goods and services as well as the conditions under which many are employed, may induce increasing numbers to favour small-scale production. New technology may also help by introducing new ways of producing on a small scale and the growth of the 'informal economy' recently has also largely been a growth in small-scale enterprise.

He argues that an adequate conceptualisation of the current position of the petite bourgeoisie requires it to be seen as 'embedded within a general process of capital accumulation' (Scase 1982: 157) and not as a marginal grouping. The stratum is important in offering non-meritocratic opportunities for upward mobility and as a safety net for those falling from higher levels in the economic order or those who want to opt out of the deprivations of employment in large-scale enterprise. It might be suggested, however, that the varied literature cited by Scase as constituting this third approach hardly adds up to a developed theory of the petite bourgeoisie. Indeed, some of the writers do not even mention the stratum but what they do offer are some interesting suggestions on some of the influences involved in the contemporary reproduction of the petite bourgeoisie, the subject which occupies the discussion below.

For the purposes of the analysis below, the small enterprise-owner stratum will be initially conceptualised along the minimal lines adopted by Bechhofer and Elliott (1976) but amended to state that they are members of a class distinguished by:

1   The use of a limited amount of capital to underpin their economic activities, the allocation of which is a major consideration in the formation and continuation of their economic activities.
2   The use of technologies — established or new — which are available to those with limited capital and suited to small-scale economic activities.
3   The use of non-bureaucratic organisational forms or organisational forms which exhibit bureaucratic characteristics only to the extent to which they are imposed on owner-managers by external forces such as credit agencies (banks) the state or powerful organisations such as suppliers and customers.
4   The holding of a distinct world view centred on the overriding importance of the values of autonomy and independence, of particularism in relations and a distrust and antipathy towards large-scale organisations, including the state.

The amount of capital deemed 'limited' and the upper number of employees depends on the type of economic activity. For example, in agriculture, the amount of capital embodied in a small enterprise may be very large compared to, say, the typical amount invested in a small retail outlet. The number of employees, on the other hand, will be limited to that enabling a non-bureaucratic, particularistic organisational framework to be maintained effectively.

Translating this broad conceptualisation into the quantitative is not easy because the available data are far from adequate but it may be suggested that the numbers involved are much larger than many might suppose. For example, in manufacturing there were just over 84 000 enterprises employing less than 100 people in Britain in 1979. Between them they employed 17.5 per cent of those working in manufacturing or over 1.1 million people (*Census of Production* 1979). In other areas

212

of the economy such as retailing and professional and scientific services, the proportional significance of the small enterprise is much greater than in manufacturing, measured in terms of employment. All told, one recent estimate suggests that there are about 1.5 million small businesses in Britain involving 8 million people as owner-managers, self-employed without employees or as employees, that is, well over one-third of those actively involved in the economy. Together they contribute about a quarter of the gross national product (Cross 1983).

More narrowly, the size of the self-employed and small employer stratum itself is more difficult to assess. The Department of Employment estimated that there were just over 2 million self-employed in Britain in 1981 representing almost 9 per cent of the employed labour force, the highest level since data collection started in 1959 and suggesting a sharp increase in recent years (*Employment Gazette* 1983: 55). If we add spouses and offspring it would not be unreasonable to suggest that the petite bourgeoisie stratum comprises perhaps 4 million adults and children in Britain, a sizeable proportion (about 7 per cent) of the population as a whole.

In other industrial societies such as Japan, the most economically successful of advanced industrial societies in recent decades, Anthony (1983) reports that small enterprises have a very substantial share of total employment. What is more he also reports that the number of small firms increased markedly over the period 1963–78. Elsewhere as, for example, in the EEC, the Economist Intelligence Unit reports that, although statistics are very imperfect or incomplete for some countries, the main trend has been towards small enterprises increasing in numbers and in their share of the total employed population (Economist Intelligence Unit 1983: 57). Overall, small enterprises are also responsible for a significant proportion of total output in the EEC countries.

Among free enterprise industrial societies, Britain is, in fact, the odd one out in having such a small petite bourgeoisie stratum (Economist Intelligence Unit 1983: 61; Thompson and Leyden 1983; Boissevain 1984: 26). In other words, the economic and social significance of the petite bourgeoisie in free enterprise industrial societies may be said to be substantial, a point reinforced by the above sources when they note that in several industrial societies the size of the petite bourgeoisie stratum, as well as the share of small enterprises in economic activities, has been on the increase in recent years.

Forces of production and reproduction

The economic, social and political dynamics of class formation and reproduction have become a central focus in recent sociological analysis of modern society. A social class is demarcated by several features including principally the distinctive role its economically active members play in the economy and the world view or collection of beliefs, values and attitudes shared by its members and which separate them in their own eyes and the eyes of members of other classes, from the population more generally. Membership includes not just adults, husbands and wives but offspring also for the economically non-active depend indirectly on the form of participation in the economy of the economically active and family membership increases the likelihood of shared experiences and world views.

In the limited previous analysis of the petite bourgeoisie considerable attention was given to their historical origins as a class in the formative period of industrial society and certainly this is important in explaining their initial creation as a stratum as well as some of their present beliefs and behaviour. Such analyses, however, do not explain current influences on their reproduction and survival; indeed, they distort our view of the petite bourgeoisie since the impression is generated that they are a class with a past but no present or future. Clearly, this cannot be so — if a class continues to survive and even expand, it must be assumed that there are contemporary forces of production at work and analysis should focus carefully on what these are. We may divide the forces reproducing the contemporary petite bourgeoisie broadly into three kinds — economic, political and social and cultural.

Economic forces

Economically, the petite bourgeoisie is conventionally seen as occupying a marginal role but on any close examination this view seems untenable. Economists, in particular, have reinforced this view both in the ways in which they have concentrated their analysis and theorising on large enterprises and a macro view of the economy. As the statistical data in the previous section demonstrated, a more balanced view would give small-scale economic activities a much more central role even in advanced industrial economies seen as dominated by large corporations such as the United States (Miller 1975).

A recent fashionable approach to the problem of situating the petite bourgeoisie in the modern economy is that of the dual economy thesis. There are a number of versions of this (Hodson and Kaufman 1982)

214

but those explicitly concerned with the petite bourgeoisie often distinguished between the 'traditional' and 'modern' sectors of the economy. The traditional sector is seen as made up of small farmers and small business owners who operate in labour-intensive, simple-technology economic activities, mainly employing those who, for one reason or another, are unattractive to the large employer. The traditional sector is under constant pressure from the modern sector of the economy, made up of large-scale, capital-intensive firms able to operate at higher levels of efficiency than any small enterprise. The traditional sector survives because large firms have not got around to invading smaller pockets of the market or because profit opportunities are not particularly great or because, politically, it serves their interests to allow small producers to survive so preserving a semblance of competition.

As a thesis, this possesses truth but it is far from complete or accurate. As Berger has argued (1980: 90–1) the 'withering away' of the petite bourgeoisie enterprise implied by this view of the small enterprise is pervasive but difficult to demonstrate rigorously. Small size, labour intensivity, low capital, particularistic management, family ownership (and family labour) and older technology, do not, by themselves, necessarily add up to low efficiency as measured by the economist's orthodox criteria. Moreover, many so-called 'traditional' elements are frequently found in enterprises which, on other grounds, would be placed firmly in the modern sector.

For example, doubts have been expressed on whether profitability and size unambiguously go together to favour the large enterprise (Whittington 1980). Among the factors stressed previously by economists as favouring large enterprises over their smaller counter-parts were economies of scale, but more recently it has been recognised that economies of scale are difficult to measure and more attention needs to be paid to diseconomies of scale, particularly outside manufacturing. This becomes more important when it is remembered that deindustrialisation in advanced industrial societies shifts the balance of economic activities towards areas where the minimum size for profitable operation is likely to be lower than in manufacturing or primary industry.

But this small versus large approach to the analysis of the role of the small enterprise in the modern economy also tends to neglect relations between the two types of enterprise. In practice, the small firm frequently does not compete with the large firm but is integrated into a larger network of economic activities in which both play a role. This is perhaps most clearly exemplified in Japan where small firms are predominantly subcontractors of large firms and the whole economy is structured on this form of relationship between small and large firms. The structure of the economy itself, therefore, becomes a source of production and reproduction of the petite bourgeoisie.

Japan is sometimes regarded as atypical of capitalist industrial societies and, hence, many might doubt the wider applicability of the above analysis. But in the United Kingdom and the United States, for example, it is possible to discern ways in which small firms and large firms are integrated into the economy in other than a simple competitive fashion. Rainnie (1984), in an analysis of the clothing industry in Britain, suggested that small firms have a close and dependent relationship with large firms and especially large retailers such as Marks and Spencer. A large number of dependent suppliers allows large, high street retailers to respond rapidly to changes in fashion in a way that would not be possible if they manufactured their products for themselves. The key to these relations is that in the increasingly highly competitive and uncertain economic environment faced by *large* firms, the latter respond by creating dependent relations with a host of small producers.

More generally, Boissevain (1984) argues that large firms are decentralising to lower labour costs and reduce industrial conflict. Not only are wages lower in smaller units but fringe benefit and safety costs are also reduced. Trade unions find it more difficult to organise small establishments and workers find it more difficult to mount collective action where employment is spread over a large number of small establishments. Large firms may decentralise by creating more branch establishments but subcontracting and creating dependent relations with nominally independent producers may have even greater attractions.

Another facet of long-term relations between small and large firms is explored by Rothwell (1984) who shows how small firms play a key role in the emergence of new technologies. He shows with reference to the development of the semiconductor and computer aided design industries that small firms played a distinct role in certain periods of the industry–product life-cycle. This role was sometimes bank-rolled by large firms while, at other times, small firms pioneered innovations in ways large firms had ignored, though later large firms sometimes took over the market created by small firms. In other words, the suggestion here is that the relationship between the small firm and the large firm is part of a continuing cycle of product and market innovation with each playing an essential part in the whole.

A further economic element in the production of the petite bourgeoisie which has received a lot of attention recently concerns changes in lifestyle and consumption patterns. Large-scale enterprise produces a wide range of goods and services meeting mass demand. But for many consumers the desirability of a good or service turns on its rarity or luxury status. Its consumption gives a special psychological satisfaction because it is rare. As soon as it becomes widespread it ceases to be what Hirsch (1977) called a 'positional good'. Such goods were, in his view, becoming increasingly important in the consumption patterns in advanced industrial societies since large firms tended to standardise patterns of consumption. The demand for something 'different' or exclusive offers great opportunities for small firms and the process by which such demands are generated is partly an outcome of large firm activities.

In discussing the economic sources of the production and reproduction of the petite bourgeoisie, the emphasis has been on demonstrating that small enterprises are an integral part of any advanced industrial economy and in opposing the view that they are residual and doomed to disappear. The analysis has been partial since the economic forces involved are highly complex but, by demonstrating some of the key ways in which small-scale economic activities are integral to a modern economy, the previous overemphasis on the decline in economic opportunities for the small firm in recent years has been corrected. Rather than a steady and inevitable decline, the more accurate picture might be of declining opportunities being replaced by new opportunities for small businesses and their overall role remaining of crucial economic importance.

Political forces

Politically, the petite bourgeoisie in Britain, unlike in other advanced industrial societies (Berger and Piore 1980, Chapter 4; Conway 1981, for example) has been a fragmented, politically impotent group, at least until recently. However, direct political organisation and representation are not the sole ways in which a stratum exercises political influence to ensure its survival. The attitudes of the state and the effects of state intervention in the economy will also have effects on the fate of the petite bourgeoisie. Also relevant are relations between the petite bourgeoisie and other classes and the balance of strength between the two main classes.

The importance of state influences on the survival of the petite bourgeoisie can be illustrated in a number of ways. A historical example in Britain is noted by Bechhofer and Elliott (1976: 87–8) who record how, in the 1920s and 1930s, the state promoted suburban development through subsidies for housing which benefited mainly small builders and which offered many opportunities for small business owners to set up in newly created communities. In other countries, as in Britain now, the state has developed or is developing positive policies designed to preserve or favour small enterprise (Thompson and Leyden 1983: 34–8; Anthony 1983: 75–80; Sauer 1984; Barreyre 1984).

Partly, these political influences represent a historical legacy. The petite bourgeoisie in the past influenced political parties by offering support in return for favourable treatment. Sometimes, as in France in the 1950s, the petite bourgeoisie have in effect had their own party (Berger 1981). The latter is especially likely to occur in multi-party states where proportional representation increases the importance of smaller parties. Given suitable conditions such as the emergence of political uncertainty or crisis, smaller groupings in the electorate may also become important in two-party political systems.

A major example of indirect political influence on the survival of the petite bourgeoisie is the taxation structure of modern industrial societies. The analysis of the impact of taxation is both difficult and complex but it is suggested that in recent decades it has had a major influence on the fate of the petite bourgeoisie. In Britain, and to a certain extent in other industrial societies such as the United States, changes in the taxation system in recent decades have tended to favour self-employment. The major changes involved have been twofold: a rapid increase in state expenditure and a drift towards a more regressive tax system through an increasing emphasis on indirect taxation.

The increase in state expenditure has been due to a wide range of items — increasing Welfare State expenditure, defence (including space exploration) costs as well as investment in the economic infrastructure and nationalised industries — although these have been of varying importance in different countries. These and other demands upon the state have, it has been argued, outstripped sources of revenue raising leading to what has been described as a 'fiscal crisis of the State' (O'Connor 1973; Gough 1979: 125–7). The difficulties of raising revenue have been accompanied by widespread resistance from sectors of the taxpaying population. Corporate taxpayers, for example, have reduced their contributions by manipulating their liabilities. Others have translated their resistance into political pressures for reduced taxes and political parties in Britain and the United States have won massive political victories recently by promising reduced direct taxation.

After World War II, many industrial societies adopted progressive taxation policies but recently there has been a drift towards indirect taxation. In part, this is due to a widespread belief among taxpayers that income tax, in its various forms, is more onerous than indirect tax. One result has been a gradual lowering of marginal rates of tax on higher income levels coupled with an increase in the loopholes for higher income earners to avoid tax. In Britain, for example, such loopholes include mortgage and home-improvement subsidies, employer-paid school fees and private health insurance.

In Britain, also, a big shift towards indirect taxation occurred with the introduction of VAT in 1973 which taxed a wide range of goods and especially services, previously untaxed. This brought Britain into line with her EEC partners already heavily reliant on VAT for tax revenues. One reason for this was the difficulties in collecting income tax, especially from high income earners, in many EEC countries and especially in France and Italy. Other indirect taxes recently increased in Britain include social security payments, road fund licenses and an increasing proportion of energy prices.

It may be argued that, among the groups squeezed hardest by these changes in the incidence of taxation have been the lower middle and skilled working classes, two groups who have been prime 'feeder' groups for the renewal of the petite bourgeoisie. Unable to follow higher income earners who have converted a high proportion of their earnings into untaxed payments in kind or corporate taxpayers who have arranged their accounts to minimise or eliminate taxes, some of these lower class groups have sought escape through small enterprise ownership. The latter offers abundant opportunities for avoiding taxation legitimately and illegitimately and has accompanied an enormous growth in the 'black economy' (O'Higgins 1980; Public Accounts Committee 1984) in Britain and particularly in Italy (Malone 1982; Bamford 1984).

The taxation changes discussed here are, as O'Connor (1973) and Gough (1979) among others, have argued, very much a reflection of the relations between large-scale capitalism and the state in advanced industrial societies. The impetus towards the regeneration of the petite bourgeoisie resulting from these changes is partly a by-product of the increasing ability of large enterprises and especially the trans-nationals, to avoid taxation and to off-load onto the state some of their costs such as those connected with the location of new plants, training of personnel and research and development. At the same time, the capital-intensive character of large-scale enterprise has led the state to promote small-scale enterprise to generate new employment.

Political influences on the reproduction of the petite bourgeoisie also relate to the ability of the petite bourgeoisie to organise themselves as an interest group and on their relations with other classes. In Britain, there has recently been a revival of petite-bourgeoisie-based organisations of one kind or another (McHugh 1979; Elliott *et al.* 1982) which, it may be argued, is also related to the fragmentation of other classes (Roberts *et al.* 1977; Crewe *et al.* 1977). Both the established middle class and the organised working class in Britain have lost their assertiveness and cohesion in recent years. The established or traditional middle class has been joined by various groupings which have been described as the 'new' middle class — the enlarged ranks of middle-level managers, technicians and other new professionals — which has led to a middle class fragmentation demonstrated politically. The Conservative Party, for example, the established party of the traditional middle class, has had to seek more actively the support of these new groups joining the middle class. The emergence of the Social Democratic Party is one indicator that they have not been entirely successful.

The Labour Party has, similarly, lost some of its traditional manual worker support. The jobs of the latter have been disappearing in the economic restructuring which is dissolving the heavy industry and manufacturing components of the economy. Affluence has led more manual workers to define political relations in materialistic rather than collectivist terms. Like the Conservatives, the Labour Party has not been entirely successful in recruiting the new middle class even though many of these come from manual family backgrounds.

One result of this fragmentation of class and political identities is that the petite bourgeoisie is more likely to be listened to and to have its support actively sought. The Labour Party, for instance, has consciously developed policies for the promotion of small-scale capitalism. The Labour government of 1974–9 made several concessions to petite bourgeoisie interests in successive budgets (Kay and King 1979: 171–6). The Conservatives set up a Small Business Bureau in 1976 to recruit the support of small firm owner-managers. Both parties in office have continued to appoint a junior minister in the Department of Industry with special responsibility for small firms.

Overall, therefore, the political climate for the survival of the petite bourgeoisie is probably more favourable in Britain than it has been for a very long time, perhaps since the decline of the Liberal Party in the 1920s and the emergence of a two-party system based on the interests of big business and organised labour. The changing political and class patterns of Britain over the last decade and a half demonstrate once again that any assumption of an inevitable decline of the petite bourgeoisie is questionable. Political forces of production and reproduction may well override economic influences in a given period since political decisions can create an economic climate more favourable to small-scale economic activities than would exist if market forces were allowed free play. Other industrial societies, for example France and Italy, appear to provide examples of this phenomenon.

Social and cultural forces

Social forces sustaining the petite bourgeoisie have arguably received more attention than economic influences and certainly more than the political influences discussed above. A good many studies have examined the motivational patterns of small business owners and their social backgrounds (for example, Boswell 1973; Stanworth and Curran 1973; Kets de Vries 1977; Scase and Goffee 1980, 1982). The great emphasis on autonomy and independence in the psychological make-up of the petite bourgeoisie has been related to its social background and a number of factors have been demonstrated as of some importance in the social production of the stratum.

As with the other classes, family influences are important in the maintenance and continuation of the petite bourgeoisie. Goldthorpe *et al.* (1980: 259), in their major study of social mobility in Britain, reported finding a stratum of individuals and families who embodied the tradition of self-employment and Robinson (1984) reports similarly for a wider range of societies. They might move in and out of self-employment as opportunity and failure dictated, but their per-sistence in maintaining this self-employment tradition was strongly marked. While some of this continuity occurs through the family transmitting capital between generations, the instability in occu-pational positions, including shifts from self-employed to employed status indicated by research, would suggest other factors are also important. The most likely alternative factor here is cultural traditions.

The knowledge of how to run a small enterprise is not widespread. Entry into small-scale economic activities is not catered for in con-ventional education where employment by others is implicitly assumed to be the normal destiny of most school leavers. Rather, such knowledge is likely to be embodied in a tradition which also transmits a strong commitment to the ideals of self-employment. Thus, those born into the petite bourgeoisie may take on employee status either through the influence of education or lack of capital or because of the non-viable nature of a previous involvement in self-employment. But, apparently, inherited commitment to the ideal of economic indepen-dence remains important, influencing them to rejoin the petite bourgeoisie proper at some later date.

The concept of social marginality has also been important in the examination of the forces reproducing the petite bourgeoisie. Socially marginal status is produced through discrepancies between individual characteristics and social structure and may emerge in a variety of ways (Stanworth and Curran 1973). There have always been those who, for whatever reason, fail to acquire the educational or social attributes which will enable them to use their talents and abilities fully. Education is often ineffective in allowing individuals fully to realise their potential and social background may be highly constraining for the individual wishing to enter many high-status, highly-rewarded adult roles. People in these circumstances frequently end up in the lower reaches of the middle class, in routine ill-paid white collar jobs or as manual workers. The discrepancies between their occupational roles and their perceptions of their own abilities engenders a drive towards a more congenial role. The large-scale bureaucratic organisation or public employer is increasingly universalistic in recruiting, demanding more and more formal qualifications, adding further to feelings of marginality. The creation of a small enterprise is one solution to such feelings.

Other well-documented examples of social marginality which may lead to entry into the petite bourgeoisie arise out of religious, ethnic or racial discrimination. The Jews have, historically, been an outstanding religious example of this process in Britain, Europe and the United States (Pollins 1984). But more recently a great deal of attention has been devoted to Asian small business owners both in Britain and elsewhere (Ward and Jenkins 1984) although it is easy to exaggerate the extent to which Asians have joined the petite bourgeoisie.

Finally, the female small business owner may also be seen as exemplifying elements of social marginality. Women have frequently been denied opportunites to reach middle and higher-level roles in business but this mattered little when most were confined to the home. More recently, however, notions of achievement and independence have been introduced into women's self-conceptions but whether the employment system is capable of fully meeting this change is debatable. Increases in the number of divorces means that many women find themselves having to support themselves and often children: self-employment is one solution to these problems (Scase and Goffee 1983).

It should be stressed that several of the above social forces producing the petite bourgeoisie not only show little indication of declining but, indeed, seem on the increase. Participation in formal education at the tertiary level remains restricted. In Britain, for example, less than 15 per cent of the relevant age cohort goes on to higher education and even in other industrial societies this proportion rarely rises above 50 per cent (Kumar 1978). Cut-backs in state welfare expenditure have affected education, denying many the opportunity of gaining further qualifications. Similarly, changes in women's roles do not appear likely to be met by an increase in employment opportunities without reductions for other groups in society.

Among the groups most likely to be 'feeder' groups for new entrants into the petite bourgeoisie there has also been a recent increase in the experience of 'deskilling' (Thompson 1983: Chapter 4). This refers to the process in which manual and routine white collar work is converted into boring, less autonomous jobs through the introduction of new technology and work procedures. Those who experience this loss of autonomy and satisfaction may be much more prone to seek self-employment as a solution. Again, these influences appear to be on the increase (mainly as a result of large enterprise management strategies, it should be noted) and may play an important part in the further generation of the petite bourgeoisie.

The cultural importance of the petite bourgeoisie for capitalist industrial society is also an important influence on their reproduction as a stratum. As Bechhofer and Elliott (1976, 1981) have pointed out, the petite bourgeoisie embodies the central values of capitalism in everyday life in a way no other class in society can, practising the values of thrift, hard work, risk-taking, entrepreneurship and experience competition more fully than other classes. Other classes may subscribe to these values in principle but, in practice, their actions and experiences often depart from them, sometimes very substantially. Ordinary employees are often highly collectivist, particularly through their commitment to trade unions, while many large firm executives are only too aware that opportunities for entrepreneurial action and risk-taking are limited and many of their day-to-day activities are dedicated to reducing rather than enhancing competition.

To the extent that the petite bourgeoisie is the carrier of key values in society, its survival becomes crucial to preserving society in its present form. Other groupings — classes, political parties, the state, big business — all sponsor its survival for its preservation of an ideal. This ideal may be distorted in the minds of the majority whose direct experience of small enterprise is very limited and may rest on a false picture of the past, of a society in which everybody was independent and where there were no all-powerful trade unions or a dominant state. But the potency of such ideals cannot be neglected in assessing the opportunities for survival of those regarded as living evidence of their reality. For the petite bourgeoisie itself these cultural ideals are a resource to be exploited in relations with others to ensure its reproduction.

Conclusions

Most discussions of the petite bourgeoisie have concentrated on issues of definition and the alleged decline of this stratum as industrial society develops. The rather unsatisfactory answers offered recently to conceptual problems have been examined briefly but the main aim has been to analyse a wide range of influences involved in the reproduction of the small enterprise owning stratum. Emphasis has been on emerging influences integral to advanced industrial society rather than those surviving from previous stages of industrialisation. Of course, this is not to argue that the survival of the petite bourgeoisie is guaranteed or will occur without struggle: no class is permanent in an absolute sense but the forces of production and reproduction identified above are fully capable of ensuring survival into the foreseeable future.

References

Anthony D. (1983). 'Japan' in D.J. Storey (ed.), *The Small Firm, an International Survey*, London, Croom Helm.

Bamford, J. (1984). 'Small Business in Italy — the Submerged Economy' in C. Levicki (ed.) *Small Business, Theory and Policy*, London, Croom Helm.

Barreyre, P. (1984). 'The Small Firm in the French Economy', in C. Levicki (ed.), *Small Business, Theory and Policy*.

Bechhofer, F. and Elliott, B. (1976). 'Persistence and Change: The Petite Bourgeoisie in Industrial Society', *European Journal of Sociology*, vol. XVIII, no. 1, pp. 74–99.

Bechhofer, F. and Elliott B. (1981). *The Petite Bourgeoisie, Comparative Studies of the Uneasy Stratum*, London, Macmillan.

Berger, S. (1980). 'The Traditional Sector in France and Italy', in S. Berger and M. Piore, *Dualism and Discontinuity in Industrial Societies*, New York, Cambridge University Press.

Berger, S. (1981). 'Regime and Interest Representation: The French Traditional Middle Classes' in S.D. Berger (ed.), *Organizing Interests in Western Europe*, Cambridge, Cambridge University Press.

Binks, M. and Coyne, J. (1983). *The Birth of Enterprise*, Hobart paper no. 98, London, Institute of Economic Affairs.

Blair, J.M. (1972). *Economic Concentration, Structure, Behaviour and Public Policy*, New York, Harcourt, Brace Jovanovich.

Boissevain, J. (1984). 'Small Entrepreneurs in Contemporary

Europe', in R. Ward and R. Jenkins (eds.), *Ethnic Communities in Business*, Cambridge, Cambridge University Press.

Bolton, J.E. (1971). *Report of the Committee of Inquiry on Small Firms* (Bolton Report), Cmnd. 4811, London, HMSO.

Boswell, J. (1973). *The Rise and Decline of Small Firms*, London, Allen and Unwin.

Conway, J.F. (1981). 'Agrarian Petit Bourgeois Responses to Capitalist Industrialization: The Case of Canada' in Bechhofer and Elliot (eds.) *The Petite Bourgeoisie, Comparative Studies of the Uneasy Stratum.*

Cooper, A.C. (1970). 'The Palo Alto Experience', *Industrial Research*, May, pp. 58–60.

Cross, M. (1983). 'The United Kingdom' in D. Storey (ed.) *The Small Firm, an International Survey*, London, Croom Helm.

Crewe, I. *et al.* (1977). 'Partisan Disalignment in Britain, 1964–74' *British Journal of Political Science*, vol. 7, no. 2, pp. 129–90.

Curran, J. (1981). 'Class Imagery, Work Environment and Community', *British Journal of Sociology*, vol. XXXII, no. 1, March, pp. 111–26.

Curran, J. and Stanworth, J. (1984) 'Small Business Research in Britain' in C. Levicki (ed.) *Small Business, Theory and Policy.*

Economist Intelligence Unit (1983). *The European Climate for Small Business, a Ten Country Survey*, London.

Elliott, B. *et al.* (1982). 'Bourgeois Social Movements in Britain: References and Responses', *Sociological Review*, vol. 30, no. 1, pp. 71–96.

Employment Gazette (1983). 'How Many Self-employed?', *Employment Gazette* , vol. 91, no. 2, pp. 55–6.

Goldthorpe, J. *et al.* (1980). *Social Mobility and the Class Structure in Modern Britain*, Oxford, Clarendon Press.

Gough, I. (1979). *The Political Economy of the Welfare State* London, Macmillan.

Hall, S. (1971). 'The "Political" and the "Economic" in Marx's Theory of Classes' in A. Hunt (ed.) *Class and Class Structure*, London, Laurence and Wishart.

Hirsch, F. (1977). *Social Limits to Growth*, London, Routledge and Kegan Paul.

Hodson, R. and Kaufman, R.L. (1982). 'Economic Dualism: A Critical Review', *American Sociological Review*, vol. 47, December, pp. 727–39.

Kay, J.A. and King, M.R. (1979). *The British Tax System*, 2nd edn, Oxford, Oxford University Press.

Kets de Vries, M.F.R. (1977). 'The Entrepreneurial Personality: A

Person at the Crossroads', *Journal of Management Studies*, vol. 14, no. 1, pp. 34–57.

Kumar, K. (1978). *Prophecy and Progress*, Harmondsworth, Penguin Books.

Malone, J.H. (1982). 'The Questionable Promise of Enterprise Zones, Lessons from England and Italy', *Urban Affairs Quarterly*, vol. 18, no. 1, pp. 19–30.

McHugh, J. (1979). 'The Self-employed and the Small Independent Entrepreneur' in R. King and N. Nugent (eds.), *Respectable Rebels, Middle Class Campaigns in Britain in the 1970s*, London, Hodder and Stoughton.

Miller, S.M. (1975). 'Notes on Neo-capitalism', *Theory and Society*, vol. 2, pp. 1–35.

O'Connor, J. (1973). *The Fiscal Crisis of the State*, New York, St Martin's Press.

O'Higgins, M. (1980) *Measuring the Black Economy*, London, Outer Circle Policy Unit.

Pollins, H. (1984). 'The Development of Jewish Business in the United Kingdom' in R. Ward and R. Jenkins (eds.), *Ethnic Communities in Business, Strategies for Economic Survival*.

Poulantzas, N. (1975). *Class in Contemporary Capitalism*, London, New Left Books.

Poulantzas, N. (1977). 'The New Petit Bourgeoisie' in A. Hunt (ed.), *Class and Class Structure*.

Public Accounts Committee (1984). *Enforcement Powers of the Revenue Department*, Thirty Fourth Report of the Public Accounts Committee, London, HMSO.

Rainnie, A.F. (1984). 'Combined and Uneven Development in the Clothing Industry: The Effects of Competition on Accumulation', *Capital and Class*, no. 22, pp. 141–56.

Riesman, D. (1950). *The Lonely Crowd; A Study of the Changing American Character*, New Haven, Conn., Yale University Press.

Roberts, K. *et al.* (1977). *The Fragmentary Class Structure*, London, Heinemann.

Robinson, R.V. (1984). 'Reproducing Class Relations in Industrial Capitalism', *American Sociological Review*, vol. 49, April, pp. 182–96.

Rothwell, R. (1984). 'The Role of Small Firms and the Emergence of New Technologies', *Omega*, vol. 12, no. 1, pp. 19–29.

Sauer, W. (1984). 'Small Firms and the German Economic Miracle', in C. Levicki (ed.), *Small Business, Theory and Policy*.

Scase, R. (1982). 'The Petite Bourgeoise and Modern Capitalism: A Consideration of Recent Theories' in A. Giddens and G. Mackenzie (eds.), *Social Class and the Division of Labour*, Cambridge, Cambridge University Press.

Scase, R. and Goffee, R. (1980). *The Real World of the Small Business Owner*, London, Croom Helm.

Scase, R. and Goffee, R. (1982). *The Entrepreneurial Middle Class*, London, Croom Helm.

Scase, R. and Goffee, R. (1983). 'Business Ownership and Women's Subordination: A preliminary Study of Female Proprietors', *Sociological Review*, vol. 31, no. 4, pp. 625–48.

Stanworth, M.J.K. and Curran, J. (1973). *Management Motivation in the Smaller Business*, Epping, Gower, 1973.

Thompson, J.H. (1983). 'The United States of America' in D. Storey (ed.), *The Small Firm, an International Survey*.

Thompson, J.H. and Leyden, D.R. (1983). 'The United States of America' in Storey (ed.), *The Small Firm*.

Tomlinson, J. (1980). 'Socialist Politics and the Small Business' in *Politics and Power I, New Perspectives on Socialist Politics*, London, Routledge and Kegan Paul.

Thompson, P. (1983). *The Nature of Work*, London, Macmillan.

Urry, J. (1973). 'Towards a Structural Theory of the Middle Class', *Acta Sociologica*, vol. 16, no. 3, pp. 175–87.

Ward R. and Jenkins R. (eds.) (1984). *Ethnic Communities in Business, Strategies for Survival*, Cambridge, Cambridge University Press.

Whittington R. (1980). 'The Profitability and Size of U.K. Companies, 1960–74', *Journal of Industrial Economics*, vol. 28, pp. 335–82.

Whyte, W.F (1960). *The Organization Man*, Harmondsworth, Penguin Books (originally published in 1956).

Wright, E.O. (1976). 'Class Boundaries in Advanced Capitalism', *New Left Review*, no. 98, pp. 3–41.

Wright, E.O. (1978). *Class, Crisis and the State*, London, New Left Books.

Wright, E.O. (1980) 'Varieties of Marxist Conceptions of Class Structure', *Politics and Society*, vol. 9, no. 3, pp 323–70.